Just Words

Just

*Moralism
and Metalanguage
in Twentieth-Century
French Fiction*

Robert W. Greene

*The Pennsylvania State University Press
University Park, Pennsylvania*

Words

PQ
673
G77
1993

Library of Congress Cataloging-in-Publication Data

Greene, Robert W., 1933–
    Just words : moralism and metalanguage in twentieth-century French
fiction / Robert W. Greene.
        p.   cm.
    Includes bibliographical references and index.
    ISBN 0-271-00899-7 (alk. paper)
    1. French fiction—20th century—History and criticism.   2. Moral
conditions in literature.   3. Ethics in literature.   4. Narration
(Rhetoric)   I. Title.
PQ673.G77   1993
843'.9109353—dc20   92-16697
                                                                              CIP

Published by The Pennsylvania State University Press,
Suite C, Barbara Building,
University Park, PA   16802-1003

To
Gene Mirabelli and Ricardo Nirenberg
and to
Judith Kramer Greene

All literary genres are artifacts, but none more blatantly so than fiction. Its very name declares its artificiality, and yet it must somehow be true to hold the interest of its readers, to tell them about experiences at once imaginary and relevant to their own lives.

—Michael Riffaterre, *Fictional Truth*

Contents

Preface

A determining constant of French literature since the time of Montaigne has been its persistent *moralisme,* its enduring preoccupation with and relentless inquiry into human frailty. Comparison with English moralistic writing perhaps can specify this constant. The well-known epigraph to La Rochefoucauld's *Maximes,* "Nos vertus ne sont le plus souvent que des vices déguisés," for example, when juxtaposed with the intent of Lord Chesterfield's letters, as formulated by Basil Willey—"to fashion a gentleman or noble person in virtuous and gentle discipline" (*The English Moralists* [London: Chatto and Windus, 1964], 11)—points to all that differentiates the seventeenth-century French aphorist from his eighteenth-century English disciple, the chasm separating the sardonic witness from the earnest pedagogue.

Another defining characteristic of French literature—and one that dates back at least as far as Rabelais, Montaigne's near coeval—has been the tendency on the part of many writers, but perhaps especially novelists, to include in their fictions passages that explicitly foreground the problematical nature of all discourse. Donald Frame, for example, summarizes the baldly contradictory approaches to reading advocated in the Prologue to *Gargantua* as follows: "Rabelais offers us two ways of reading the book and invites us to choose the second, but without canceling the first" (*François Rabelais: A Study* [New York: Harcourt Brace Jovanovich, 1977], 32). Now metalinguistic puzzles and verbally self-conscious musings like those found in *Gargantua*'s Prologue (and elsewhere in Rabelais) might seem particularly incompatible with moralistic analysis which, presumably, must utilize the least contestable, most transparent of codes. Paradoxically, however, in a number of major French novelists these apparently divergent intentions (metalinguistic versus moralistic) coexist and in fact interpenetrate to an extraordinary extent. Indeed, it is almost as if any sustained *examen de conscience* in French fiction must inevitably involve a coincident scrutiny of the instrument used for conducting the cool soul-searching.

No doubt because it is more consistently self-conscious than that of any previous era, the fiction of twentieth-century France seems to illustrate this convergence with special brilliance. Accordingly, over the past dozen years, I have explored the interpenetration of moralistic analysis and metalinguistic commentary in selected prose narratives by some of the most universally admired French novelists of our century: Gide, Proust, Malraux, Camus, Duras, and Sarraute. Surprisingly, this domain has been largely neglected by recent criticism. The present examination of the apparent marriage of moralistic analysis and metalinguistic commentary in certain twentieth-century French narratives will, I hope, fill an intriguing scholarly void.

From time to time, I shall use insights gleaned from the theoretically oriented writings of poststructuralism. My overriding aim in this study, however, is to combine practical criticism with literary history, to offer close readings of a specific sequence of prose texts. The choice of fictions treated in these pages, while obviously neither exhaustive nor definitive, is far from arbitrary. In every instance, as noted above, the novelist is by general consensus a major writer. Treated as three consecutive pairs, moreover, these novelists reflect three distinct phases in the evolution of prose narrative in twentieth-century France: the fiction of High Modernism (1900–1920), the fiction of commitment (1930–50), and the fiction of/after the *nouveau roman* (1960–80). Hence the selection, and the groupings, proposed here.

Earlier versions of Chapters 2 through 7 of this book have appeared as journal articles: Chapter 2, *French Forum*, 12 (January 1987), 75–91; Chapter 3, *Contemporary Literature*, 25 (Summer 1984), 136–55; Chapter 4, *Modern Language Quarterly*, 46 (June 1985), 161–80; Chapter 5, *French Studies*, 34 (October 1980), 422–33; Chapter 6, *Romanic Review*, 80 (January 1989), 131–48; Chapter 7, *Novel*, 16 (Spring 1983), 197–214. I should like to thank the editors of the above-named journals for allowing me to reprint these articles, now substantially revised, in the present study.

A number of individuals and organizations contributed to the preparation of this book. Both the research and the writing were facilitated by a fellowship from the National Endowment for the Humanities and by grants-in-aid from the Research Foundation of the State University of New York, for which I should like to express my heartfelt appreciation. During the last decade and a half, my students at the State University of New York, Albany, proved to be excellent traveling companions as we ventured down some of the highways and byways of modern French fiction. I am grateful to them for their curiosity, their attentiveness, and their enthusiasm. Warm thanks go as well to Leslie Abend Callahan who, with seemingly inexhaustible skill, patience, and good humor, typed an early draft of the whole study into a word-processor, making all subsequent revision considerably easier to implement than would otherwise have been the case. Likewise, I am obliged to Philip Winsor, Cherene Holland, and their colleagues at Penn State Press for their interest in the manuscript, and their wise counsel and expertise in seeing it through to print.

In carrying out my project, I was indeed fortunate to have had the support of the following distinguished scholars: Robert Alter, Peter Brooks, Mary Ann Caws, Renée Riese Hubert, Neal Oxenhandler, and Michael Riffaterre. It is as much a pleasure as an honor to acknowledge my indebtedness to them.

I am especially beholden to Dennis Porter, Richard Stamelman, and Steven Winspur, who read the entire manuscript and made extremely helpful comments and suggestions. Their generosity, perception, and tact were, and remain, a source of inspiration for me.

Finally, a word about the persons named on the dedication page of this book. The first two demonstrated unflagging forbearance, lent a sympathetic ear, and provided constant encouragement, as this study took shape over far too many years. In return for their unwavering faith, I can offer only my abiding affection and eternal gratitude. The third person named on the dedication page was the book's guiding spirit from the start to finish. To her my debt is boundless.

Introduction

One

Moralism and Metalanguage in French Literature

By every relevant measure, the perennial if generally unremarked-upon collaboration of moralism and metalanguage in French literature finds its most compelling expression in twentieth-century fiction. Why this should be so must of course remain forever beyond the reach of certain knowledge, for the obvious reason that the manifold historical factors shaping outcomes such as this one interact in ways so subtle as to defy sure analysis. On the other hand, any serious consideration, however schematic and speculative, of those aspects of French literature that affect the traditions in question and their convergence, will at the very least situate that collaboration, as well as its flowering in modern French fiction, within an authentic, hence illuminating, cultural and conceptual context. Accordingly, in this introductory chapter, I propose to examine the workings of moralism and metalanguage in French letters, mindful that the former notion, precisely because it is so often taken as a given by readers of French literature, deserves a systematic if not necessarily lengthy review.

For etymological reasons first of all, an aura of ambiguity surrounds the French word *moraliste.* As Jules Brody has observed, the

same Latin noun, *mos,* engendered "deux dérivés, *moeurs* et *morales,* et deux sens différents: le relatif et l'arbitraire d'une part, et le
permanent et l'absolu de l'autre."[1] In keeping with this semantic bi-
furcation, moralistic writing in France has concerned itself with
manners, the foibles of a society, *and* with permanent ethical values
and universal psychological truths. On the other hand, as scholars
have often noted, in French moralistic writing, analysis and description usually win out over reproof and prescription (or proscription),
bemused observation over chastisement and edification. Odette de
Mourgues exemplifies this viewpoint:

> The French moralist studies man within the world of nature
> and reason in a non-metaphysical, non-reflexive way. More-
> over, he is not a *moralisateur* and has no system of ethics to
> propound. He is content to examine man's behaviour (includ-
> ing man's moral attitudes) as it is, with some kind of clear-
> sighted objectivity.... Although he is interested in moral
> issues, since they are an integral part of man's social behav-
> iour, he is not concerned to reform humanity and can dis-
> tance himself from the ethics of a given society, relieved of
> the immediate task of edifying his readers.[2]

Thus, a detached, almost clinical gaze typifies the approach of
French moralists, who generally refrain from pedagogical imperative
or outright prohibition. Nevertheless, as may be extrapolated from
Brody's point, a kind of righteous nostalgia, perhaps inevitably, can
cling to even the most cynical *réflexion,* for irony never totally deflects the French moralist's normative impulse.

Louis Van Delft's concise but comprehensive definition of *le moraliste classique* identifies the principal currents of meaning and
questions of form that the term encompasses: "Nous appelerons
moraliste l'écrivain qui traite des moeurs et (ou) s'adonne à l'ana-
lyse, en ne s'interdisant pas de rappeler des normes; qui adopte très
généralement pour forme soit le traité, soit le fragment; dont l'attitude consiste à se maintenir avant tout à hauteur d'homme, du fait

---

1. Jules Brody, "La Bruyère: le style d'un moraliste," *CAIEF* 30 (1978): 152.
2. Odette de Mourgues, *Two French Moralists: La Rochefoucauld and La Bruyère* (Cambridge: Cambridge University Press, 1978), 4, 173–74.

du vif intérêt qu'il porte au vécu."[3] In his erudite, astringent reappraisal of the seventeenth-century French moralist, and of the ramifying traditions that have grown up around this neoclassical model, Van Delft draws out the implications of his definition. As becomes obvious over the course of his study, the spectrum of types that French moralists successively (and at times simultaneously) embody runs the gamut from preacher to teacher to unmasker to observer to contemplator. Still, certain invariant aspects of this class of writer (and of writing) emerge from Van Delft's inquiry. He observes, for example, concerning the moralist: "Il impose moins qu'il ne propose. Il est, à proprement parler, un directeur de conscience laïc" (302). As for the moralist's native habitat, "la province du moraliste," according to Van Delft, "se situe à la lisière de trois grands domaines, la religion, la science et la littérature" (337). But no doubt the principal thread tying French moralists together is their common ancestry; Van Delft maintains that all trace their origins to Socrates, specifically to his ideal of *gnôthi seauton* (335). Thus, in heeding their Master's precept, French moralists turn observation into contemplation, focusing ultimately on themselves.

Chamfort, the great moralist of the French Revolution, Van Delft notes, possessed the lucidity necessary for understanding this destiny. The author of *Maximes et anecdotes* was one of the first French writers to use the term appropriately when outlining French literary history, to apply it to figures and concerns now automatically thought of as constituting the mainstream of French moralism: "Montaigne, La Rochefoucauld et La Bruyère sont les premiers de nos écrivains moralistes et peut-être aussi ceux qui ont le mieux connu le coeur humain." Chamfort also knew that the true contemplative, the genuine sage, following La Fontaine's Socratic injunction: "Apprendre à se connaître est le premier des soins," finally comes full circle in his odyssey of the human heart: "L'homme du monde, l'ami de la fortune, même l'amant de la gloire, tracent tous devant eux une ligne directe qui le conduit à un terme inconnu. Le sage, l'ami de lui-même, décrit une ligne circulaire, dont l'extrémité le ramène à lui."[4]

3. Louis Van Delft, *Le Moraliste classique: essai de définition et de typologie* (Geneva: Librairie Droz, 1982), 108.

4. Chamfort passages quoted in Van Delft, *Le Moraliste classique,* 29–30, 335–36.

In this perspective, "Know Thyself" becomes the common denominator, the one irreducible element of all French moralistic writing. And the French moralist emerges, in Van Delft's astute characterization, as a "directeur de conscience laïc," a secular counterpart to the religious confessor. On reflection, Van Delft's insightful remark leads one to suspect that the phenomenon of *moralisme* in French literature may well have come into being in direct response to the crisis in faith that had been steadily tightening its grip on French intellectual life ever since Montaigne's time.

As devised and perfected by La Rochefoucauld, the maxim is generally considered the moralistic genre par excellence. La Rochefoucauld transformed the juridical *maxima sententia*, a directly stated, widely recognized rule of conduct, into a penetrating judgment of human nature, couched usually in paradoxical language. The cool, concise, universally applicable maxim outlived La Rochefoucauld, but over time the impulse generating it gave rise to longer, more richly textured, more bitingly ironic forms such as the *anecdote*, which increasingly tended to eclipse the maxim. Eventually, the brief, lapidary, neoclassical genre lost its appeal for most, but by no means all, French writers, as the broad moralistic current in French literature invaded the realm of the novel. I shall return to this last point later in this chapter.

First, however, I should like to consider the practice of a twentieth-century writer, Pierre Reverdy, whose maxims constitute eloquent proof of the continuing vitality into our own era of the quintessential genre within the moralistic tradition. A glance at several of Reverdy's maxims will show the extent to which the seventeenth-century master guided the twentieth-century poet's composing hand. It may also provide reasons why this literary form should hold a special attraction for poets, as well as for any writer alert to what his/her occupation entails, who is scrupulously self-aware while engaged in the act of writing.

Le Gant de crin, Reverdy's 1927 volume of notes and aphorisms that bears the apt epigraph "Je ne pense pas, je note,"[5] includes maxims that could conceivably have come from the pen of La Rochefoucauld himself. Like his model, the poet is clearly capable of

5. Pierre Reverdy, *Le Gant de crin* (Paris: Plon, 1927), 1. Subsequent page references to this work are in the body of the study, in parentheses.

producing maxims that are almost perfectly balanced semantically, syntactically and rhythmically:

15/16 La course au flambeau de la postérité est une duperie / contre laquelle devrait au moins se révolter notre égoïsme. (86)

15/16 Une opinion est un sentiment étroitement personnel / auquel nous donnons l'importance d'une vérité universelle. (95)

Reverdy underlines the antithesis in the second maxim (*senti-ment... personnel / vérité universelle*) by placing the antonymic words in rhyming position. Elsewhere he uses paronymic repetition, a favorite device of La Rochefoucauld, in the rhythmically stressed position:

14/12 Celui qui connaît sa faiblesse est réellement plus fort / que ce-lui qui croit aveuglément à sa force. (92)

The pattern of unstable balance is another stylistic feature common to La Rochefoucauld and Reverdy. By setting the bulk of the word/thought matter in the first of the maxim's two parts, the poet heightens the effect of the surprise ending:

11/4 On est plus durement prisonnier de la haine / que de l'amour. (94)

13/8 On appelle défauts ce qui, chez les gens, nous déplaît, / et qualités ce qui nous flatte. (115)

With these two maxims, Reverdy uses the device of antithesis of abstractions in typical La Rochefoucauld fashion: *haine* versus *amour* and *défauts* versus *qualités.*

The other basic structural pattern found in La Rochefoucauld, the ternary form, is similarly employed by Reverdy:

9/8/5 La pudeur accompagnée d'orgeuil / produit parfois les mêmes mouvements / que la modestie. (84)

In this maxim, as in the very first one quoted above, Reverdy uses a mitigating term ("au moins" earlier, "parfois" here) in the same way as La Rochefoucauld, that is, not only to lighten the pessimism but to introduce veiled irony and achieve rhythmical balance as well.

In the final analysis, Reverdy's somber maxims convey an oddly satisfying message to readers. It has been suggested that the charm of La Rochefoucauld's maxims stems largely from their structure and flow, that it is the poet in La Rochefoucauld who, with patterns of rhythmic, syntactic, and semantic balance, combined with strategically deployed qualifiers, softens even while monumentalizing the harsh truths he is offering. This view seems equally appropriate for *Le Gant de crin* where, again, the dynamic "equation" dimension of a maxim distracts readers from its *pointe,* gives the maxim's operating aesthetic equal status with its ethical component. An entry from Reverdy's 1948 volume of notes and aphorisms, *Le Livre de mon bord,* captures the inherent mutuality or reciprocity, for certain French writers, of inner (moral) and outer (formal, writerly) concerns: "L'éthique, c'est l'esthétique du dedans."[6]

Also palpable in Reverdy, as in La Rochefoucauld and, for that matter, in every strict practitioner of the maxim form, is a highly self-conscious scriptural superego. Thus, if a flawed human nature is the ostensible subject of all maxims modeled after La Rochefoucauld's, the choice of this particular form implies an obsessive preoccupation on the author's part with the problematics of writing, and suggests that the maxim's hidden subject across the centuries is the endless working through of the problems involved in its composition. One is reminded here, almost inevitably, of Roland Barthes's famous distinction between the *écrivant* and the *écrivain,* between the naive, "transitive," message-driven writer, on the one hand, and the knowing, "intransitive," perpetually self-regarding writer, on the other—between the word's clerk or scribe and its priest.[7] For perhaps more successfully than any other writer, the molder of maxims disfigures or collapses these two categories, by engaging in a scriptural activity that is both teleologically determined and characterized by unrelenting self-monitoring. In this limited sense, moralism and metalanguage may already be collaborating in French literary texts of the neoclassical age.

Chamfort stands out in the history of French moralism following the neoclassical period because of his genius for blending passion

6. Pierre Reverdy, *Le Livre de mon bord* (Paris: Mercure de France, 1948), 154.
7. Roland Barthes, *Essais critiques* (Paris: Seuil, 1964), 151–52.

with percipience in his writings. In a mostly condemnatory piece on La Rochefoucauld, La Bruyère, Vauvenargues, and Chamfort, Francis Jeanson sums up their work as "la dénonciation systématique d'une nature humaine tarée."[8] By this judgment, Jeanson is of course agreeing with the nowadays widely held, quasi-official view of the French moralists, especially French moralists of the late seventeenth century. Once his discussion reaches Chamfort, however, Jeanson's tone abruptly changes. He manifestly and unequivocally admires the moralist of the Revolution, "qui se garde de moraliser" and who, "affranchi de toute précaution et de tout calcul ... se livre sans réserve au hasard de ses observations" (103–4). Jeanson then proceeds to assert that "Chamfort ne s'attaque pas à quelque 'nature humaine,' c'est *aux hommes* qu'il en veut" (105). At issue here is what René Girard more than three decades ago called "the false morality of essence which Sartre would like to see all of us abandon."[9] For Jeanson, the fundamental essentialism of the earlier three moralists is exposed for what it is by Chamfort's incipient existentialism, his capacity to pose moral questions in utterly concrete terms, caught "in situation," far from the factitious solidity of universals.

Jeanson, moreover, is hardly alone among twentieth-century writers in his preference for Chamfort over the other great moralists of France's past. For example, in an interview with Paul Guth, published to coincide with the appearance of *En vrac* (1956), Reverdy's third (and last) volume of notes and aphorisms, the poet declared, and not insignificantly given his near-perfect, La Rochefoucauld-like maxims of earlier times: "A force de l'avoir lu et commenté, j'ai chez moi un Descartes complètement désossé. Comme un La Bruyère, comme un La Rochefoucauld, auquel, maintenant, je préfère Chamfort."[10] Samuel Beckett turned several Chamfort maxims into poems.[11] E. M. Cioran, possibly France's greatest living *moraliste*, has written approvingly of Beckett's fascination with Chamfort.[12]

8. Francis Jeanson, *Lignes de départ* (Paris: Seuil, 1963), 72. Subsequent page references to this work are in the body of the study, in parentheses.

9. René Girard, "Existentialism and Criticism," in *Sartre: A Collection of Critical Essays*, ed. Edith Kern (Englewood Cliffs, N.J.: Prentice-Hall, 1962), 122. [Girard's essay first appeared in *Yale French Studies* 16 (Winter 1955–56): 45–52.]

10. Quoted in Paul Guth, "Pour Pierre Reverdy, poète du présent, l'homme est imperfectible jusqu'à l'infini," *Le Figaro littéraire* 524 (5 May 1956), 4.

11. Samuel Beckett, *Collected Poems in English and French* (New York: Grove, 1977), 122–37. ["Huit Maximes," in English verse, appear under the heading "Long After Chamfort."]

12. E. M. Cioran, *Exercices d'admiration: essais et portraits* (Paris: Gallimard, 1986), 107.

But no doubt the most thought-provoking paean to Chamfort by a twentieth-century French writer is Camus's preface to an edition of Chamfort's *Maximes et anecdotes* published in 1944.[13] In this consistently stimulating, unabashedly partisan, but never tendentious piece, Camus praises Chamfort for the far-reaching innovations he brought to moralistic writing, including his rejection of the sweeping generalization (7), and frozen portraiture, in favor of open-ended, dramatic depictions (10).

Camus's perhaps most telling comments about Chamfort touch on matters of literary genre or form that are alluded to in the second of the three parts of Louis Van Delft's definition of the neoclassical moralist—"qui adopte très généralement pour forme soit le traité, soit le fragment." The rubrics regularly applied to Chamfort's oeuvre, including those used in the edition prefaced by Camus—*caractères, anecdotes, maximes, pensées*—would tend to support Van Delft's rough taxonomy (an approximateness made inevitable by the taxonomy's brevity). In other editions of Chamfort, one finds analogous headings: *réflexions générales, petits dialogues philosophiques, axiomes, principes de morale, portraits.*[14] This nomenclature, in its aggregate, tends to ascribe considerable, if not complete, generic autonomy to French moralistic writing. On the other hand, anyone familiar with French literature knows the opposite to be the case. Thus, for example, one is hardly surprised to find Madame de Lafayette, Prévost, Constant and Fromentin, or even Stendhal and Gide, or indeed Camus himself, identified as moralists. In other words, French moralism indisputably, and long ago, fled the confines of the *maxime* and the *réflexion,* even if such brief textual vehicles typify it and have carried some of its most memorable formulations.

The great range of forms (and their seemingly endless proliferation) exploited by French moralists down through the centuries may explain, in part at least, Camus's palpable dissatisfaction with La Roche-

13. Camus's essay has been reprinted most recently in the "Collection Folio" edition of Chamfort's moralistic writings; see Chamfort, *Produits de la civilisation perfectionnée: maximes et pensées, caractères et anecdotes,* with preface by Albert Camus, introduction and notes by Geneviève Renaux (Paris: Gallimard, 1982), 5–15. Subsequent page references to this volume are in the body of the study, in parentheses.

14. See, e.g., the headings in Chamfort, *Maximes et anecdotes,* with preface by Albert Camus (Paris: Nouvel Office d'Edition, 1963) and Chamfort, *Oeuvres. Texte intégral des Produits de la civilisation perfectionée (maximes et anecdotes),* with introduction by Claude Roy (Paris: Le Club français du livre, 1960).

foucauld's *maxime* (6). Significantly, Camus places Chamfort in a totally different class from La Rochefoucauld: "Or l'intérêt de
Chamfort est qu'il n'écrit pas de maximes, à quelques exceptions
près" (7). Like Jeanson, Camus is much impressed by Chamfort's
seizing upon the specific details of individual lives: "Il fait penser
d'abord à Stendhal qui est allé chercher comme lui l'homme où il se
trouvait, c'est-à-dire dans la société et la vérité où elle se cache, dans
ses traits particuliers... et il est possible sans paradoxe de parler de
Chamfort comme d'un romancier. Car mille traits... finissent par
composer chez lui une sorte de roman inorganisé... inavoué" (8).
That he is willing to go to such lengths in order to confer the title of
novelist on Chamfort reflects Camus's conviction, also articulated
in his preface to the *Maximes et anecdotes,* that "nos plus grands
moralistes ne sont pas des faiseurs de maximes, ce sont des
romanciers" (5).

In the end, Camus's claims for Chamfort bring us face to face with
an inescapable reality, the plurality of forms to which French moralism has given rise ever since La Rochefoucauld's time (and before).
Although not always comfortable with this reality—the protean
quality of French moralistic writing—students of the subject, including such distinguished ones as Van Delft, have had to concede that its
very breadth and variability, while frustrating for those seeking to
define the phenomenon, have contributed enormously to establishing its dominance within French literature.

Implicit in all of the foregoing, and so unself-consciously present
as to seem a given, lurks the assumption, by now unquestioned, that
one of the most striking constants in French literature is its powerful
moralistic strain, its obsessive, continuous exploration of human
frailty. Within this single strain, moreover, two distinct if occasionally
overlapping currents coexist, one broad, the other narrow. On the
one hand, there are the dramatist-moralists, the novelist-moralists,
the essayist-moralists and the poet-moralists; on the other, there are
the deliberately economical moralists, the purists, the distillers,
those who offer their potion neat, in brief, self-contained forms like
the maxim.

To French moralists, of both broad and narrow persuasion, sooner
or later the individual human being becomes the measure of everything human, which brings us to the third (and last) component of
Van Delft's definition of the moralist, the notion of particularism:

"l'écrivain . . . dont l'attitude consiste à se maintenir avant tout à hauteur d'homme, du fait du vif intérêt qu'il porte au vécu." Whether leaning to the cosmic or the quotidian, whether practicing brief, undiluted forms like the maxim, or longer, mixed ones like the novel, all concentrate, ultimately, not on the divine or on some idealized version of themselves, but on the whole human continuum in all its splendid, miserable variety ("l'attitude consiste à se maintenir avant tout à hauteur d'homme").

When the multifarious scriptural activities of all of these writers are viewed conspectually, across century and form, Chamfort, especially in his searing, detailed *anecdotes,* becomes a kind of two-way prism, refracting and mediating everything. After Chamfort, French moralism will fan out to include the narratives of Stendhal, Flaubert, and Proust, but without forsaking its original concerns. Looking back through Chamfort, we see French moralism again expanding, this time to take in, besides such obvious "narrow" practitioners as La Rochefoucauld and La Bruyère, the likes of Madame de Lafayette and Montaigne.

The following two Chamfort *anecdotes,* chosen almost at random in his oeuvre, typify the radiant, suggestive power of his writing:

> 1. Voici une anecdote que j'ai ouï conter à M. de Clermont-Tonnerre sur le baron de Breteuil. Le baron, qui s'intéressait à M. de Clermont-Tonnerre, le grondait de ce qu'il ne se montrait pas assez dans le monde. "J'ai trop peu de fortune," répondit M. de Clermont. "Il faut emprunter: vous payerez avec votre nom." "Mais, si je meurs?" "Vous ne mourrez pas." "Je l'espère; mais si cela arrivait?" "Eh bien, vous mourriez avec des dettes, comme tant d'autres." "Je ne veux pas mourir banqueroutier." "Monsieur, il faut aller dans le monde: avec votre nom, vous devez arriver à tout. Ah! si j'avais eu votre nom!" "Voyez à quoi il me sert." "C'est votre faute. Moi, j'ai emprunté; vous voyez le chemin que j'ai fait, moi qui ne suis qu'un *pied-plat.*" Ce mot fut répété deux ou trois fois, à la grande surprise de l'auditeur, qui ne pouvait pas comprendre qu'on parlât ainsi de soi-même.

> 2. Une femme avait un procès au parlement de Dijon. Elle vint à Paris, sollicita M. le garde des sceaux de vouloir bien écrire,

en sa faveur, un mot qui lui ferait gagner un procès très juste; le garde des sceaux la refusa. La comtesse Talleyrand prenait intérêt à cette femme; elle en parla au garde des sceaux: nouveau refus. Mme de Talleyrand en fit parler par la reine; autre refus. Mme de Talleyrand se souvint que le garde des sceaux caressait beaucoup l'abbé de Périgord, son fils; elle fit écrire par lui: refus très bien tourné. Cette femme, désespérée, résolut de faire une tentative, et d'aller à Versailles. Le lendemain, elle part; l'incommodité de la voiture publique l'engage à descendre à Sèvres, et à faire le reste de la route à pied. Un homme lui offre de la mener par un chemin plus agréable et qui abrège; elle accepte et lui conte son histoire. Cet homme lui dit: "Vous aurez demain ce que vous demandez." Elle le regarde et reste confondue. Elle va chez le garde des sceaux, est refusée encore, veut partir. L'homme l'engage à coucher à Versailles; et le lendemain matin lui apporte le papier qu'elle demandait. C'était un commis d'un commis, nommé M. Etienne.[15]

Both of the very brief *anecdotes* above, it will be noted, thematize insistent repetition, which creates the illusion of greater length and substance than either text actually possesses. Also, thanks to this device, we have the distinct impression of having stepped "barefoot into reality," in the words of Wallace Stevens, of having entered the realm of *le vécu* with all of its dailiness, all of its ordinary redundancies. In both texts we thus sense the presence of teeming life located just out of sight or beyond hearing. In each case, clearly, we are confronting, in embryonic, schematic form, the makings of a tale, if not indeed of an entire novel.

But the differences between the two texts, or, more precisely, their complementarity, may be more interesting in the end than their similarities. The first *anecdote,* in announcing its genre, exhibits a degree of textual self-consciousness rare even for Chamfort. Also, the interlocutors in this text are drawn from French history (the

15. Chamfort, *Produits de la civilisation perfectionnée,* "Collection Folio," 196–97; 199–200. It is perhaps worth recalling that Chamfort wrote a prize-winning *éloge* in honor of La Fontaine who, a century earlier, had practiced that miniature narrative/moralist verse form, the *fable,* with a sophistication unparalleled since Aesop's time; in this connection, see Claude Arnaud, *Chamfort* (Paris: Robert Laffont, 1988), 80–81.

baron de Breteuil in fact turns up in several of Chamfort's *anec-dotes*), while the central figure in the second *anecdote* remains un-identified, which raises the possibility of invention, of fiction, however verisimilar the story being told. The first text, practically a *saynète* (comic playlet), consists largely in the dialogue between Breteuil and Clermont, while the second, dominated by narrated ac-tion and indirect discourse, contains only one direct quotation: "Vous aurez demain ce que vous demandez," which is uttered by the obscure, virtually anonymous clerk of a clerk, Monsieur Etienne.

The first text turns inward, toward character, while the second faces out onto the public sphere, toward behavior and mores, polit-ical power and influence, both real, within one's grasp, and imag-ined, merely sought or desired. The first *anecdote* offers a subtle, comparative (and contrastive) study of *amour-propre* and the price exacted by burning ambition in the currency of self-abasement. The second presents a fleeting yet revealing glimpse into the nether-world of influence peddling (or its counterfeit) in high places, the capriciousness of favors given and received in such circles, and for-tune's ironic, all-determining role in these matters, as here in the form of the spontaneous act of kindness performed by a lowly stranger, who elects to help a powerless woman with only her just cause to speak for her. Between them, these two *anecdotes* suggest a maxim by La Rochefoucauld fleshed out and a novel by Stendhal or Flaubert sketched out. In this sense, Chamfort prefigures the novel's eventual takeover of the larger *moraliste* enterprise.

Chamfort's perennial "modernity" as a moralist also reveals itself in his critical self-awareness, his readiness to acknowledge the limits of the maxim. As Geoffrey Bennington has reminded us, Chamfort declared the form and its users guilty of "the falsity of over-generalisation." In Chamfort's own words, quoted by Bennington: "Les moralistes, ainsi que les philosophes qui ont fait des systèmes en physique ou en métaphysique, ont trop généralisé, ont trop mul-tiplié les maximes."[16] Bennington further comments that in the lengthy liminal text of his "Maximes Générales," Chamfort positions the maxim, in terms of logic, "at the end of a process of induction" rather than at the start of such a process, and, although "a result

---

16. Geoffrey Bennington, *Sententiousness and the Novel: Laying Down the Law in Eighteenth-Century French Fiction* (Cambridge: Cambridge University Press, 1985), 24. Sub-sequent page references to this work are in the body of the study, in parentheses.

rather than its beginning . . . it cannot be invoked dogmatically as absolute truth" (26). Guided by Bennington's gloss of Chamfort's text, we can perceive not only a "change in the status of the maxim" (25), but also a radical foregrounding of this primary vehicle of neoclassical moralists, and a questioning of its oracular, conclusive thrust. Possibly for the first time, a typically hardheaded writer of maxims includes in his inventory of humanity's weaknesses one of the basic tools he employs when plying his moralist's trade.

Chamfort's lucidity in this area makes us curious to know whether other French moralists were capable of reappraising their scriptural routines and procedures. A brief excursus into the role of self-consciousness within the moralistic tradition in French letters can shed light on just this point.

Doubtless some of the maxim's limitations or drawbacks, including those noted by Chamfort, derive from its roots in speech and social intercourse. As Peter Brooks has pointed out: "The idea of publishing a collection of maxims occurs only after one has essayed and polished them in conversations in a drawing room."[17] He attributes special significance to the fact that the little world of the salon, in which La Rochefoucauld's maxims were honed, was for all practical purposes autonomous, self-sufficient, cut off from the great world beyond its walls. Specifically, Brooks adduces a direct correlation between the maxim's source, its self-contained milieu of origin, and its regulating, excluding, restrictive power: "La Rochefoucauld finds meaning in his world, and gives meaning to his world, by a language which actively mimes the world's enclosure, which defines and fixes limits" (64–65). The correspondence that Brooks perceives between La Rochefoucauld's setting and his writing, leads us to suspect that Chamfort's malaise with the maxim's tendency to foreclose on intractable life may have induced him to try other, more open forms, like the *anecdote*, for rendering that life.

In a broader sense, however, we may simply be addressing here an element in French moralistic writing (of the "narrow" variety) that, in one fashion or another, has accompanied it ever since its inception, namely, its scriptural self-consciousness. We have already seen, for example, in our consideration of several perfectly fashioned

---

17. Peter Brooks, *The Novel of Worldliness: Crébillon, Marivaux, Laclos, Stendhal* (Princeton: Princeton University Press, 1969), 66. Subsequent page references to this work are in the body of the study, in parentheses.

neoclassical maxims by Reverdy, how the form itself implies an almost exquisite degree of self-monitoring on the author's part. In
addition, from the start maxims were, as Brooks has reminded us, an
inherently oral form, in that they were first spoken, then refined in
salon banter, and only later published. Aesthetic concerns, therefore,
must have always weighed as heavily on the maxim sayer/writer's
mind as ethical ones, considerations of style as urgently as those of
psychology, wit as much as wisdom. Thus it was perhaps inevitable
that the *moraliste* tradition in French letters would eventually ac-
quire a patently metalinguistic component.

If La Rochefoucauld's misgivings about his moralist's tools are less
exclusively centered on the maxim than Chamfort's, they are no less
real than Chamfort's. According to Odette de Mourgues, La Rochefoucauld's *Réflexion 16* is one of his most illuminating texts for us to
consider in this regard, being obsessively concerned "with definitions and classifications yet stat[ing] the fallacy of the classifying process. It is carefully and brilliantly written, but even so the writer
questions the value of the written word. . . . La Rochefoucauld's skepticism about the reliability of words . . . seems to extend to all the
terms he has to use."[18] In this same *Réflexion,* La Rochefoucauld also
contends, in keeping with the oral origins of his maxims, that the
many ways in which one can enunciate a handful of semantically
similar phrases cannot be reproduced exactly in writing, which can
never capture all the nuances available to the speaker of such
phrases.[19]

Roland Barthes, in his critique of the *Maximes,* takes La Rochefoucauld's "skepticism about the reliability of words" a giant step further. Barthes's essays on La Rochefoucauld and La Bruyère may be
the first ever on these foundation figures of French *moralisme* to
call attention to the boomerang effect accompanying the maxim (or
portrait) writer's demystifying maneuver. He observes the unavoidable circularity that connects La Rochefoucauld's reservations about
humanity with his doubts about himself as an expounder of these
reservations: "La démystification infinie que les *Maximes* mettent
en scène ne pouvait laisser à l'écart (et à l'abri) le faiseur de ma-

---

18. Odette de Mourgues, *Two French Moralists,* 13.
19. See François de La Rochefoucauld, *Oeuvres complètes,* ed. L. Martin-Chauffier and
J. Marchand (Paris: Gallimard, 1964), 527–30, esp. 529.

ximes lui-même."[20] Barthes detects an even larger measure of critical self-awareness in La Rochefoucauld's disciple, La Bruyère,
deeming the opening chapter of *Les Caractères,* entitled "Des ouvrages de l'esprit," its author's definition of his entire undertaking:
"au niveau du discours." Barthes asserts: "Il semble que La Bruyère
ait très consciemment mené une certaine réflexion sur l'être de
cette parole singulière que nous appelons aujourd'hui littérature."
And he marvels that La Bruyère should devote "au livre tout un
chapitre de son oeuvre, et ce chapitre est le premier, comme si toute
réflexion sur l'homme devait d'abord fonder en principe la parole
qui la porte."[21] Thus, according to Barthes, nothing is taken for
granted by La Bruyère, least of all the language in which the por-
traitist couches his "réflexion sur l'homme." Reading Barthes on La
Rochefoucauld and La Bruyère together, one infers that for these
writers at least, interrogating the human heart involves interrogating
human speech, that moralistic analysis and metalinguistic commentary of necessity go hand in hand.

But long before his seventeenth-century successors were to
achieve such an amalgam, Montaigne, the initiatory figure in Chamfort's historical schematic of French moralistic writing, had already
fused concerns of the heart with those of the tongue. Montaigne's
tentative, digressive, highly allusive style testifies to the presence in
his *Essais* of a scriptural consciousness deeply sensitive to and wary
about its own comportment. Besides the effect of continuous self-
correction that the *Essais* as a whole create, moreover, there are specific passages, here and there throughout the work, in which the
essayist expresses grave doubts about language as a reliable medium
of communication. The conclusion of "De l'incertitude de nostre
jugement," which is typical in this regard, has Montaigne paraphras-
ing (as is his wont) a text from classical antiquity, while explicitly
relating the inevitable uncertainty of human reasoning with the
fated errancy of humans speaking: "Nous raisonnons hazardeuse-
ment et inconsiderément, dict Timaeus en Platon, par ce que,
comme nous, nos discours ont grand participation au hasard."[22]

20. Roland Barthes, *Le Degré zéro de l'écriture, suivi de Nouveaux Essais critiques* (Paris: Seuil, 1972), 86.
21. Roland Barthes, *Essais critiques* 235.
22. Michel de Montaigne, *Essais,* ed. Maurice Rat (Paris: Garnier Frères, 1952), 1:319.

Another of Montaigne's seventeenth-century disciples, if on the oblique, is Molière, whom Paul Bénichou, in his classic *Morales du grand siècle,* calls one of the "trois moralistes les plus grands de ce siècle."[23] For Bénichou, Molière (and not, significantly, La Bruyère) dramatizes "une morale mondaine, à la fois sans illusions et sans angoisse, qui nous refuse la grandeur sans nous ôter la confiance" (11). Still, Bénichou's admiration for Molière does not prevent him from acknowledging the essential validity of Rousseau's celebrated attack (in his *Lettre sur les spectacles*) on *Le Misanthrope,* whose opening scene, it will be recalled, consists in the virtually formal debate between Alceste and Philinte on the question of how best to live in this world, while taking fully into account the incurable failings of human nature. Partisan of Molière though he is, Bénichou observes that "Rousseau . . . décrit, lui-même, avec une justice et une pénétration plus fréquentes chez lui qu'on ne veut bien le dire, les circonstances affectives souvent déplorables de la misanthropie même vertueuse" (352), and he ends his treatment of the Rousseau-Molière controversy with the following categorical declaration concerning Rousseau: "On peut lui reprocher son système de morale, mais non son manque de clairvoyance" (352 n. 1).

Before breaking off our discussion of Molière, however, we should note that France's greatest comic playwright had his own generous share of critical self-awareness, as is attested in his polemical plays, *La Critique de l'Ecole des femmes* and *L'Impromptu de Versailles.* Molière's theater as a whole, moreover, would surely support Lionel Abel's provocative claim in *Metatheatre* that "after Hamlet it would be difficult for any playwright to make us respect any character lacking dramatic consciousness."[24] Further, in Molière, such "dramatic consciousness" can even impinge on a character's view of the words he or she utters. As Judd Hubert has reminded us, language is explicitly problematized in at least four of Molière's plays: *Dom Juan, Le Bourgeois Gentilhomme, Les Femmes savantes,* and *Le Malade imaginaire.*[25] More generally, as Hubert contends, "words . . . appear

23. Paul Bénichou, *Morales du grand siècle* (Paris: Gallimard, 1948), 11. Subsequent page references to this work are in the body of the study, in parentheses.

24. Lionel Abel, *Metatheatre: A New View of Dramatic Form* (New York: Hill and Wang, 1963), 58.

25. Judd D. Hubert, *Molière and the Comedy of Intellect* (Berkeley and Los Angeles: University of California Press, 1962), 118–22, 222–26, 241–44, 255–57. Subsequent page references to this work are in the body of the study, in parentheses.

in all of Molière's comedies as the greatest enemies of the action and the staunchest upholders of convention. As such, they fare scarcely better than reasoning" (118). Thus in Molière, as in Montaigne before him, inadequacies of reasoning and those of speech are seen to correspond. In both writers, but especially in the playwright, continuity obtains between a fundamentally flawed inner faculty and its principal outward manifestation, language.

Rousseau has also been explicitly linked (e.g., in Van Delft) to the tradition of moralism in French letters.[26] But what makes Rousseau's oeuvre especially pertinent in the present circumstances, besides, as we have just noted, the critique of Molière's moralism that Jean-Jacques included in his *Lettre sur les spectacles*, is his rigorous if highly speculative *Essai sur l'origine des langues*, as well as his startlingly personal apologias, *Les Confessions* and *Les Rêveries d'un promeneur solitaire*. In the *Essai*, the object of intense scholarly scrutiny in recent decades,[27] Rousseau displays a profound grasp of the centrality of the linguistic factor in any sustained inquiry into the rise of human society and the nature of the human condition. In *Les Confessions* and *Les Rêveries*, on the other hand, he embarks on a search for self-understanding and self-validation that will chart a course for others to follow in the future. In these works, Rousseau obscures the frontiers between autobiography, fiction and the essay, while enlarging the terrain of each. He states, for example, in his *Première Promenade*: "Je fais la même entreprise que Montaigne, mais avec un but tout contraire au sien: car il n'écrivait ses *Essais* que pour les autres, et je n'écris mes rêveries que pour moi."[28] As for the *Confessions*, here the recurrent dramatization of the author's persona continually underscores the text's fictive dimension. A comparable drift toward the imaginative marks the *Essai*, as when Rousseau argues for the figurative as opposed to the literal origins of speech by positing a primitive man alone in the forest who, on first

26. Van Delft, *Le Moraliste classique*, 12.

27. See Jacques Derrida, *De la grammatologie* (Paris: Minuit, 1967), 235–378; Paul de Man's analysis of both Rousseau's text and Derrida's commentary in *Blindness and Insight: Essays in the Rhetoric of Contemporary Criticism* (New York: Oxford University Press, 1971), 11–141; and Gerald L. Bruns's critique of both Derrida and de Man on Rousseau in *Inventions: Writing, Textuality and Understanding in Literary History* (New Haven: Yale University Press, 1982), 88–107.

28. Jean-Jacques Rousseau, *Les Rêveries du promeneur solitaire*, ed. Samuel de Sacy (Paris: Gallimard, 1965), 37.

encountering his own kind, in a spontaneous cry of terror calls them "giants"; only later, after his fear has subsided, does he call them "men."[29]

In his idiosyncratic way, Rousseau may be as instructive a figure as Chamfort for our appreciation of the emergent confluence of moralism and metalanguage in French letters. Like his contemporary, Rousseau preferred solitude to society, and seemed bent on exposing, in a cluster of genres, the vices of humans living in society. Unlike Chamfort, however, Rousseau wrote a lengthy separate essay on the nature and provenance of speech, which concludes rather gloomily on the low level to which language has now purportedly fallen. If he himself did not fully coordinate his bleak dissection of human society with his dark speculations about human speech, points of contact between the two concerns can nonetheless be located in his oeuvre—one thinks immediately of his *Discours sur l'origine de l'inégalité*, in which the two foci occasionally intersect.[30] In any event, Rousseau's richly imagined, elaborately developed disquisitions on both subjects may well have enabled future French writers, specifically novelists, to merge the two activities in their fictions, in pursuit of parallel and, perhaps, corresponding defects. Working (unwittingly) in tandem with Chamfort's phalanxlike *anecdotes,* Rousseau, through his extremely varied writings, advanced the joint cause of moralism and metalanguage along a broad, interconnected textual front.

It was not until the mid-nineteenth century, however, in a novel that is in some ways the natural fulfillment of the promise represented by Montaigne, La Rochefoucauld, La Bruyère, Chamfort, and Rousseau together, that moralism and metalanguage would overtly collaborate in French literature. The site of the joint venture would be *Madame Bovary,* where Flaubert conducts a twofold exploration with a panache and verve all his own. (In the present context, it is surely worth noting that many editions of Flaubert's masterpiece carry on the title page the subtitle "moeurs de province.") In this, the centerpiece of the narrative canon in post-Romantic French literature, the novelist achieves a perfect blend of moralistic analysis

29. See Jean-Jacques Rousseau, *Essai sur l'origine des langues* (Paris: Bibliothèque du graphe, 1967). [A pamphlet reprinted from A. Belin's 1817 edition of Rousseau's works.]

30. See Jean-Jacques Rousseau, *Discours sur l'origine et les fondements de l'inégalité,* ed. Bertrand de Jouvenel (Paris: Gallimard, 1965), 63–70.

and metalinguistic commentary. Throughout his text, Flaubert co-ordinates a character's degree of moral callousness with his or her measure of linguistic obtuseness. Emma alone transgresses this "law" of correlative values. That she remains unaware of the controlling effect of all utterance yet manages to avoid the implicit moral censure that everywhere else in the novel is reserved for such stupidity, serves merely to emphasize that she is acting heroically in a situation in which the oppressive, foreclosing weight of clichés and the flaws of human character become sides of the same coin, produce similarly tragic results.

Flaubert's interest in clichés asserted itself early on and stayed with him until the end of his days. Almost everywhere, for example, in the posthumously published *Bouvard et Pécuchet* and *Le Dictionnaire des idées reçues,* one finds evidence of a profound fascination with clichés—clichés of language, of thought, and of behavior. These works also make plain the novelist's disgust with humanity's blindness to, and meanness of spirit because of, the web of bromides in which it is ensnared. But a full quarter of a century before writing *Bouvard et Pécuchet,* Flaubert was already drawn irresistibly to the cliché, as an inspection of the variorum edition of *Madame Bovary* reveals; many of the passages cut from the novel in the course of its laborious composition are the hackneyed obiter dicta of Bovary *père* and Homais.[31] A decade earlier still, Flaubert's obsessive concern with the paralyzing incrustations of verbal habit shows up in his letters, where he often juggles a variety of conventionalized voices (a trait of his that became particularly apparent with the publication of volume 1 of the unexpurgated *Correspondance* in 1973). For example, in a letter to Ernest Chevalier written in July 1844, when Flaubert was only twenty-two, the tone shifts abruptly from award-ceremony speechifying to classic schoolboy obscenity, with the letter's signatory, Flaubert himself, obviously in command of both voices, as well as of the shifts between them.[32]

31. See Gustave Flaubert, *Madame Bovary, nouvelle version précédée des scénarios inédits,* ed. Jean Pommier and Gabrielle Leleu (Paris: Corti, 1949). For a brief but suggestive characterization of the excisions that Flaubert made in his manuscript while preparing it for publication, see John Porter Houston, *Fictional Technique in France, 1802–1927* (Baton Rouge: Louisiana State University Press, 1972), 71–72.

32. Gustave Flaubert, *Correspondance, I (janvier 1830 à avril 1851),* ed. Jean Bruneau (Paris: Gallimard, 1973), 211–12.

As a stylistic device in his fiction, this coupling of discordant voices or codes reaches perhaps its highest point in the celebrated *comices agricoles* section of *Madame Bovary*, where Rodolphe seeks to seduce Emma with a string of Romantic clichés. By way of counterpoint, it will be recalled, congratulatory bombast accompanying the distribution of prizes wafts up to the lovers from the square below their window, sporadically interrupting, and unwittingly (as it were) commenting upon Rodolphe's ardent jargon. Unlike the rhetorical situation of the letter, however, now it is not a signature, but the mere interweaving of conflicting yet oddly complementary recitations that betrays the presence of an ironic viewer or narrator.[33]

Through his depiction of the druggist Homais, the most treacherous and cliché-prone figure in the novel, especially of Homais's relationship with the priest Bournisien, Flaubert renders his harshest judgment of bourgeois society. It is this world that would stifle the threat to the established order that Emma's refractory, self-destructive, profoundly unsettling comportment represents. Until Emma's wake, Homais and Bournisien are shown to be unyielding adversaries, ideological enemies to the death. Together, they constitute a variation on the theme of the perennial tug-of-war in France between *curé* and *instituteur*. As such, they symbolize the rival claims of France's Christian and Republican heritages, those warring historical currents that between them, according to conventional wisdom, define or specify what France is and that, though inimical, join in common cause during her hour of need (as is illustrated, for instance, in Louis Aragon's Resistance poem "La Rose et le réséda"). It is this quasi-sacred, semi-official myth of France that Flaubert explodes at Emma's wake, with the startling, eerily inevitable *entente cordiale* of priest and druggist.

An ambience of claustrophobic misogyny permeates Emma's world, and becomes almost palpable at the moment of her death. There, as throughout her life, the parameters of her consciousness are defined by a combination of sacred and profane texts, scripts that ratify Emma's sense of herself as a sensual, fallen woman, a transgressor of patriarchal laws, thus a living validation of misogynistic clichés. The last words she hears are the prayers of the priest per-

---

33. Gustave Flaubert, *Madame Bovary*, ed. Claudine Gothot-Mersch (Paris: Garnier, 1971), 145–55. Subsequent page references to this work are in the body of the study, in parentheses.

forming the final cleansing sacrament of Extreme Unction, and, moments later, the vaguely salacious ditty of the blind beggar. Recognizing the beggar's song, Emma sits bolt upright on her death bed, cries "L'Aveugle!" and with her very last breath laughs "d'un rire atroce, frénétique, désespéré" (332). In the end, the grace of ironic vision saves her, or comes as close to doing so as is required by the demands of heroism in literature.

In yet another of the cruel ironies that abound in *Madame Bovary,* Justin, who worships Emma, is the one who gives her access to the arsenic with which she kills herself. But when he sees her eating the poison (instead of merely taking some to exterminate rats, her declared purpose in asking for it), Justin cries out "Arrêtez!" (320) and tries, unsuccessfully, to stop her. Justin's shouted command in this circumstance is one of his extremely rare utterances in the novel. Most of the time by far, he remains in the background, a shadowy, silent, nearly aphasic figure of pubescent longing. He is in love with Emma, but his is the unnoticed, inarticulate attachment of the early adolescent to the mature woman.

Like that other mooning adolescent, Chérubin in *Le Mariage de Figaro,* Justin is fascinated by everything about the object of his adoration, including articles of her clothing. And as with Chérubin, whose part, significantly, is traditionally played by a woman, there is a great deal of indeterminancy in Justin's sexuality (in variation on the theme of shifting sexuality embodied by Emma). For example, when the apprentice pharmacist faints "like a woman" at the sight of blood, Homais, his employer and master, chastizes him: "Il faudra pourtant garder son sangfroid, raisonner, se montrer homme . . . !" (133). But Justin will never "se montrer homme," just as he will almost never speak, since to be a man in *Madame Bovary* means to speak with ease and in so doing join Emma's oppressors. Clearly, as Leo Bersani has observed, "Flaubert reserves his deepest sympathy for the dumb."[34] Justin's immense, unspoken love for Emma is that of a child, a speechless Chérubin, a diffident male still uncompromised by the language of men. Long before *Bouvard et Pécuchet* and *Le Dictionnaire des idées reçues* saw print, *Madame Bovary* dramatized Flaubert's abiding conviction that humanity's gravest flaw flowed from its dullest need, the thick, imperious, unassuageable desire (of

34. Leo Bersani, *Balzac to Beckett: Center and Circumference in French Fiction* (New York: Oxford University Press, 1970), 170.

adult males, real or would-be) to make definitive statements, to formulate conclusions.[35]

One of the ironies involved in recognizing that *Madame Bovary*
supersedes previous avatars of French moralism, arises from the fact
that this tradition, in its "narrow" variety especially, at times exhibits
a strong antifemale bias, a legacy no doubt of medieval *gauloiserie,*
reinforced and frozen in place by the Querelle des Femmes of Rabelais's time. Many a *maxime,* a *portrait* or an *anecdote,* for example,
today simply dismay by their arrant misogyny. But thanks precisely
to the interplay of its moralistic and metalinguistic elements, *Madame Bovary* rejects out of hand this dubious aspect of the *moraliste* heritage. Instead, the novel shows that Emma suffers and dies in
fact because she is a woman struggling to live according to codes
that have been devised (quite literally dictated) by tyrannical, lout-
ish males. As Dennis Porter has observed: "The mode as well as the
choice of Emma's death constitute a bitter comment on male
sexuality."[36] Proper names even textually spell out the basic conflict
between woman (victim) and man (victimizer) in Flaubert's novel.
As Naomi Schor writes: "The structuring opposition of the novel
is . . . none other than Emma vs. Homais, a fundamental opposition
half-expressed, half-concealed by their names, which should be read
'Femm(a) vs. Hom(ais)—*Femme* (Woman) vs. *Homme* (Man).' "[37]
Thus, in, through, and by its very words, *Madame Bovary* proves
(among other things) that feminism and moralism need not be hostile, mutually exclusive currents in French literature. On the contrary, they collaborate very effectively indeed, especially when the
role of language as such is accorded the recognition it deserves.

In Chapters 2 through 7, I explore further combinations and per-
mutations of moralistic analysis and metalinguistic commentary in a
particular sequence of twentieth-century French narratives. As
chance would have it, the titles of the first and the last texts considered here, *L'Immoraliste* (1902) and *L'Usage de la parole* (1980),

35. "L'ineptie consiste à vouloir conclure," Flaubert once wrote to Louis Bouilhet; see
Charles Carlut, *La Correspondance de Flaubert: étude et répertoire critique* (Columbus: Ohio
State University Press, 1968), 599.

36. Dennis Porter, "*Madame Bovary* and the Question of Pleasure," in *Flaubert and Post-
modernism,* ed. Naomi Schor and Henry F. Majewski (Lincoln: University of Nebraska Press,
1984), 134.

37. Naomi Schor, *Breaking the Chain: Women, Theory and French Realist Fiction* (New
York: Columbia University Press, 1985), 12.

evoke the conceptual framework for the entire study, its dual preoccupation with ethics and/or manners and with words. Along the way,
Gide, Proust, Malraux, Camus, Duras, and Sarraute, each in his or her
own fashion, move ceaselessly back and forth between auscultations
of the heart and diagnoses of the tongue.

The first two novelists studied, Gide and Proust, reflect the exploratory, self-regarding aesthetic of High Modernism that permeated advanced artistic circles, in France and elsewhere, during the early
decades of this century. With these writers, as will be demonstrated
in some detail, moralism and metalanguage work together through,
for instance, the interplay of learned citation, self-quotation, and/or
repetition. The next two texts examined, *La Condition humaine*
and *La Peste,* illustrate a fundamentally different approach to the
writer's art in France, the notion of commitment in literature, the
belief that fiction especially can dramatize and possibly even influence sociopolitical realities, an approach that reached its peak during the 1930s and 1940s. Here, laconism, eloquence, silence,
dialogue, polyphony, and other metalinguistic devices and themes,
operate within a textual setting that is thoroughly *moralisé.* The last
two writers considered, Duras and Sarraute, represent still another
change in the status and function of the novel in twentieth-century
France: the shift into the postmodernist mode, an aesthetic whose
immediate precipitant (and incarnation) was the "nouveau roman"
that arose in the late 1950s, and which seems to have assimilated and
(at times) transcended the values and innovations of modernism.
Here, the blanks that can occur in conversation, as well as conversation itself (and, indeed, "subconversation"), are foregrounded, to
telling analytical effect. With all six novelists, as we shall discover, a
pitiless moralist and a merciless scriptor inhabit the same skin.

Chapter 8 concludes the study by elucidating important interconnections among the texts studied, such as, for example, the ways in
which a feminist outlook can be seen to inform novels as apparently
different as *Madame Bovary, La Condition humaine,* and *Le
Ravissement de Lol V. Stein.* Primarily, however, in this final chapter,
I briefly reexamine the narratives and novelists I have treated in the
earlier chapters, while identifying moralistic and metalinguistic preoccupations both within and among the pairs of writers involved.

All of the extremely varied narratives explored in this book oblige
readers to plumb the depths of the same fundamental, either/or

question: Are the words the novelist is using adequate to his or her elusive subject, the human condition—are they pertinent, accurate, invariably fair, unflinchingly honest—or, rather, do the novelist's words execute essentially formal maneuvers, engaging our interest through their patterns, not their reach? Simply put, are the novelist's words *just,* or are they *just* words? And what about a possible third, synthesizing option? These questions, posed directly here, underlie the inquiry conducted in the following chapters.

Part One

French Fiction
in the Modernist Age
(1900–1920)

Two

Fading (Sacred) Texts
and Dying (Guiding) Voices
in Gide's Early *Récits*

In recent decades, even amateur readers of fiction
have found it increasingly difficult to ignore the strategies employed
and the conventions observed in the narrative texts engaging their
attention. Virtually everywhere in fiction, moreover, but perhaps especially in post-*nouveau roman* France, the so-called traditional or
Balzacian novel has steadily lost ground, as has the novel reader's all-
too-comfortable illusion of apprehending a verisimilar moral universe in a reliable mirror of words. Accompanying this profound
change in the way in which novels are both written and read, critics
have more and more treated the genre as a "closed-circuit poesis
rather than [a] mimesis."[1] Accordingly, in their studies they have
with growing exclusivity sought to identify intertextual relationships or to track semiotic "laws" in action rather than to elucidate
the social, psychological, or other thematic concerns informing a particular piece of prose fiction. For novelists, critics, and readers alike,
experimentation and exploration within the genre have gradually

---

1. Robert Alter, *Motives for Fiction* (Cambridge: Harvard University Press, 1984), 11.

taken precedence over any recognizably human experience an individual novel may conjure up or reflect.

This fundamental shift in what had been the novel's apparent center of gravity since the mid-nineteenth century has of course not met with universal acceptance, especially in the United States. For example, impatient with the propensity of so much postmodern fiction to let its seams show, so to speak, John Updike has remarked: "While the novel as a form certainly asks for, and can absorb, a great deal of experimentation, it must at some point achieve self-forgetfulness and let pure event take over."[2] The author of *Rabbit Is Rich* and *Hugging the Shore* obviously feels that in fiction sentences *qua* sentences must inevitably yield pride of place to events and situations. Robert Alter, an astute and sympathetic critic of self-consciousness in fiction, has reminded us that flaunted artifice and blatant experimentation in the genre date back through Sterne and Diderot to Cervantes, and thus can scarcely be thought to have originated with Nabokov, Robbe-Grillet, or John Barth. The two great traditions in fiction, the self-conscious (or reflexive) and the realist, Alter further notes, have coexisted quite nicely since the *Quixote,* and often within the same work, each mode enriching and even grounding the other. He persuasively argues that some of the most compelling postmodern novels are intermittently illusionist, shot through with real-seeming if fragmentary human worlds. Like Updike, Alter clearly believes that self-forgetfulness must at least sporadically eclipse self-consciousness in a work of fiction if that work of fiction is to come to life as something more fully involving than a death-denying game of words.[3] I would suggest that André Gide, especially in his early *récits,* combines the reflexive and the realist narrative modes in ways that are particularly vivifying for the texts in question and that

2. John Updike, *New Yorker* (22 July 1985): 87 (in a review of Julian Barnes, *Flaubert's Parrot* [Knopf]). In the closing sentences of another of his essay-reviews in the *New Yorker,* this time of several works of fiction and autobiography by Michel Tournier, Updike pinpoints a major source of his irritation with (what he sees as) an excess of self-consciousness in a particular sector of recent fiction: "The novelist must be thoughtless, to some degree, in submitting to the world's facts; he must be naive enough, as it were, to let the facts flow through him and unreflectingly quicken recognition and emotion in his readers. And this the French find difficult to do" (*New Yorker* [10 July 1989]: 96).

3. See Alter, *Motives for Fiction,* 3–31; see also Alter's earlier study of the subject, *Partial Magic: The Novel as a Self-Conscious Genre* (Berkeley and Los Angeles: University of California Press, 1975), ix–xvi.

tend to validate, *bien avant la lettre,* both Updike's and Alter's manifest desire to incorporate self-consciousness in some larger perspective for the writing and reading of fiction.

With his highly self-conscious *soties* and his ambitious experimen-
tal novel *Les Faux-Monnayeurs,* together with his theoretical statements on art and literature, Gide probably contributed more than
any other French writer of his day to paving the way for the radical
specularity of the *nouveau roman* and its successors.[4] At the same
time, however, in his *récits* it is almost as if he anticipated, in order
to counter in advance as it were, the self-regarding orientation—if
not to say fixation—of so much French fiction since the 1950s. Considered on the one hand "a central figure in the development of
modern fictional self-consciousness"[5] and on the other as "obsédé
de morale,"[6] Gide embodies, especially in his earlier *récits,* that fusion or synthesis put forward by Roger Shattuck as an ideal, the
writer who can "reconcile the two undeniable extremes of art: its
urgent, realistic depiction of human life and its retreat to a self-
reflexive realm of language, forms and ideas."[7] The *récits* that Gide
published between 1902 and 1919—*L'Immoraliste, La Porte étroite,
Isabelle,* and *La Symphonie pastorale*—show the novelist attaining
on four quite different occasions a well-nigh perfect blend of "story"
(with its textual self-obliviousness) and "discourse" (with its textual
self-absorption). Throughout each of these narratives, metafictional
elements interpenetrate with an extended exposé of a specific human vice or weakness. Moreover, in these fictions writing per se is
both continually foregrounded and found wanting, while moralistic
analysis is undertaken repeatedly but always in vain. This pairing of
failed probings into the purely verbal and the strictly ethical may in
fact constitute the defining characteristic of the Gidian *récit.* Such, at
least, is the hypothesis that I propose to examine here with reference
to the novelist's earliest *récits, L'Immoraliste* (1902) and *La Porte
étroite* (1909).

4. For a discussion of Gide's contribution to the conditions that gave rise to the *nouveau
roman,* see Jean Ricardou, *Le Nouveau Roman* (Paris: Seuil, 1973), esp. 47–50. See also in this
connection Lucien Dällenbach, *Le Récit spéculaire: essai sur la mise en abyme* (Paris: Editions
du Seuil, 1977), 15–55.

5. Alter, *Partial Magic,* 159.

6. André Malraux, "Préface," *Cahiers André Gide* (Paris: Gallimard, 1973), 4:xxiii.

7. Roger Shattuck, *The Innocent Eye: On Modern Literature and the Arts* (New York: Farrar,
Straus and Giroux, 1984), 352.

When Gide claimed that France excelled not in the novel but in the realm of moralists, he was at once rehearsing a critical commonplace and revealing his own predilections as both a writer and a reader. He admired La Bruyère's *Les Caractères* enough to toy with the idea of attempting to rewrite it. Other figures he singled out for special praise in this regard bear further witness to the esteem in which he held France's "classical moment"—Montaigne, Pascal, Molière, Bossuet, La Fontaine, Corneille, and Racine.[8] The affinity he felt with the moralistic current in French letters was thus not only knowingly rooted, it was also sufficiently wide-ranging to encompass more forms than just the *maxime,* the *portrait,* and the *pensée.* His narrative practice, first and foremost his *récits,* would in fact incline one to imagine Gide's readily agreeing with Camus's assertion, included in the latter's preface to Chamfort's *Maximes et anecdotes,* that "Nos plus grands moralistes ne sont pas des faiseurs de maximes, ce sont des romanciers. Qu'est-ce qu'un moraliste en effet? Disons seulement que c'est un homme qui a la passion du coeur humain."[9] For both Camus and Gide, moralistic analysis would fare best in the commodious and yet rigourously focused—what Malraux might have called the "monographic"[10]—form of the *récit.* Is it only by chance that the title of Gide's first *récit* is *L'Immoraliste?* Given his critical sophistication and self-awareness in such matters, it seems far more likely that he chose his title with a view to linking his text antiphrastically with the whole *moraliste* tradition in French literature.

In the main part of *L'Immoraliste,* it will be recalled, a certain Michel, a young Frenchman now living in North Africa, gives an account of the last three years of his life to three friends he has summoned to his side, an account that, while never quite shading off into a confession, hovers somewhere among autobiography, *examen de conscience,* apologia, and manifesto. Through it, Michel, the "immoralist" of the title, emerges as a genuine moralist in Camus's sense of the term; that is, "un homme qui a la passion du coeur humain," be it only of his own heart.

8. André Gide, *Pretexts: Reflections on Literature and Morality,* trans. Justin O'Brien (New York: Meridian Books, 1959), 243–50, 294.

9. Albert Camus, "Préface" to Chamfort, *Maximes et anecdotes* (Paris: Nouvel Office d'Edition, 1963), 6. [This "Préface" was first published in 1944 by Editions Dac in Monaco.]

10. Malraux, "Préface," xxii.

Michel expresses his desire to uncover a deeper, purer, more authentic version of his self in terms of a scholar's efforts to read an older, truer, now obscured piece of writing: "Et je me comparais aux palimpsestes; je goûtais la joie du savant, qui, sous les écritures plus récentes, découvre, sur un même papier, un texte très ancien infiniment plus précieux. Quel était-il, ce texte occulté? Pour le lire, ne fallait-il pas tout d'abord effacer les textes récents?"[11] This striking analogy, which presides in one way or another over the entire narrative, is even richer and more suggestive than it might at first seem. For Michel compares himself and his search for self-knowledge *both* to palimpsests (parchments containing in the same space more than one text, with later ones written literally over now-obliterated earlier ones, including an *Urtext*) and to the paleographer who deciphers or at least glimpses, through the added-on layers of writing, that precious original inscription. Michel thus presents himself in this trope as both the multilayered set of writings and its cryptographer, as both the texts read and the texts' reader.

His quest begins with a ritual purging. Here and elsewhere in the narrative, Michel equates his erudition in particular and his formation more generally with artificial constraints imposed upon his "être authentique" (398) from without. Images of rebirth, renewal, and reawakening abound, always connoting a sloughing off of impedimenta, a casting aside of the shackles of culture and book learning. When Michel has his beard shaved off, for example, he intends the gesture to signify his "morale changée" (402), his stripping away the confining armor of a stultifying education, ethical and philological, moral and linguistic. Classical antiquity, ancient languages and civilizations, his areas of special interest as a scholar, are rejected. He now claims that "chaque jour croissait en moi le confus sentiment de richesses intactes, que couvraient, cachaient, étouffaient les cultures, les décences, les morales" (457). According to Michel, study and learning elide language, culture, and moral code, inasmuch as all three disciplines are internalized at the same time. All three must therefore be purged, thrown off at the same time.

Near the start of his quest for a stripped-down, essential self, Michel rereads three sentences from the *Odyssey* and finds "un

11. André Gide, *Romans: récits et soties, oeuvres lyriques,* ed. Yvonne Davet and Jean-Jacques Thierry, with introduction by Maurice Nadeau (Paris: Gallimard, 1958), 399. Subsequent page references to this work are in the body of the study, in parentheses.

aliment suffisant dans leur rhythme" (391), the sensual pleasure afforded him by their sheer musicality, not their meaning, satisfying him completely. Later, words pale to insignificance next to deeds. A trunk filled with books, dragged along on Michel's (and his wife Marceline's) return trip to North Africa, remains unopened. Above all, he wants to stop living the life of a "chartiste" (403), even though family background and formal training have destined him to view everything, including his own life, through the eyes of "un chartiste," a specialist in decoding ancient manuscripts and documents. He will thus liken his true self to the primordial script of a palimpsest; his task, in his own words, will be to erase recent texts ("effacer les textes récents") so that his original text-self, "aux caractères effacés" (399) might reappear. (Somewhat paradoxically, we note, erasures are expected to recover what has been erased.)

As Michel's narrative unfolds, it becomes quite obvious to the reader, if only partially and intermittently to Michel, that this *Urtext* of the self he is so ardently seeking is composed of unadulterated ego; it is a Nietzschean nightmare of a being, a self-willed, self-obsessed destroyer, an extravagant amalgam of the worst features of the Romantic hero. From time to time Michel catches fleeting, oblique sight of the regressive, brutish nature of his project, as when he speaks of it as "ce tragique élan vers un état plus sauvage" (407). For the most part, however, he goes about the business of self-cleansing and self-decipherment in a state of mind approaching solipsism. Through a succession of inverted preferences, he sheds the cloak of dedicated scholar and devoted husband for something more primitive. He chooses Africa over Europe, the barbarian invaders over the civilized Romans, the present over the past, the air of life over the dust of books, desert over oasis, spontaneity over the planned, the senses over the intellect. Eventually his reversals of old habits, values, and preferences include transgressions of accepted social norms and received moral codes. Self-indulgence replaces concern for others. Poaching on his own land by night with the amoral dregs of the local population supplants attending to the needs of his farmlands by day with reliable and available helpers. Gradually he drops the mask of heterosexual commitment in marriage and lets his heretofore repressed homosexual impulses shape his behavior.

Michel tries embracing the philosophy of the sinister mentor figure, Ménalque, namely, total freedom from social covenant and responsibility. But, finally, what does this avail him? Not very much, it would seem. At the end of his narrative he twice begs his friends to take him away with them, admitting that a paralyzing abulia has come over him: "Quelque chose en ma volonté s'est brisé" (471). But can he also acknowledge the (at least passive) role he played in his wife's death? And has he in fact gained access to his true self, does he at last know himself? His final words oblige us to answer both of these questions in the negative. He refuses, for example, to recognize his attachment to "le petit Ali" (472) for the homoerotic infatuation that it is. And in a characteristically semilucid moment he says: "Parfois j'ai peur que ce que j'ai supprimé ne se venge" (471). Like Mallarmé's hubristic "Pitre châtié," but less clearly, less completely, Michel senses, also too late, that his "fard"—in his case his entire intellectual and moral baggage—"était tout [son] sacre."

On one level, that of the story, Michel's narrative suggests that the human heart lies buried beneath incrustations of habit, especially verbal, book-learned habit, of which we should be infinitely suspicious. The story also shows that our supposedly true self, hidden under all these "outer" accretions and conventions, may be so unstable and lawless that, in trying to reach it, we risk unleashing destructive forces beyond our ken or control. The palimpsest seems the perfect metaphor for rendering this thematic structure, with the more recent but always already fading layers of writing corresponding to the necessarily precarious rules governing what we at any given time consider to be civilized society, the *Urtext* corresponding to the amorphous, doubtless unrecoverable, violent but sacred originating *Verbum*, and an individual life, Michel's, recapitulating in reverse the entire ascent of man, all of human history.

The enduring appeal, the monumentality (in Michael Riffaterre's sense of that term) of *L'Immoraliste*, however, derives from the way in which its thematics or "story" (or "énoncé"), as just outlined, interacts with its textuality or "discourse" (or "énonciation"), a phenomenon I should now like to explore, however briefly. In an analysis of Gide's first two *récits*, Albert Sonnenfeld refers, appropriately, to "the fearful symmetry of *L'Immoraliste*."[12] The excessive symmetry of Gide's *récit*, the great care given to such matters as

12. Albert Sonnenfeld, "On Readers and Reading in *La Porte étroite* and *L'Immoraliste*," *Romanic Review* 67 (May 1976): 172.

balance, parallelism, and contrast, calls attention to the text itself as a construct, as something made, fabricated. For example, the *Odyssey* is mentioned twice, once toward the beginning of Michel's narrative and again toward the end. On the first of these occasions Michel reads several sentences from the epic, while on the second it is not even opened. In an almost perfect parallel, the same passage from Scripture is quoted by Michel two different times, again, once toward the beginning of his narrative and once toward the end. Initially Michel *reads* the biblical verse, but on the later occasion he merely tries to remember it and is able to recollect only part of it. Then there is the obvious numerological bias of Michel's narrative, with its use (i.e., its abuse) of the mystical three and its multiples. It has been *three* years since Michel has seen his *three* friends. He rereads exactly *three* sentences from the *Odyssey.* His narrative is divided into *three* parts, with part one containing *nine* chapters, part two *three* chapters and part three *one* chapter. The crucial palimpsest analogy appears in chapter *six* of part one. There is also the inordinate number of rather facile oppositions, some of which have already been noted. To that list one could add the Catholic-Protestant polarity (which also turns up in other Gide *récits*), life versus death, reading versus being, monologue versus dialogue, male versus female, dead languages versus living languages, cold versus warmth, and so forth.

Finally, there are the patently implausible circumstances surrounding the provenance and nature of Michel's account of his life. A letter addressed to the prime minister of France by the prime minister's brother, which serves as a preamble to Michel's account, tells us, among other things, that the letter-writer (one of the three friends called to Michel's side to hear his story) functioned as Michel's scribe, copying down his words as they were spoken. Critics have pointed out that Michel's scribe would have needed a prodigious supply of paper, ink, and mental alertness to have carried out his Herculean recording task successfully.[13] As for Michel, in spite of his announcing his intention to "raconter [sa] vie, simplement" (372),

---

13. See Sonnenfeld, "On Readers," 182, and G. W. Ireland, "Le jeu des 'je' dans deux récits gidiens" in *Actes du Colloque André Gide (Toronto 1975)*, ed. Jacques Cotnam, Andrew Oliver, and C. D. E. Tolton (Paris: Minard, 1979), 69–80. For a broader discussion of the lack of verisimilitude in *L'Immoraliste,* see Arthur E. Babcock, *Portraits of Artists: Reflexivity in Gidean Fiction, 1902–1946* (York, S.C.: French Literature Publications, 1982), 15–27.

he would have to have been an unbelievably gifted oral stylist and rhetorician to have imparted to his tale the polish, nuance, and shapeliness it so manifestly possesses. Furthermore, the particular revisions that Gide made in the letter-preamble while composing it, as critics have also noted,[14] diminish rather than enhance the verisimilitude of Michel's utterance.

These essentially textual factors and features, along with others (e.g., the scribe's hesitation as to whether or not he should actually send Michel's narrative to his brother; the preface that Gide included in all editions of *L'Immoraliste* after the first, according to which the novelist would exempt Michel's tale from moral judgment, primarily on aesthetic grounds) have the effect of problematizing *L'Immoraliste*, of underscoring its artifice and autonomy, hence of stressing its "discourse" and, in the process, of undermining any exclusive focus we might be tempted to bring to bear on its "story." In the end, it becomes virtually impossible for readers not to wonder how story and discourse might be collaborating in Gide's *récit*. As long as he keeps on talking, Michel can perhaps sustain the fiction of an innocent self; at the very least, he can make his listeners postpone final judgment of his conduct. And even after he stops talking, as we have seen from the letter-preamble, his scribe remains perplexed, uncertain as to how he should interpret and respond to Michel's tale, and whether or not he should actually forward his transcription of it to his brother. The scribe's uncertainty regarding Michel's narrative also surfaces within it, shortly before the end, when Michel falls silent for a time. During this pause, the scribe notes down his private reaction to what he has heard, from which it is clear that for him Michel remains an opaque, inscrutable presence: "Je ne distingue pas en lui, même à présent, la part d'orgueil, de force, de sécheresse ou de pudeur" (471).

In his preface to *L'Immoraliste*, Gide distances himself from those who insist on choosing, for example, between *Le Misanthrope's* Alceste and Philinte when the latter debate the question of how best to live in human society, given the failings of human nature. In an attenuated echo of Flaubert's brusque contention that "l'inéptie consiste à vouloir conclure,"[15] Gide asserts: "Je ne prétends pas, certes,

---

14. See, for example, Babcock, *Portraits of Artists*, 16–17.
15. Charles Carlut, *La Correspondance de Flaubert: étude et répertoire critique* (Columbus:

que la neutralité (j'allais dire: *l'indécision*) soit signe sûr d'un grand esprit; mais je crois que maints grands esprits ont beaucoup répugné à ... conclure—et que bien poser un problème n'est pas le supposer d'avance résolu" (367). The ellipses before the word "conclure" in this passage convey, ironically (and iconically), Gide's reluctance, precisely, to conclude. And they remind us that this is exactly how Michel's narrative (and the book) ends—hesitantly, speculatively, decidedly not decisively: "Peut-être a-t-elle un peu raison ... " (472). The undecidable thus reigns supreme. Michel's voice trails off and dies, having decided on nothing. (The word "indécision," we recall, is emphasized by means of italics in the preface.)

In seeking the text of his true self, Michel eventually refuses even to open one of the great originating texts of Western civilization, Homer's *Odyssey*. As for the Bible, another basic text for the archetypically learned Michel, eventually he remembers only a few of the lines from it that he once thought he would never forget. As the sacred texts fade from his consciousness, Michel is deprived of their certitudes. His sole guide now is his own dying voice, by which he can provide himself with only the dubious reassurance of provisional innocence.

The interdependence of palimpsest and paleographer in *L'Immoraliste*, indeed their fusion in the figure of Michel, may be seen as a metaphor for the marriage of story and discourse in Gide's text, in the sense that each completes the other. Similarly, Michel recounts his life while his friend records the utterance, speaker and scribe needing each other for their mutual actualization. Michel's failed attempt to turn his glance fully back on himself, and thus to see the entire truth of his life, is mirrored in his inability to finish his story, to push it to a conclusion. Similarly, the absence of concluding remarks by the scribe deprives the book of the formally framed closure that the scribe's letter-preamble encourages us to anticipate. On the other hand, Gide's preface, written long after everything in the body of the *récit* was written, including scribal preamble and Michel's narrative, closes *L'Immoraliste* in no doubt the only way it can be closed, stressing from the outset the necessary inconclusiveness and the inevitable undecidability of this text and this life—and, possibly, of all texts and all lives.

Ohio State University Press, 1968), 599.

A more subtle kind of undecidability characterizes Gide's next *récit*, *La Porte étroite*, where moralistic and metalinguistic elements combine in an even more complex fashion than they do in *L'Immoraliste*. If anything, Gide's celebrated Socratic dictum: "Bien comprendre qui l'on est,"[16] appears to haunt his second *récit* even more pervasively than it does his first. Now it is not a question of just one character, Michel, seeking self-understanding, but of two, Jerome and Alissa. And although Gide himself seemed to think of the narratives interchangeably, or at least, as complementary, with the excessive individualism of Michel answering, so to speak, the excessive mysticism or self-abnegation of Alissa,[17] critics have demonstrated that in fact *La Porte étroite* shows considerable development on Gide's part in his handling of his chosen narrative form.[18] All of the questions that arose in connection with his first *récit* arise again regarding his second, but less schematically and more compellingly now than before.

From early on quotation is conspicuous in *La Porte étroite*. The title, for example, as the text's epigraph reveals, comes straight from the Gospel according to Luke. In a sense, the narrative itself consists of one long quotation, Jerome's first-person written account of his perpetually thwarted and eventually doomed love for his cousin Alissa. Jerome's "memoir," in turn, virtually bristles with quotations—from the Bible, from letters and conversations, from literary giants like Dante (quoted in Italian), Shakespeare (quoted in English), Goethe (in French translation), from such popular works of religious piety as the *Imitation de Jésus-Christ* and *Internelle Consolacion*, from Racine, Pascal, and Baudelaire, not to mention the briefer references to Swinburne, Malebranche, Leibniz, Shelley, Byron, Keats, Hugo, and Ronsard.

But by far the longest "quotation" in Jerome's account appears just before its end in the form of a two-part, fifteen-page insert that Jerome has stitched together from entries in Alissa's diary (581–95). Perhaps not surprisingly, this lengthy citation, interspersed with explanatory remarks by Jerome and containing its own quotations

---

16. Quoted and characterized as "un leitmotiv dans l'oeuvre d'André Gide" by Maurice Nadeau in his introduction to Gide, *Romans,* xxviii.

17. See Gide, *Romans,* 1546, 1549.

18. See, for example, Sonnenfeld, "On Readers," 172–80, and Babcock, *Portraits of Artists,* 29–47.

(from letters, from the Bible, from La Bruyère, Pascal, etc.), functions more effectively than any of the shorter quotations as a foil for Jerome's account, as a corrective for the narrative in which it is embedded. In *Rashomon* style, Alissa's journal, truncated though it is, gives readers an alternative version of the very same abortive love story that Jerome's memoir as a whole is recounting. I shall come back to this crucial point.

Positioned near the end of Jerome's account, Alissa's journal (or, more precisely, those parts of it that Jerome elects to quote) undermines what little faith we may still have in Jerome's lucidity, if not his veracity. This is doubly ironic since Jerome himself is our source for Alissa's journal and since he has sought from the very start to establish his credibility as an honest and objective if perhaps naive witness to his own life. From his opening paragraph, Jerome pointedly adopts a straightforward, unmeddling stance vis-à-vis his utterance:

> D'autres en auraient pu faire un livre; mais l'histoire que je raconte ici, j'ai mis toute ma force à la vivre et ma vertu s'y est usée. J'écrirai donc très simplement mes souvenirs, et s'ils sont en lambeaux par endroits, je n'aurai recours à aucune invention pour les rapiécer ou les joindre; l'effort que j'apporterais à leur apprêt gênerait le dernier plaisir que j'espère trouver à les dire. (495)

The thrust of this passage, especially its operative clause "J'écrirai donc très simplement mes souvenirs," recalls its near equivalent at the beginning of Michel's account of his life in *L'Immoraliste:* "[J]e vais vous raconter ma vie, simplement, sans modestie et sans orgueil, plus simplement que si je parlais à moi-même" (372). Later in his narrative Jerome will refer to his "simple récit" (566). Like Michel in *L'Immoraliste,* Jerome on still other occasions will claim that he is merely transcribing conversations as they occurred, neither adding nor subtracting anything. And when he introduces his selections from Alissa's diary, he asserts: "Je les transcris sans commentaires" (580). Perhaps his slyest assurance that he is offering us the undoctored truth comes with the last word in his first paragraph, "dire," which underscores the oral, hence quasi-citational status of the narrative, and at the same time implies that we are reading merely recorded speech. And what could be less calculating, less duplicitous than speech, especially simple, unedited speech?

But is Jerome's account of his life really as impartial as he would have us believe? The interplay of narrative and quotation peculiar to *La Porte étroite* would suggest that it is not. On four separate occasions when introducing passages taken from Alissa's letters or diary, Jerome makes it quite clear that the quoted material has been drawn from a larger source, one to which he alone has access. We also notice, Jerome's assertion to the contrary notwithstanding ("Je les transcris sans commentaires"), that in fact he intersperses his extracts from Alissa's journal with comments, comments that serve to emphasize that he is including only selections from his source. Further, we can hardly fail to observe that while Alissa often speaks of Jerome's letters to her, only one such letter is quoted, and it by Jerome, who identifies it as a copy of a letter he sent to Alissa. Less significant in the present circumstances than the letter's addressee or its contents is the fact that Jerome kept a copy of it—a "double" (560) he calls it (perhaps not insignificantly in view of his obsession with "simple")—which he can now insert in his narrative as a means of buttressing his argument. All of these instances draw attention to Jerome's status as the sole, unreflective, and rather arbitrary redactor of the entire text that we are reading.

One of the major ironies in *La Porte étroite*, given the prominence of quotation within it, is the extent to which in this text quotation fails to perform its traditional function, that of guarantor or support or illustration for the larger discourse in which it is included. Although Jerome's purpose in writing his account remains murky, certainly implicit in his narrative is a desire for self-knowledge and, undoubtedly, a desire for self-exculpation (in, for example, the death of Alissa). Thus once again we are dealing with a text that partakes of several distinct modes—self-portrait, apologia, *examen de conscience*, and so forth. Yet, in all of these modes and purposes Jerome's account is foredoomed, largely because of his obtuse, obsessive concern to produce a "simple récit," to establish and maintain a univocal, strictly constative discourse. It is as if Jerome assumes that purity of heart correlates with linguistic naïveté, that an inability or a refusal to accept verbal ambiguity, to acknowledge the shifts constantly taking place in speech and writing between literal and figurative, as well as between constative and performative, will protect him from guilt. It is as if he unconsciously identifies with such noble if benighted souls as Félicité in Flaubert's *Un Coeur simple* or Billy Budd in Melville's tale. Félicité, it will be recalled, invariably merges sign with referent—a lamb in a sheepfold with Agnus Dei; Loulou, her stuffed parrot, with the Holy Ghost; a map of Havana with the real place where, if she looks closely enough, she can spot her nephew's house. Melville, for his part, stresses Billy's "straightforward simplicity," noting that "to deal in double meanings and insinuations of any sort was quite foreign to him." Both Félicité and Billy read everything at face value, both are literal-minded in the extreme, and this is what saves them, what keeps them innocent. Perhaps Jerome chooses simplicity of utterance because he knows instinctively what it signifies, even though, as in the case of Billy Budd, "innocence was his blinder."[19]

Alissa, too, longs for simplicity. Like the princesse de Clèves, the literary heroine she no doubt most resembles, Alissa is so disturbed by Eros, in the form of an unyielding *inclination,* that in evading its tentacles, she gravitates toward the univalent, unchanging simplicity of perfect *repos,* Thanatos. Along the way, she gradually loses faith in the readings, sacred and profane, that she and Jerome once shared and from which they once drew guidance and inspiration. Even Pascal is eventually banished from her bookshelf, replaced, to Jerome's horror, by "d'insignificants petits ouvrages de piété vulgaire." Alissa justifies her new choice of reading matter as follows: "Ce sont là d'humbles âmes qui causent avec moi simplement." In them she knows that she will encounter "aucun piège du beau langage" (569). She has given up reading the *Imitation de Jésus-Christ* in Latin. She goes so far as to put away for good a work that was once a spiritual mainstay for her, *Internelle Consolacion,* on the grounds that "cette ancienne langue m'amusait fort, mais me distrayait et la joie payenne que j'y goûte n'a rien à voir avec l'édification que je me proposais d'y chercher" (588–89). Now only Scripture will do, and the simpler the passage the better. Like Jerome from the beginning of his narrative, but always with more lucidity, Alissa increasingly wishes to by-

19. For my approach to this aspect of *La Porte étroite,* I am indebted to Barbara Johnson's brilliant deconstruction of *Billy Budd;* see "Melville's Fist: The Execution of *Billy Budd*" in her *The Critical Difference: Essays in the Contemporary Rhetoric of Reading* (Baltimore: Johns Hopkins University Press, 1980), 79–109. My quotations from Melville's tale are taken from Johnson's essay.

pass the figurative and the performative in language and deal only with the literal and the constative, with language as a *simple* (i.e., one-dimensional) vehicle of communication.

Alissa's flight from the complexities of love and language leads her to withdraw from society and to depend more and more for spiritual sustenance on her diary, which she wishes to consider an "instrument de perfectionnement" (582). Aspiring to "la sainteté" (564), she climbs the ladder of ascesis, pursues the progressive purification of her soul. In the process, she voices opinions that sound increasingly Jansenistic, even quietistic, labels, moreover, that she explicitly declines to repudiate (570). All the while, she moves ever closer to Manichaeanism, using terms like "vertu" (repeatedly), "progressive" and "perfectionnement" in ways that call up the spectre of Catharism, of *credentes* and *perfecti* marching ever upward toward complete detachment from things earthly. And, as if to convince Jerome of the absolute purity of her motives, she tells him that she prefers to remain in doubt regarding any divine joy she might ultimately obtain because of her commitment: "Je veux qu'elle [la félicité] demeure incertaine afin que tout soupçon de marché soit écarté. C'est par noblesse naturelle, non par espoir de récompense, que l'âme éprise de Dieu va s'enfoncer dans la vertu" (570). Thus her ascesis will be gratuitous, unmotivated in the traditional sense, free from such contaminating complications as bargains or pacts with God. In short, her dedication to the goal of saintliness will be utterly and perfectly simple.

Alissa's pursuit of perfect simplicity, however, is doomed from the start. In the first place, the energy she expends in controlling her *inclination* takes an enormous toll on her health, sapping nearly all of her strength, moral and physical. Second, Jerome's passivity toward her deprives Alissa of, on the one hand, the support she would need to embrace the anchorite's life completely, and, on the other, the encouragement she would need to accept her sexual feelings for Jerome. But perhaps the principal cause of Alissa's failure to achieve her goal of unalloyed happiness in union with God, relates to the complex nature of *her* temperament as compared to Jerome's. Where the latter contends that he is recounting his life with neither embellishment nor distortion, that is, through a purely constative medium, Alissa has no such illusions about the twofold nature of language, its constative and performative aspects, hence about the potential for duplicity in even the sparest, most cautiously self-regarding utterance.

When making entries in her diary, Alissa monitors her jottings for signs of "un affreux retour d'égoïsme" (582). Immediately after discussing her sadness, she dissects her discussion for its possible component of "coquetterie," and expresses the hope "que ce journal ne soit pas le complaisant miroir devant lequel mon âme s'apprête" (583). Like Michel in *L'Immoraliste*, who observes that "on ne peut à la fois être sincère et le paraître" (422), Alissa is painfully aware of the doubts, ambiguities, and unsettling disjunctions that besiege the staunchest of striving souls. She is all too familiar with the discrepancies that separate appearance from reality, the desire for purity from the double-dealing rhetoric we can deploy in formulating that desire. In reflex action, she recoils in horror from "le trop écrire" (583). She understands only too well that the very instrument she has chosen for carrying out her sacred quest, keeping a journal, can at any moment betray her: "Voilà plus de six semaines que je n'ai pas rouvert ce cahier. Le mois dernier, en en relisant quelques pages, j'y avais surpris un absurde, un coupable souci de bien écrire.... J'ai déchiré toutes les pages qui m'ont paru *bien écrites*" (587–88). Clearly Alissa's exacerbated lucidity, the remorseless gaze she focuses upon herself, at times slides into agonizing self-criticism. In the end, her relentless review of her every thought, word, deed, and diary entry, her fanatic contemplative's conscientiousness, her scrupulosity, will destroy her.

How unlike Jerome she is in this regard. The absence of such merciless self-scrutiny in his case, indeed his seemingly invincible ignorance regarding himself, his inner life, and the inherently problematic nature of all discourse, saves him from precisely the kind of anguish that torments Alissa. Although capable of keeping a "double" of at least one of his letters to Alissa, he seems incapable of really doubling-back, of retracing his steps in order to reexamine his life and move beyond a simple, linear retelling of it. If Alissa holds off from commiting herself to him partly out of fear that he may one day stop loving her, she is not entirely unjustified in having such fears. In one of his last visits to her, Jerome's heart by his own admission turns to ice when he sees the change wrought in her physical appearance by time, a change he refers to (not for the first time) as a "dépoétisation." Now, however, he adds to that chilling noun the adjective "affreuse" and interprets her physical deterioration as a "retour au naturel" (573). He speculates that her former beauty probably existed only in his beholder's eye, derived from his "poétisation" of her "naturel," from his having made an idol of her. Without the scrim of bedazzlement to filter out her flaws, for the first time he sees Alissa clearly, so he thinks, and realizes that he no longer desires her. The callousness, self-deception, and disingenuousness suffusing this passage come as a shock to readers.

But who exactly are Jerome's readers? The Gide scholar Arthur Babcock has noted: "On nine occasions Jerome addresses a *vous* in his narrative. Whereas this *vous* is once identified as Lucile Bucolin and once as Alissa, the seven remaining passages offer no clue as to the reader's identity."[20] By contrast, there is never any doubt about the intended reader of Alissa's journal or her letters, even one that she addressed to her (and Jerome's) Aunt Félicie—virtually everything she writes is for Jerome's eyes only. As to her purpose, we know that she wrote at least her diary as an aid in her ascesis. On the other hand, the ambiguity surrounding the identity of Jerome's readers only replicates the ambiguity that attends his purpose in writing his account. Paradoxically, therefore, while he goes to great lengths to persuade his readers that his text will carry nothing but the simple, unvarnished truth, he remains exceedingly vague about both his reasons for writing it and the intended audience for it. Possibly he senses that his vagueness in these areas shields him, at least for a time, from moral judgment (in subtle variation, perhaps, on Michel's tactic for delaying judgment of *his* conduct in *L'Immoraliste*).

Obviously, Jerome's view of himself as a writer differs radically from Alissa's, especially from Alissa's self-concept as author of her journal. In terms of Roland Barthes's famous distinction, the former is an *écrivant* while the latter is an *écrivain*. To recall Barthes's definitions:

> Ce qui définit l'écrivant, c'est que son projet de communication est *naïf:* il n'admet pas que son message se retourne et se ferme sur lui-même, et qu'on puisse y lire, d'une façon diacritique, autre chose que ce qu'il veut dire: quel écrivant supporterait que l'on psychanalyse son écriture? Il considère que

> sa parole met fin à une ambiguïté du monde, institue une ex-
> plication irréversible . . . alors que pour l'écrivain . . . c'est
> tout le contraire: il sait bien que sa parole, intransitive par
> choix et par labeur, inaugure une ambiguïté, même si elle se
> donne pour péremptoire.[21]

The profound difference in outlook between *écrivant* Jerome and
écrivain Alissa explains much of the disharmony that exists between
the former's narrative and the latter's journal. If the narrative reveals
how confused and mystified Jerome eventually becomes because of
Alissa's acts of avoidance, the journal shows how Alissa's successive
withdrawals might constitute an entirely reasonable response on her
part to Jerome's hesitations. In spite of their close family ties and
their many shared readings, they neither speak nor write the same
language. Alissa seems eventually to intuit this and she gradually for-
sakes the books that she and Jerome virtually learned by heart.

In one of her last diary entries, written shortly before her death,
Alissa, after noting that now she has only the Bible to read, then af-
firms "mais aujourd'hui, plus haut que les paroles que j'y lis, résonne
en moi ce sanglot éperdu de Pascal: 'Tout ce qui n'est pas Dieu ne
peut pas remplir mon attente'" (594). Thus long after she has
stopped reading him, Pascal's dolorous words still reverberate in her
memory, searing her consciousness with their unquenchable thirst
for the divine and their uncompromising rejection of the human. Explicitly, textually surfacing here is the thematics of waiting, specifically of "full" waiting versus "empty" waiting, of hope versus despair,
which runs through *La Porte étroite* from the beginning—in, for example, Jerome's ineluctably declining expectations regarding Alissa,
as well as in hers regarding him.

Against this thematic backdrop, the writer whom Alissa cannot
forget, the writer for whom things earthly provide only empty waiting, Pascal, evokes his opposite, Corneille, the writer of great expectations par excellence, of full waiting, the writer Alissa cannot
remember. Midway through *La Porte étroite,* Alissa sends a letter to
her (and Jerome's) Aunt Félicie, a letter that Alissa really intends for
Jerome, and that she no doubt expects her aunt, eager to foster their
love, will send on to Jerome. In this letter, Alissa quotes several lines

---

21. Roland Barthes, *Essais Critiques* (Paris: Seuil, 1964), 151–52.

from Racine's fourth *Cantique spirituel,* which she erroneously attributes to Corneille (543). Aunt Félicie does forward the letter to Jerome, who shows it to his friend Abel who, in turn, points out to Jerome the mistaken attribution. Shortly thereafter, in a letter to Jerome, Alissa corrects her mistake, and does so in a manner that suggests she suspects Jerome has read the original letter. The rather large amount of attention paid to a small error caused, it would seem, by a mere memory lapse, highlights both Alissa's coquettishness and Racine's profoundly spiritual (one is tempted to say "Pascalian") canticle, which is quoted at considerable length in Alissa's letter to Jerome (545–46).

Quite possibly, however, the emphasis placed here on a mistake, a gap in Alissa's memory, serves yet another purpose. Corneille, "le Grand Corneille," the great unquoted writer in a book that is filled with quotations, has evidently already faded from Alissa's consciousness. Long before she removes Pascal, Racine, the *Imitation* and the rest from the library she and Jerome assembled with such care, Corneille, author of *Le Cid* and *Polyeucte,* those mastertexts of hope, of full waiting, will have disappeared from the bookshelf of her mind. Through his wished-for (by Alissa) presence but his actual absence, Corneille represents Alissa's always fading hope as the already forgotten first item in the long list of cherished texts she must inevitably consign to oblivion. Long before the *récit*'s desolate finale, Corneille's absent presence sitting squarely in the middle of *La Porte étroite* foreshadows that finale—Alissa's bleak, lonely death in a state of utter despair, empty waiting. Decades before Beckett, Gide thus exploited, for all its power as an aesthetic foil, the thematics of hope coming down to our beleaguered century from the glorious birth of French tragedy.

In view of what Corneille's absence at its center may signify, the *mise en abyme* structure of *La Porte étroite* seems particularly appropriate. The missing (because named but not quoted) writer at the heart of the *récit* functions as an objective correlative for the great textual emptiness that is located where a great textual fullness ought to be found. As already noted, Alissa's diary with its own quotations replicates in miniature the *récit*'s larger narrative with *its* quotations. Moreover, the letters and conversations quoted by Jerome also contain frequent quotations. In the end *La Porte étroite* gives readers the unmistakable impression that texts always enclose other texts, and that the act of quotation involves an infinite regression, an endless quest for an original, authenticating citation. When one considers that the sacred texts cited by Alissa in the long run lose their consoling efficacy for her (her abandonment of *Internelle Consolacion* may be deemed emblematic in this regard) and that the extracts from her diary that form Jerome's longest quotation subvert rather than support *his* position, one realizes that the search for the perfect textual source from which to quote can lead to a vanishing point, an imploding void. In *La Porte étroite,* that black hole in texts is named Corneille. (Perhaps we are glimpsing here a more dispersed and more elaborate version of the palimpsest figure that we have seen structuring *L'Immoraliste.*)

Jerome devotes the final pages of his narrative to an account of the visit he paid to Alissa's sister Juliette a decade after Alissa's death. Stolid dolt that he is, throughout his visit, as indeed throughout his life heretofore, he remains insensible to the suffering that Juliette's unrequited love for him has caused her ever since their adolescence. His visit to Juliette thus underscores Jerome's dull, unchanging obtuseness, in stark contrast to Alissa's downward spiral into despair, during which she let fall away, one after another, the sacred texts and guiding voices of her youth. As *La Porte étroite* comes to an end, we come to see that Jerome's entire account and Alissa's journal constitute not harmonious, mutually supportive parts of a textual whole but, rather, mutually contradictory, if not mutually exclusive, pieces of writing. In the end, nothing has been resolved, no one has been reconciled and a kind of generalized dissonance prevails. That Jerome's narrative physically encloses Alissa's journal gives the text only the appearance, not the reality, of a framing close. Like *L'Immoraliste, La Porte étroite* thus concludes, ironically, without closing, and, once again, discourse collaborates with story to achieve this effect.

As may be inferred from the foregoing, Gide's earliest *récits* blend moralistic analysis and metalinguistic commentary with a finesse that, in hindsight, makes these novellas touchstones of such fusions. Both the palimpsest figure presiding over *L'Immoraliste* and the learned or pious quotations informing *La Porte étroite* perform essentially the same function, that of foregrounding blocks of monumentalized discourse, and it is precisely through these high-profile rhetorical devices and flourishes that both novellas dramatize timeless human failings, complementary versions of our inescapable amour propre. In Gide, clearly, moralist and scriptor work hand in glove.

Sartre once remarked: "Au fond Gide cherche à se surprendre dans les moments où il ne sait pas qu'il s'observe."[22] Indeed, antithetical though these impulses may be, extreme self-awareness and complete self-obliviousness, working in concert on both the ethical and the aesthetic levels, shape Gide's imagination and generate much of his fiction, perhaps especially in his *récits*. In these gracefully pointed prose tales, "pure event," to use John Updike's term, never quite takes over from figuration, and vice versa. *L'Immoraliste* and *La Porte étroite* may even embody that ideal accommodation between exigent artistic concern and urgent moral vision that Roger Shattuck sees as a major desideratum for art: in both *récits* the flaws in the teller match the flaws in the tale perfectly.

22. Quoted as the epigraph to *Album Gide,* ed. Philippe Clerc and Maurice Nadeau (Paris: Gallimard, 1985).

Quotation, Repetition, and Ethical Competence in Proust's *Un Amour de Swann*

C ritics have begun to explore the complex, funda-
mental roles played by quotation and repetition in *A la recherche du
temps perdu.*[1] So far, however, little of this relatively new approach

---

1. The phenomenon of self-quotation in *A la recherche* as a whole has been examined by
Luzius Keller in "L'Autocitation chez Proust," *Modern Language Notes* 95 (May 1980): 1033–
48. As he makes clear early in his study, Keller is concerned almost exclusively with the question of "l'autocitation à la fois au niveau du narrateur et au niveau de l'auteur" (1035) in *A la
recherche.* It is perhaps also worth noting here that Keller's penetrating article opens with a
rapid survey of previous studies that have touched, if only glancingly, on the stylistic implications of quotation in Proust. Most notable among such earlier studies is Jacques Nathan's *Citations, références et allusions de Proust dans "A la recherche du temps perdu"* (Paris: Nizet,
1953), even though, as Keller points out, "le but que Nathan s'est proposé est différent du
nôtre. Dans ce répertoire, il s'agissait avant tout de relever et d'identifier les citations et de les
mettre en rapport avec la situation biographique dans laquelle Proust s'est occupé des auteurs
cités" (1034).

As for the various forms of repetition that occur throughout *A la recherche,* Gérard Genette,
in *Narrative Discourse: An Essay in Method,* trans. Jane E. Lewin (Ithaca: Cornell University
Press, 1980), has observed that "no novelistic work . . . has ever put the iterative to a use comparable—in textual scope, in thematic importance, in degree of technical elaboration—to
Proust's use of it in the *Recherche du temps perdu*" (117). Regarding quotation, itself a form
of repetition, Antoine Compagnon in *La Seconde Main, ou le travail de la citation* (Paris:
Seuil, 1979), makes, in passing, even larger claims for *its* role in the composition of *A la*

to Proust's great novel has focused on its most famous segment, *Un Amour de Swann,* even though quotation and repetition, under various guises, are pervasive in this emblematic early section of *A la recherche.* More important for my purposes here, the extensive use in *Un Amour de Swann* of these basic modes of scriptural emphasis seems closely linked to Proust's profoundly *moraliste* vision.[2] Purely verbal and strictly ethical concerns and competencies, moreover, correlate highly in *Un Amour* and, through their convergence, appear to engage a number of its dominant themes and techniques— snobbery, the religion of art, the transformation of confusion into at least partial understanding, and binary opposition in a host of forms. Thus, with Proust, as with Gide, although in other ways and for different ends, quotation performs a basic, generative function.

Italics and quotation marks setting off consecrated commonplaces highlight the more absurd elements of the human comedy depicted in *Un Amour:* Madame Verdurin's papal diction and her snobbery, Odette's English phrases and her blind quest for *le chic,* Swann's privately minted language of love and his self-deception. Most blatant is Doctor Cottard's pathetic *arrivisme,* which he blithely displays in his misfired puns and his general incapacity to distinguish between literal and figurative expression. These examples, of course, suggest that by the way in which it fuses verbal self-consciousness and moral

---

recherche, noting that the device of quotation allows Proust to assemble his text from already written fragments, cutouts, which he simply arranges, pastes together: "Proust . . . comparait volontiers son travail lorsqu'il épinglait de-ci de-là ses 'paperoles,' à celui du couturier qui bâtit une robe plutôt qu'à celui de l'architecte ou du constructeur des cathédrales" (17).

Regarding the question of quotation and repetition in Proust generally, see Richard Macksey's introduction to Marcel Proust, *On Reading Ruskin,* ed. and trans. Jean Autret, William Burford, and Phillip J. Wolfe (New Haven: Yale University Press, 1987), xiii–liii.

2. Peter Brooks, in *The Novel of Worldliness: Crébillon, Marivaux, Laclos, Stendhal* (Princeton: Princeton University Press, 1969), no doubt expresses the viewpoint of many in his comments on Proust, *moraliste:* "One can feel the way the *moraliste* tradition informs the glance that narrator and protagonist turn toward the Faubourg Saint-Germain in an effort to comprehend individual roles and to master social structure" (285). The critic's inclusive but precise definition of "the *moraliste* tradition" is also helpful in the present context: "the *moraliste* tradition, using that term in its most general sense: the line of worldly literature, conversational and social in its origins, hard-headed in its attitudes, directed toward an exploration and definition of man in the social medium, which was pursued in memoirs, letters, aphorisms, reflections, histories, and on the stage in the 1660's and 70's" (60). See also in this connection Richard Macksey's comment in his introduction to Marcel Proust, *On Reading Ruskin* (New Haven: Yale University Press, 1987): "Throughout his artistic career Proust was a stern if paradoxical moralist" (xiv).

censure for satirical purposes, *Un Amour* is quite traditional. On the other hand, in his narrative Proust combines metalanguage and moralism in extremely subtle ways too, and to nontraditional, if not to say original, ends. It is precisely because of this combining that *Un Amour de Swann* makes strong claims on our attention. It does so, moreover, despite the status of *Un Amour* as a "flashback" within *A la recherche du temps perdu*—albeit a flashback that is the length of a novel and, for all practical purposes, fully self-contained.[3]

In the opening paragraph of *Un Amour de Swann*, Proust places quotation marks around a number of words and phrases and around one entire sentence, all remarks made at Mme Verdurin's salon, presumably by Mme Verdurin herself, at least initially:

> Pour faire partie du petit "noyau," du "petit groupe," du "petit clan" des Verdurin, une condition était suffisante mais elle était nécessaire: il fallait adhérer tacitement à un Credo dont un des articles était que le jeune pianiste protégé par Mme Verdurin cette année-là et dont elle disait: "Ça ne devrait pas être permis de savoir jouer Wagner comme ça!," "enfonçait" à la fois Planté et Rubinstein et que le docteur Cottard avait plus de diagnostic que Potain. Toute "nouvelle recrue" à qui les Verdurin ne pouvaient pas persuader que les soirées des gens qui n'allaient pas chez eux étaient ennuyeuses comme la pluie, se voyait immédiatement exclue. Les femmes étant à cet égard plus rebelles que les hommes à déposer toute curiosité mondaine et l'envie de se renseigner par soi-même sur l'agrément des autres salons, et les Verdurin sentant d'autre part que cet esprit d'examen et de démon de frivolité pouvait par contagion devenir fatal à l'orthodoxie de la petite église, ils avaient été amenés à rejeter successivement tous les "fidèles" du sexe féminin.[4]

---

3. Roger Shattuck's remarks, in *Marcel Proust* (New York: Viking, 1974), on *Un Amour's* virtual autonomy as a work of fiction epitomize the views of many Proust readers: "The first two sections of Proust's novel, 'Combray' and 'Swann in Love,' can stand separately and have earned many admirers" (2); see also Eléonore N. Zimmermann, "Proust's Novel in a Novel: *Un amour de Swann,*" *Modern Language Review* 68 (1973): 551–58.

4. Marcel Proust, *A la recherche du temps perdu,* ed. Pierre Clarac and André Ferré (Paris: Gallimard, 1954), 1:188. Subsequent page references to this work are in the body of the study, in parentheses.

The quoted remarks, working in concert with the implied quotations, stereotypical expressions, and other pat phrases that are also contained in this overture to *Un Amour,* create an amusing extended metaphor in which Mme Verdurin becomes a supreme cult leader empowered to expel from her group those who fail to adhere strictly to its tenets. The principal article of faith of this new religion requires its followers to believe all salons but Mme Verdurin's worthy only of their scorn. By underscoring—via the use of explicit and implicit citation—the trite, self-aggrandizing chatter of Mme Verdurin's salon, Proust mocks, at the very outset of this narrative, the pretensions of the milieu that he will dissect in this section of *A la recherche,* and thus presents the theme of snobbery ahead of all others.

Far more than snobbery is at issue here, however, as a closer look at the paragraph just quoted reveals. First of all, a marked shift in tone distinguishes the direct from the implied quotations, with the latter, even as they contribute to the extended metaphor, undercutting its suggestiveness by virtue of an excess of detail and explicitness. What was merely latent or potential papal (i.e., excommunicating) diction in the direct quotations, becomes all too manifest in the indirect. The middle clauses of the first sentence typify this heavy-handedness ("une condition était suffisante mais elle était nécessaire: il fallait adhérer tacitement à un Credo dont un des articles..."), as do several phrases in the paragraph's last sentence: "toute curiosité mondaine," "cet esprit d'examen," "ce démon de frivolité," "l'orthodoxie de la petite église." So insistent does the metaphor become in these phrases that we begin to suspect Mme Verdurin of not being the implied speaker here. Rather, in *style indirect libre* fashion, we are now no doubt hearing the narrator's voice commenting ironically on Mme Verdurin's self-inflating talk by reprising and exaggerating it. On the other hand, we cannot be sure about this, since Mme Verdurin herself hardly shrinks from the overemphasis of that variant of repetition, redundancy ("Pour faire partie du petit 'noyau,' du 'petit groupe,' du 'petit clan'..."). Furthermore, Mme Verdurin is virtually tone-deaf to her own speech, as her use of the vulgarism "enfonçait" and the tired (hence boring!) simile "ennuyeuses comme la pluie"—which though lacking inverted commas is plainly attributable to Mme Verdurin—attests. The lofty and the banal, the quick and the dead, mix freely in her conversation without her being aware of it.

At this point one might reasonably object that while these observations indicate the extent of Mme Verdurin's literally laughable, rather all-too-prickly social pretensions, they leave us exactly where we started, reflecting on the twin themes of snobbery and social exclusion. In fact, however, we have moved considerably beyond that subject and are now dealing with a major component of *Un Amour*'s thematics, the notions of inner confusion and self-deception. The lingering ambiguity that attends the speaker's identity in several of the implied quotations, combined with the unwitting wide swings in Mme Verdurin's tone, prefigures the lack of clarity and rigor that will characterize Swann's inner life. In this sense, the opening paragraph of *Un Amour,* particularly the workings of quotation—direct and implied—and repetition within it, perfectly foreshadows what comes after it: the steady unfolding of the consequences of spiritual flabbiness and self-delusion.

Such reflections lead almost inevitably to the larger question of the ties that bind the first paragraph of *Un Amour* to the rest of the narrative. The extended metaphor in which Mme Verdurin becomes a kind of pope allows Proust to satirize the petty snobbery and pretentiousness of Mme Verdurin's set, and the surplus of terms that overload the metaphor, found in the indirect quotations, constitutes the chief vehicle of the ironic commentary. In its very elaborateness, however, the metaphor makes another, more important contribution to the narrative: it introduces the code that will be used for formulating the essentially spiritual truth that Swann dimly perceives in *Un Amour* and that the narrator of *A la recherche* eventually sees quite clearly. I am alluding, of course, to their discovery of the redemptive powers of art.[5]

The notions of a sacred hierarchy, of the pious *cénacle,* of righteous exclusion and self-discipline, combined with unconscious philistinism, transposed onto the aesthetic plane, structure *Un Amour de Swann* to its core, and they do so in an entirely positive,

---

5. The narrator's realization of art's capacity to take us beyond ourselves and to put us in contact with "la vraie vie" is explicitly set forth in *Le Temps retrouvé;* see Marcel Proust, *A la recherche du temps perdu,* ed. Pierre Clarac and André Ferré (Paris: Gallimard, 1954), 3:895–96.

non-ironic way. The religious lexicon of the opening paragraph is thus overdetermined, functioning as it does simultaneously on at least two different levels and for at least two distinct purposes. It announces both the surface theme of snobbery and the deep theme of the religion of art. In this perspective, the key term in the paragraph becomes the one common noun in it that is capitalized and hence foregrounded the most, "Credo." Precisely, the narrator's most profound beliefs are the basic "subject" of *Un Amour de Swann*—as they are of the entire *A la recherche*—and his Act of Faith in art will, in the end, displace such false gods as snobbery, social climbing, and even love. So if normative, catechistic language is flaunted in the opening paragraph, this is done not only for reasons of satire, but also because value judgments pervade the narrative as a whole. According to these judgments, the highest good in life is art, in whose name proscription, reproof, and moral censure may justifiably be employed. The ethical, the spiritual, and the aesthetic are thus interwoven throughout *Un Amour de Swann,* as are the comical and the more serious aspects of the narrative.

The figure of Dr. Cottard illustrates this interpenetration with special éclat. The most grotesquely comical personage in *Un Amour,* he is also its least admirable and as such plays an extremely serious role in the narrative. Though invariably—if inadvertently—funny, he does not retain our sympathy for very long; his insatiable need for social acceptance has long since stifled any propensity he may ever have had for compassion vis-à-vis others or lucidity regarding himself. Also, his posture of abject submission before Mme Verdurin's various "papal bulls" seems so craven as to discredit him completely as even a possible locus of value. Moreover, in relation to the other characters, including faithless Odette, he seems to represent a kind of moral baseline, absolute zero on *Un Amour's* ethical barometer; no other figure in the narrative has given himself over quite so unconditionally to the job of learning the ground rules of the milieu to which he has recently gained access.

The doctor's basic misapprehension of the complex nature of verbal communication constitutes the butt of Proust's humor in *Un Amour.* Cottard is fascinated by the waywardness of language and at the same time utterly bewildered by it. Appropriately enough, therefore, his greatest fear is of being found out, of having his linguistic naïveté exposed to the habitués of Mme Verdurin's salon. Accordingly, he protects himself, in the immediate situation of a conversation, by always wearing a tentative, knowing smirk, in case the remark just made by his interlocutor should turn out to have been facetious. For the long term, he is constantly informing himself about the exact meaning of idioms, figures of speech, and proper names—to no avail, however, since "il prenait tout au pied de la lettre" (201). Thus, for example, to the sporadic displeasure of Mme Verdurin, the good doctor takes her pro forma self-denigrations at face value and unwittingly offends her by agreeing with her.

Every one of his speaking appearances in the narrative but the last draws attention to Cottard's invincible ignorance concerning the problematics of discourse. And even in his final intervention, a benighted preoccupation with his own words is suggested: " 'Mais, est-ce que nous ne verrons pas M. Swann ce soir? Il est bien *ce qu'on appelle* un ami personnel du . . .' " (289, emphasis added). When Mme Verdurin cuts him off with " 'Mais j'espère bien que non,' " his cowering acceptance of this, her latest excommunication from the circle of the faithful, is rendered in a metaphor that likens the precipitous decline in Cottard's powers of articulate utterance to the terrified, mechanically bowing, tightly controlled withdrawal of the meekest of subjects from the presence of his angry sovereign: "baissant d'un air ému et peureux son nez dans son assiette, il se contenta de répondre: 'Ah! -ah! -ah! -ah! -ah!' en traversant à reculons, dans sa retraite repliée en bon ordre jusqu'au fond de lui-même, le long d'une gamme descendante, tout le registre de sa voix. Et il ne fut plus question de Swann chez les Verdurin" (289). Significantly, just as Swann's name will never be mentioned again at the Verdurins', Cottard's voice, emptied first of meaning and then sound by Mme Verdurin's interjected command—thinly disguised as a wish—will never be heard again in *Un Amour.* (Cottard is named on only one further occasion in the narrative, shortly before the end, and then only in connection with Swann's unexpectedly running into Mme Cottard on a Paris omnibus.) In other words, Swann's "official" expulsion from the Verdurins' and Cottard's virtual disappearance from the narrative occur simultaneously, in departures yoked and formalized in the text by the dying, repeated gutturals "Ah! -ah! -ah! -ah! -ah!" appearing in quotation marks. It is as if Cottard's cowardly retreat into silence/absence and Swann's humiliating exclusion, including the taboo attached to the mere saying of his name, were aspects of the same thing. Or, more precisely, it is as if the two men's separate destinies and distinct characters ultimately converged through their coincident dismissals, their shared banishment into the dark night of the unuttered.

It is my contention that there are indeed several points of contact between these two otherwise contrary figures. I propose that a bond of structural similarity links them: if Swann may be considered an incomplete harbinger of the narrator,[6] Cottard, in caricatural fashion, can be seen as a cruder version of Swann. In this perspective, the former represents a heightening of the latter, an exaggeration which both distorts and instructs, simplifies and at the same time illuminates. Gazing through the prism of Cottard, we see Swann's weaknesses writ large. If the doctor, in spite of his dogged efforts, never masters the jargon of Mme Verdurin's salon, Swann, for his part, continually exploits his considerable verbal resources to screen himself from the truth about Odette and to turn her, through ennobling citation, into something worthy of his love: "Le mot d' 'oeuvre florentine' rendit un grand service à Swann. Il lui permit, comme un titre, de faire pénétrer l'image d'Odette dans un monde de rêves où elle n'avait pas eu accès jusqu'ici et où elle s'imprégna de noblesse" (224). Where, concerning the workings of language, the one (Cottard) is presented as both fanatically curious and hopelessly obtuse, the other (Swann) seems supremely gifted and utterly self-deceiving.

Although homologous at key points in their makeup, in other areas Cottard and Swann differ enormously. For example, if the correlation between linguistic and ethical incompetence is blatant in the case of Cottard, with Swann it is subtle and complex. While the latter is usually attuned to the slightest nuance in social banter, when Odette is involved, his alertness to discordant turns of phrase and inappropriate tonal shifts falters. He disregards what his cultivated senses report to him about Odette's coarse-grained speech and, without fully realizing what he is doing, fabricates his love for her out of a confusion. He is not attracted to her type but his inclination to abulia and the soft, directionless life he has slipped into make him vulnerable to her patently manipulative flattery. Bored and inert, his

---

6. See in this connection, for example, Marcel Muller, *Préfiguration et structure romanesque dans "A la recherche du temps perdu"* (Lexington, Ky.: French Forum, 1979), 21; see also Germaine Brée, *Marcel Proust and Deliverance from Time* (New Brunswick: Rutgers University Press, 1955), 152ff.

normally discriminating responsiveness to the myriad ways in which people speak has become dulled. In a lazy conflation, he merges Odette's image with a haunting sonata by Vinteuil and his favorite Botticelli fresco.

Swann is drawn to the beauty of art and has intimations of its transcendent powers, but the pleasure that he derives from music and painting, though far greater than that of any other character in *Un Amour*—not counting, of course, the narrator—can never be transformed into permanent knowledge; his insights in this realm remain partial and fleeting. One suspects that could he but listen to Odette's words with the same attentiveness that he reserves for Vinteuil's sonata, his understanding of both would be deepened. Still, that Swann should have even limited vision in art, and thence life, places him on a higher plane, intellectually, than, say, the Verdurins, Odette, Forcheville, or, to be sure, Cottard. Furthermore, the degree of his moral superiority to each of these figures corresponds exactly to the degree in which his sensitivity to language exceeds theirs. Thus, his distance in both regards is greatest, paradoxically, from his homologue, Cottard.

Binary opposition, involving characters who converge on one level and diverge on another, abounds in *Un Amour.* Besides Swann and Cottard, there is the case of Swann and Forcheville. The latter enters the narrative in a passage that enumerates important differences between him and Swann. Forcheville—and the paragraph in question—is introduced as follows: "Quelle différence avec un 'nouveau' qu'Odette leur avait demandé d'inviter...!" (250). Particularly striking in this opening—in addition to the by now familiar quotation marks around a term drawn from the ritualized code of Mme Verdurin's salon—and especially appropriate to the Forcheville-Swann relationship, is the baldly binary nature of the opposition between the two figures; they are, so to speak, officially declared to be the same and yet different. Just as Swann, not long before, was a "nouveau" being brought to the Verdurins' by Odette, now it is Forcheville who has that honor (the replication or similarity). But the controlling rubric for the pair comes with the paragraph's first two words, the exclamation "Quelle différence...!" (the basic polarity). Forcheville knows instinctively, it would seem, how to play up to Mme Verdurin's philistinism, a skill that Swann never acquired, partly out of principle but more so out of a kind of torpor. Sensing the irritation that defenseless Saniette, the old archivist who haunts the Verdurin soirées, continually provokes in their hostess, Forcheville, like a predatory animal, moves in for the kill. He gives the archivist such a tongue-lashing that the poor wretch is reduced to tears and obliged to flee the Verdurin house, never to return. As we look back over Forcheville's conduct up to this point, we realize that his act of scapegoating in this circumstance is but the last step in his initiation into the Verdurin circle. With it, he ratifies Mme Verdurin's intolerance, spitefulness, and periodic need to purge her little group, through the ritual of expulsion, of "ennuyeux." By paying her the compliment of imitation in this crucial realm, Forcheville guarantees himself a permanent place in her group.

Forcheville's ability to "fit in" with the Verdurins is evident on his first evening in their home, long before his "exécution" of Saniette (a deed, apparently, of which Odette completely approved). It reveals itself in his general comportment at table, but especially in his patterns of speech and in his reactions to the ways in which others speak. As readers encountering a new character, we of course have no prior knowledge of Forcheville's speech habits. On the other hand, we soon learn that he is the comte de Forcheville, that he is the brother-in-law of gentle, well-bred Saniette, and that he and Swann have moved in the same predominantly aristocratic circles. These facts lead us to expect a generally comparable level of language from the two men, with due allowance made of course for differences in taste and temperament. What we find, however, is a large discrepancy between them in this domain, for Forcheville's conversation is in fact much closer in tone and substance to Odette's and Mme Verdurin's than it is to Swann's. It is fawning, rough, and approximate where Swann's is courteous, polished, and precise. Inevitably, a specific inference suggests itself to us; a verbal chameleon, Forcheville seems to have taken on, without plan or effort, the linguistic coloration of his new surroundings. He consistently and unintentionally misnames the self-important Professor Brichot "Bréchot," he teases Swann in crass, inappropriate terms and, at a single stroke, flatters Mme Verdurin in her *arrivisme* and Odette in her Anglophilia by congratulating the former for "le petit 'speech' du peintre" (257), with the English borrowing signaling to the latter his unqualified embrace of her pretensions to *le chic.* In overpraising Mme Cottard's wit, Brichot's intelligence, and the painter's eloquence, Forcheville makes plain that he is in his element, linguistically speaking, at the Verdurins', something that Swann would never be.

The apparent ease with which Forcheville joins the facile, formulaic, and at times gross conversation of the Verdurin salon establishes both his kinship with Odette, Mme Verdurin, and Cottard, and his distance from Swann, Mme Cottard, and Saniette. To his credit— even though it bespeaks passive rather than active inner strength— Swann refrains from taking part in the mean-spirited gossip of the salon. Instead, except when talking seriously about art, he chooses mild protest, evasion, or silence. Mme Cottard, too, normally remains mute at the Verdurin gatherings and elsewhere, and when she does speak, she displays modest wit and true generosity (see 255– 56, 377). Hence the following provisional conclusion: in *Un Amour,* the presence (or absence) of fluent, unmonitored and (in the case of Cottard) unrelievedly gauche talk, signifies the copresence (or co-absence) of callousness and cruelty.

Although necessarily schematic, this axiom finds strong support in the characterization of Saniette, who embodies the literary topos of the innocent stammerer: "Saniette ... avait dans la bouche, en parlant, une bouillie qui était adorable parce qu'on sentait qu'elle trahissait moins un défaut de la langue qu'une qualité de l'âme, comme un reste de l'innocence du premier âge qu'il n'avait jamais perdue. Toutes les consonnes qu'il ne pouvait prononcer figuraient comme autant de duretés dont il était incapable" (203). Thus, in *Un Amour,* evil linked to glibness (Forcheville) drives out goodness wedded to impaired speech (Saniette). If Cottard, by his repeated vain attempts to penetrate the mystery of language, foregrounds the problematics of discourse, Forcheville and Saniette, viewed together, dramatize the dangers inherent in dropping the quotation marks with which, figuratively speaking, Cottard has surrounded all words. For they demonstrate that when the trammeled tongue is freed, it will trip, not lightly along the heart's byways, but in mindless hammer blows on the soul. Put more abstractly, the Forcheville-Saniette conflict— brothers-in-law in conflict, hence another binary opposition— shows that when speakers lose their hesitancy and diffidence, their critical self-awareness, when the sense of always citing earlier speakers abandons them, brutishness is at hand.

Swann's special friendship with the princesse des Laumes, the future duchesse de Guermantes, revealed in the long climax of *Un Amour,* gives us yet another insight into the role of citation in

Proust's narrative. The Princess belongs to the aristocratic circle that Swann frequented before he was caught in the Verdurins' web. During an evening musicale held at Mme de Saint-Euverte's, the two meet, purely by chance. It is their first encounter since before the onset of Swann's consuming passion for Odette. As this pivotal section of the narrative progresses, Swann and the Princess emerge as virtual soul-mates on one level and, on another, as barely distant relatives.

The Princess dominates "la coterie Guermantes," the group that Mme Verdurin most despises, envies, and seeks to emulate. But she is clearly both more secure socially and more sophisticated linguistically than Mme Verdurin. These traits, coupled here as elsewhere in the narrative, are quickly but sharply etched in the case of the Princess. In her conversation with General de Froberville, she makes fun of the sound of Mme de Cambremer's name in very particular fashion: "ce n'est pas *euphonique,* ajouta-t-elle en détachant le mot euphonique comme s'il était entre guillemets, petite affectation de débit qui était particulière à la coterie Guermantes" (377). Her verbal mannerism in this circumstance reminds us of Swann's gentle mockery of the pianist's aunt during his first evening at the Verdurins': "Je voulais dire qu'elle ne me semblait pas 'éminente,' ajouta-t-il en détachant cet adjectif" (204). This shared affectation—the use, as it were, of oral italics or quotation marks—places Swann and the Princess on the same rarefied verbal plane, hence in the same social world. Their solidarity, moreover, is unmistakable in the narrator's assertion that they speak, literally, the same language (342). When Swann first catches sight of the Princess, who has been patiently waiting for his glance to turn in her direction, the phatic moment of recognition and complicity, the exchange of signs, is instantaneous. He immediately falls into the arch yet intimate teasing he had so often indulged in with her in the past, and she answers in kind, to their mutual delight. If most of their sparkling repartee passes over the heads of their auditors, so much the better. For Swann and the Princess, their bantering forms a saving oasis in a desert of clichés. Conversation, skillfully, knowingly, lovingly conducted is at once their common bond, the dialect of their tribe, and their liberation from an otherwise oppressive social situation. Through self-citation and self-parody, they momentarily rise above their bleak, linguistically impoverished surroundings.

But if Swann and the Princess, by the sheer force of their verbal grace, soar above the whispering schemers, seducers, and sycophants swirling around them at Mme de Saint-Euverte's, eventually in these climactic pages Swann alone emerges as a truly superior being. He alone experiences the catharsis and illumination that only art can provide. Just as he is about to leave, the concert resumes with the playing of Vinteuil's sonata. Once again, before he can escape the heartrending reminder, he hears "l'air national" (218) of his and Odette's love. This time, however, the music frees him, purges him, lets him partake of Vinteuil's suffering and at the same time understand and begin to accept a hard truth, that "le sentiment qu'Odette avait eu pour lui ne renaîtrait jamais" (353). He alone among the assembled listeners is able to receive "la petite phrase" of the sonata for what it is, as profoundly sacred in character and almost magical in its powers. He alone appreciates the essentially spiritual import of the ceremony in which "la petite phrase" functions as the hushed, ineffable consecration, the *sanctus, sanctus, sanctus.* For the others in attendance, all represented in the reaction of the comtesse de Monteriender, the sonata is merely "prodigieux," unmatched by anything "depuis les tables tournantes," hence only spiritualist in nature.

But "la petite phrase" has another possible application in *Un Amour,* one involving the most important foregrounding of language through quotation marks in the entire narrative. Together Swann and Odette coin the expression "faire catleya" (234)—a term that means literally "to make orchid" and that appears in the text in quotation marks—as their private metaphor for "faire l'amour." Serge Doubrovsky has proposed that the coinage be construed as Swann's scriptural counterpart to Vinteuil's "petite phrase."[7] I would contend that from at least one perspective "faire catleya" *is* "la petite phrase."

Doubrovsky's intriguing rapprochement is more than justified, it seems to me, by specific elements in the text of *Un Amour.* It will be recalled that Swann falls in love with Odette when he associates her with Vinteuil's sonata and identifies her with the depiction of Zipporah, daughter of Jethro, wife of Moses, in Botticelli's fresco in the Sistine Chapel. Both works of art, beloved by Swann, merge in his mind with Odette, shielding him from the truth about her, namely,

7. Serge Doubrovsky, "Faire catleya," *Poétique,* no. 37 (February 1979), 111–25, esp. 125.

that she has not a single attribute that appeals to him. Similarly, the phrase "faire catleya," protects Swann from having to face a void, that in love-making, in the act of physical possession, "l'on ne possède rien" (234). The words "faire catleya," Zipporah in Botticelli's fresco, and "la petite phrase" in Vinteuil's sonata thus all conspire to create and maintain an illusion for Swann, that of a desirable, attainable, and even "ownable" Odette.

Of the two artworks, Vinteuil's sonata, especially "la petite phrase," is the more intimately tied to the expression "faire catleya." The term "la petite phrase" can mean, depending on context, either "the little sentence" or "the short musical phrase," with the former meaning having far greater currency in the language than the latter. Consequently, a degree of residual semantic interference occurs each of the many times that readers encounter the term in the text, interference that effectively restores to the term, if only for an instant, its first or higher-frequency meaning. The term "la petite phrase" in *Un Amour* thus conveys, subliminally, the idea or possibility of a sentence, albeit a sentence without specific content. (One is reminded here of Valéry's celebrated avowal that in composing "Le Cimetière marin" he started with simply a beat, a measure, the rhythmic figure of the decasyllabic line, quite empty of words or filled only with meaningless syllables.)[8]

Supporting the standard or usual semantic thrust of the term in question is the stress placed by Proust, from the term's very first mention in the text, on the imagined visual-graphic form of the musical phrase (208). Soon enough the display of shape and color takes on a specifically scriptural character. Before "la petite phrase" can escape, Swann captures it in his mind's eye as a form of writing, as "une transcription sommaire et provisoire" having the qualities of "la graphie, la valeur expressive . . . du dessin, de l'architecture, de la pensée" (209). And so "la petite phrase" enters the narrative, somewhat tautologically, in the imaginary raiment of a written sentence.

The data provided about the melodic dimension of "la petite phrase" forge even stronger, more conspicuous links between it and "faire catleya." In the pivotal section of the narrative that describes Swann's final hearing of Vinteuil's sonata—at Mme de Saint-Euverte's—we learn that "la petite phrase" comprises a sequence of

8. Paul Valéry, *Oeuvres,* ed. Jean Hytier (Paris: Gallimard, 1957), 1:1503.

five notes barely separated from one another in pitch, two of which are constantly repeated (349). This, it so happens, would be an entirely appropriate way of *singing* the words "faire catleya." The five syllables of the phrase, when sung—"e" in "faire," normally mute, is sounded in verse or song—would correspond to the five tightly intervaled notes and the word "faire" to the two repeated ones. In light of these considerations, and since "la petite phrase" is "the national anthem" of Swann's and Odette's love, "faire catleya" could certainly qualify as the unsung lyrics to the musical phrase that Swann finds so mysteriously haunting.

For Swann, the expression "faire catleya"—in the coining of which his role was apparently larger than Odette's—enables him to view himself as a true creator, an *artiste* instead of a mere *collectionneur.*[9] He imagines Odette bedecked in orchids in an earthly paradise, yet ready to "sortir d'entre leurs larges pétales mauves" (234) so as to participate with him in an unprecedented pleasure of his devising. To his chagrin, however, only when he begins to strip away such illusions and fantasies—thanks, ironically, to "la petite phrase"—will Swann start to free himself from the bondage that "faire catleya" in reality represents for him. His final illumination in this domain, his full, bitter realization of his self-deception, comes with *Un Amour's* last sentence which, fittingly enough, is a direct quotation from Swann's anguished reflections on the matter: " 'Dire que j'ai gâché des années de ma vie, que j'ai voulu mourir, que j'ai eu mon plus grand amour, pour une femme qui ne me plaisait pas, qui n'était pas mon genre!' " (382).

The use of quotation in the last third of the narrative paves the way for this mournful close. In the latter part of *Un Amour,* the reprise of quoted remarks—of remarks by Odette especially—often serves to contrast the different situations in which the same phrase arises, to shed light on the changed value that is conferred on an utterance by the passage of time and by the new context in which it finds itself. In the later sections of the narrative, for example, the repetition of a quoted phrase often indicates the distance Swann has

9. Swann's self-serving tendency to play down the difference between an *artiste* and a *collectionneur,* while at the same time identifying himself more with the former than with the latter, is made abundantly clear in the text; see 224, 239. In the final analysis, of course, as Doubrovsky has reminded us, in *Un Amour* "le collectionneur est le frère ennemi de l'artiste" (120). Thus once again Proust is employing the device of binary opposition.

covered, the halting progress he has made toward disenchantment. The recurrence of citation, in other words, becomes in *Un Amour* both the sign and the means of a gradual, somber revelation.

Before proceeding with this exploration of repetition's function in *Un Amour*, however, we must back up a step so as to identify the type of remark that is generally quoted in the first place. Normally, quotations in *Un Amour* epitomize the speaker; they consist of statements that the speaker frequently or usually makes. Thus when the typical or oft-stated is repeated, as occurs in the latter parts of the narrative, repetition does not merely replicate but rather multiplies an earlier utterance. Accordingly, the rhetoric of *Un Amour* enacts or mimes the very idea of the habitual; repetition of citation becomes the sturdy icon of habit, a great structuring theme of *A la recherche du temps perdu* as a whole.[10]

The dialectics of habit and surprise, of indifference and jealousy, sloth and pain, delusion and revelation, zigzag through *Un Amour* like a mighty underground river, cracking its smooth, nearly monolithic surface from time to time in the jarring repetition of a habitual remark appearing in quotation marks. A single example can illustrate the effect that these repetitions have on the narrative. Long after Odette has ceased to love him, Swann looks back longingly on better days: "Dans ce temps-là, à tout ce qu'il disait, elle répondait avec admiration: 'Vous, vous ne serez jamais comme tout le monde'" (319). (Her exact words much earlier were: "Vous êtes un être si à part. C'est cela que j'ai aimé d'abord en vous, j'ai bien senti que vous n'étiez pas comme tout le monde" [198].) Proust then deftly establishes a new, drastically altered context for the remark by having Swann meditate on Odette's current variant of her former encomium: "Maintenant, à toutes les paroles de Swann, elle répondait d'un ton parfois irrité, parfois indulgent: 'Ah! tu ne seras donc jamais comme tout le monde!'" (320). As if she were addressing a spoiled child ("*tu* ne seras *donc* jamais"), Odette is impatient, exasperated, mildly contemptuous. Passion's urgent timbre, whether or not it was ever sincere, has long since left her voice. Despite the radical tonal shift

---

10. Samuel Beckett, in his seminal 1931 monograph on *A la recherche*, was among the first to stress the importance of habit in Proust's novel; see Samuel Beckett, *Proust* (New York: Grove, 1957), passim. See also Howard Moss's remarks on this subject in *The Magic Lantern of Marcel Proust* (Boston: Godine, 1963), 105ff.

distinguishing Odette's former from her current declaration to Swann that he will never be like everyone else, both versions of her remark are presented as habitual on her part ("Dans ce temps-là, à tout ce qu'il disait"; "Maintenant, à toutes les paroles de Swann"). Habit and surprise, the known and the novel, thus interact dialectically here. Both declarations are habitual and almost identical lexically, but their respective circumstances, hence their messages, could hardly be more different.

As is obvious by now, we are dealing here with a device—repetition—that is homologous to one we have already seen operating in *Un Amour*: binary opposition. Indeed, the dialectical movement that repetition brings to the narrative fits into a larger pattern, in that the notions of sameness and difference, and the ceaseless interplay between them, permeate *Un Amour*, where they appear to constitute its most basic stylistic trait. A continuous transformation of like into unlike and back again expresses itself in the guise of redundancy, tautology, binary opposition and, perhaps most tellingly, repetition, but repetition, as we have noted, of a specific nature, of habitual utterances foregrounded in the text by quotation marks.

During Swann's final conversation with Odette, two interlocking repetitions of this type compress into a few pages the generally gradual change from cozy illusion to shattering lucidity that characterizes Swann's awakening. After seemingly interminable coaxing, Swann finally persuades Odette to satisfy his gnawing curiosity about any sexual encounters she may have had with women (one of the allegations of Odette's past debauchery that are contained in an anonymous letter to Swann). Although clearly at her wit's end because of Swann's persistent cajoling, Odette still manages to combine disingenuousness with callous, misplaced casualness in her eventual response: "Mais je n'en sais rien, moi, s'écria-t-elle avec colère, peut-être il y a très longtemps, sans me rendre compte de ce que je faisais, peut-être deux ou trois fois" (363). In spite of his growing suspicions about her murky previous life, Swann, unprepared for harsh reality, is dismayed if not savaged by Odette's confession, especially by her unabashed flippancy: "peut-être deux ou trois fois." In the pages following Odette's offhand reply, the phrase "deux ou trois fois," within quotes, reappears, reverberating in Swann's consciousness no fewer than five times, each repetition throbbing like a spasm of mounting pain as the enormity of all that Odette has admitted to him, wittingly and unwittingly, stabs ever more deeply into his heart.

Through a supreme effort of will, however, Swann maintains his composure. But desperate now to know if any of Odette's homosexual adventures have taken place during their love affair, he presses her to tell him how recently she has engaged in such activity. Again, she at first refuses to talk about the subject. She soon relents, however, and proceeds to recount an incident that did in fact occur during their liaison. In relating what she said to her seductress on that occasion, she speaks to Swann in a manner that is intended to minimize both the gravity of the episode and her part in it: "Je lui ai dit: 'Cette blague!' je savais bien où elle voulait en venir" (366). Her words, of course, have precisely the opposite effect on Swann from the one desired, and he is even worse off spiritually and morally than he was after her first avowal. The expression "Cette blague!" (still in quotation marks) then recurs at irregular intervals in the ensuing paragraphs, having the same devastating impact on Swann that the phrase "deux ou trois fois" had just before, that is, echoing in his brain like pulsations of pain from a severe, increasingly discomforting injury. At one point he mulls over the tormenting expressions together and observes that even in memory, unspoken, each word "tenait son couteau et lui en portait un nouveau coup" (367). The successive crescendos in enlightenment thus run together to compound Swann's misery.

For the narrative as a whole, the expression "Cette blague!" is doubtless the more important of the two repeated phrases. Odette has uttered it once before—at the Verdurins' during Forcheville's first evening there—which means that it qualifies as a genuine repetition, one linking an earlier to a later section of Un Amour. In its earlier appearance especially, the expletive "Cette blague!" also typifies Odette's coarse manner of speaking, and in that sense may be considered an habitual remark by her. Prophetically, at the Verdurin dinner she aimed the dismissive vulgarism at Swann, and in so doing allied herself with Forcheville in mocking what they perceived to be intellectual pretentiousness on her lover's part. Although her words are not set off by quotation marks on that first occasion, they are nonetheless highlighted on the page; no sooner has Odette spoken when Cottard makes a clumsy attempt at wordplay: "Blague à tabac?

demanda le docteur" (260). Cottard's failed pun calls attention to Odette's utterance as such, thereby assigning to it, so to speak, belated quotation marks or italics. Once again a single utterance that is both typical of its speaker and foregrounded in the text turns up in widely separated parts of the narrative and in palpably different contexts. In the early context Swann is merely mocked by the phrase, but in the later he is humiliated by it and obliged to accept a painful truth.

The two, slightly overlapping sequences of repetition—of "deux ou trois fois" and "Cette blague!"—reflect, in speeded-up, compacted fashion, both the general texture of *Un Amour de Swann* and its overall structure. The salient textural feature of Proust's narrative consists in the periodic alternation between, on the one hand, predominantly long, complex, frequently convoluted, yet always fluently deployed passages of narration, analysis, and description, and, on the other, dramatic scenes of varying length; between stretches of interior monologue, in which the narrator's consciousness seems to merge with Swann's much of the time, and interludes of dialogue involving either large social gatherings or only Swann and Odette. Within each of these rather commodious categories of discourse, quoted or italicized words, phrases, and occasionally whole sentences intrude upon the flow from time to time, furnishing to the parts an alternation not unlike the one characterizing the whole. The words thus isolated for emphasis usually have special resonance and relevance for Swann's fate, which brings us to the matter of *Un Amour*'s overall structure as a work of fiction. Pared to its essentials, Proust's narrative tracks Swann's inexorable drift toward enlightenment, his reluctant advance from the lazy denial of truth to awful, agonizing knowledge. The sequences of repetition we have been discussing, therefore, reproduce on a microcontextual scale the texture and structure of the principal components of *Un Amour,* as well as those of the whole narrative.[11] Thus, the acquisition of ethical competence, of critical self-awareness, and the concomitant shedding of

11. That Proust was alert to precisely these stylistic devices—the fusion of narrator's and protagonist's consciousness in *style indirect libre,* the maintenance or the disruption of narrative flow through the avoidance or the use of quotation marks—is evident from his essay on Flaubert's style; see Marcel Proust, "A propos du 'style' de Flaubert," in *Contre Saint-Beuve, précédé de Pastiches et mélanges et suivi de Essais et articles,* ed. Pierre Clarac and Yves Sandre (Paris: Gallimard, 1971), 590.

self-deception, proceed apace in *Un Amour* with the playing out of these sequences of repetition.

In light of the foregoing, the sequences of repetition in question emerge as perfect *mises en abyme,* stark mirror images in miniature of the entire *Un Amour de Swann.* An ironic speculative conclusion now suggests itself: could Swann have but viewed Odette and their affair as not unique in his life, but instead as eminently replaceable and repeatable, could he have but exclaimed—and meant—about his mistress and his loves "Cette blague!" and "deux ou trois fois" as thoughtlessly as Odette had blurted out these same words, he would no doubt have been spared the horror of discovering that he had wasted the best years of his life on a woman who was not even his type. But then, the first word in *Un Amour's* title, initiatory, capitalized, and further emphasized on the title page by white space above and below, governs all the succeeding words, there and in the body of the narrative, if only by antiphrasis. For the word "one" (*Un*), together with its inevitable companions, the ideas of uniqueness and primal unity, literally launches the narrative, a text that by its recurrent use of quotation and other forms of repetition continually undercuts, even while validating, the very notions of origin and oneness. In Proust, the act of returning, mediated through recursive discourse, remains the only forward motion that counts, that redeems, that saves lives from utter waste and time from irretrievable loss.

Part Two

The Fiction
of Commitment
(1930–1950)

Women and Words in Malraux's
La Condition humaine

Two apparently unrelated but in fact convergent concerns lie at the heart of *La Condition humaine*: the virtually insurmountable difficulties inherent in verbal communication and the state of permanent oppression characterizing woman's fate. The first of these concerns has often been remarked upon, if only in passing, by Malraux scholars, and was even acknowledged by the writer himself.[1] The second, however, has so far attracted little critical attention.[2] Moreover, to date, the crucial link between the two concerns (one metalinguistic, the other moralistic) has gone entirely unnoticed. But the relative reticence of critics regarding the feminist

---

1. See, for example, Denis Boak, *André Malraux* (Oxford: Clarendon, 1968), 70; Gaëtan Picon, *Malraux par lui-même* (Paris: Editions du Seuil, 1953), 69. Jean Lacouture, *André Malraux*, trans. Alan Sheridan (New York: Pantheon Books, 1975), 146–47. For Malraux's own observations on the subject, see *Les Voix du silence* (Paris: Gallimard, 1951), 628.

2. Only a few studies focus on the way in which Malraux depicts women: e.g., Micheline Herz, "Woman's Fate," *YFS* 18 (1957): 7–19; Martine de Courcel, "Ses personnages féminins," in *André Malraux*, ed. Michel Cazenave (Paris: Editions de l'Herne, 1982), 138–49; Susan Rubin Suleiman, "Malraux's Women: a Re-Vision," in *Witnessing André Malraux: Visions and Re-Visions*, ed. Brian Thompson and Carl A. Viggiani (Middletown: Wesleyan University Press, 1984), 140–58.

implications of Malraux's fictional masterpiece, and their silence regarding the relationship of these implications to the problematizing of speech in *La Condition humaine,* can perhaps be understood in light of the novel's focus on "amour viril," the strong sense of bonding that characterizes the friendship of its male protagonists. For the Hemingwayesque, "men's club" ambience of much of the text and the adroit use in it of elliptical narrative techniques reminiscent of film (particularly in passages devoted to the depiction of violent action), with the attendant illusion of unmediated vision that such techniques foster,[3] no doubt distract readers from the novel's reflective dimension, from its probings into (for example) the feminine condition and the limits of language—in short, from the moral and intellectual explorations occurring within or alongside the gripping adventure story.

Actually, as critics have long maintained, the "adventure story" in *La Condition humaine* functions as only a foil for its more contemplative moments, for the endless search for truth and meaning that governs the inner lives of several of its major characters.[4] On the other hand, although they are not equally weighted in terms of the novel's ultimate thrust, action and reflection follow regularly upon each other, giving the text a rhythm not unlike that found in Japanese samurai movies, where the bloodiest of battle sequences frequently alternate with scenes of quiet recollection or of subtle colloquies over tea. In this respect Malraux's novel has an "Asian" quality about it that is fully in keeping with both its principal setting, Shanghai, and its hero, the half-Japanese Kyo. Lethal revolutionary act and sustained philosophical deliberation or debate take turns advancing the narrative. But the events and circumstances leading to and flowing from the uprising in Shanghai in March 1927, though transfigured by some of the most stirring pages in twentieth-century literature,

3. For a discussion of Malraux's use of "cinematographic" techniques in his fiction, see Jean Carduner, *La Création romanesque chez Malraux* (Paris: Nizet, 1968).

4. Edmund Wilson, in an essay on Malraux published in the *New Republic* (9 August 1933), was no doubt among the first to make this oft-repeated point in print; see "André Malraux," in *Malraux: A Collection of Critical Essays,* ed. R. W. B. Lewis (Englewood Cliffs, N.J.: Prentice-Hall, 1964), 25–30. For this 1964 reprinting of his essay, which deals primarily with *Les Conquérants* and *La Condition humaine,* Wilson appended the text of a letter Malraux wrote to him in reaction to his piece, a letter in which Malraux mentions, in reference to *La Condition humaine,* his "need to convey a certain order of ethical values through fictional characters" (30; my translation).

eventually become less significant than the novel's analytical component. In the end, a Pascalian meditation on specific aspects of our human condition eclipses the powerful representation of incipient civil war in strife-torn China, the latter purpose, it turns out, having served as but a pretext for the former.[5]

Among the more important issues examined in Malraux's novel is the question of woman's place in a male-oriented world. The writer's interest in this subject dates from virtually the beginning of his career. It is broached on several occasions in his first book, *La Tentation de l'occident* (1926),[6] and is a basic constituent of two relatively early essays, one on *Lady Chatterley's Lover* (1932)[7] and the other on *Les Liaisons dangereuses* (1939).[8] But without doubt the high-water mark in his exploration of the status of women may be found in *La Condition humaine* (1933),[9] where the matter so dominates the text that the standard English translation of its title—*Man's Fate*—seems finally quite ironic, if not altogether inappropriate.

The two main female characters in *La Condition humaine,* May and Valérie, are the principal means by which the novelist dramatizes "woman's fate." In a pioneering article published over three decades ago and entitled, fittingly enough, "Woman's Fate," Micheline Herz states:

> May represents Malraux's attempt at describing a woman liberated from the "feminine" myth, liberated also from the European bourgeois tradition that curtails the development of a full personality.... May as a character is an adventure in a

5. For information about Malraux's two sojourns in the Far East during the 1920s, which gave him the settings for his first three novels (including *La Condition humaine*), see Walter G. Langlois, *André Malraux: The Indochina Adventure* (New York: Praeger, 1966), and Clara Malraux's memoirs, *Le Bruit de nos pas,* especially vol. 3, *Les Combats et les jeux* (Paris: Grasset, 1969), and vol. 4, *Voici que vient l'été* (Paris: Grasset, 1973).

6. Ileana Juilland, *Dictionnaire des idées dans l'oeuvre de André Malraux* (The Hague: Mouton, 1968), reproduces no fewer than five passages from *La Tentation de l'occident* that deal explicitly with the status of women; see 147, 149.

7. The preface to D. H. Lawrence, *L'Amant de Lady Chatterley,* trans. Roger Cornaz (Paris: Gallimard, 1932), has been published in English as "D. H. Lawrence and Eroticism: Concerning *Lady Chatterley's Lover,*" trans. Melvin Friedman, *Yale French Studies* 11 (1953): 55–58.

8. "Choderlos de Laclos," in *Tableau de la littérature française, XVIIe–XVIIIe siècles* (Paris: Gallimard, 1939), 417–28; reprinted in Choderlos de Laclos, *Les Liaisons dangereuses* (Paris: Gallimard, 1952), 5–17.

9. Quotations from *La Condition humaine* are from André Malraux, *Romans* (Paris: Gallimard, 1947).

virgin field. She represents the ideal of the times to come, a brand of woman which does not quite exist yet, at least not on a large scale. Malraux, before Simone de Beauvoir, is perhaps the first writer to attempt such a portrayal. (16)

As for Valérie, who is in some ways even more emancipated than May, she breaks off her relationship with Ferral by writing him a farewell letter that is a veritable feminist manifesto in miniature.

But feminist themes in *La Condition humaine* go beyond these striking portraits of liberated women. Observations about woman's lot are both more numerous and more pointed here than anywhere else in Malraux's fiction. Kyo, for example, reflects on "la misogynie fondamentale de presque tous les hommes" (216, surely one of the earliest occurrences of "misogynie" in a nonscientific French text). May, a medical doctor and Kyo's wife, tells him one evening of a young bride she has treated that day at the hospital who, forced to marry a wealthy old man, had tried to kill herself. May quotes the dismaying reaction of the bride's mother: "Pauvre petite! Elle avait pourtant eu presque la chance de mourir," and concludes her anecdote with the wry comment: "La chance.... Ça en dit plus long que nos discours sur l'état des femmes ici" (212).

Beneath the surface of explicit textual reference to the plight of women, feminism plays an even more pervasive role in the novel. Thematic conflicts involving solitude and solidarity, dignity and humiliation, lucidity and intoxication, which constitute the core of *La Condition humaine,* achieve a kind of resolution in its final pages through the invocation of two antithetical models of womanhood. Utterly alone, humiliated by grief to the point of paralysis, fallen back into his opium habit, the widower Gisors, father of the now dead Kyo, in conversing with his daughter-in-law for the last time, realizes that he has little taste for women like May, "pour les femmes à demi viriles." He had loved "une Japonaise parce qu'il aimait la tendresse, parce que l'amour à ses yeux n'était pas un conflit mais la contemplation confiante d'un visage aimé, l'incarnation de la plus sereine musique, —une poignante douceur" (328–29). Fondly remembering his docile, subservient wife, he daydreams for a moment of a geisha-like child-woman, a soothing embodiment of ritualized obsequiousness. Gisors's patriarchal fantasy, however, clashes with his actual interlocutor, May, a real, grieving, but vibrant adult woman who accepts the pain of the past while resolutely facing a future she is determined to help shape. At the novel's close, Gisors's reverie and May's reality thus stand opposed to each other, leaving readers with, among other things, the sense that in any genuinely broad-based attempt to overthrow injustice and oppression, the most oppressed, hence most emblematic, heroic figures must inevitably be women.

It is therefore fitting that May should have, so to speak, the last word, which, though bleak and spare, is not despairing: " 'Je ne pleure plus guère, maintenant,' dit-elle, avec un orgueil amer" (432). So the novel ends. May has suffered the loss of a beloved husband, and Gisors, that of an adored son, but only she will continue the good fight elsewhere, far from China. Moments before her brief terminal (and terminating) avowal, she had learned that her father-in-law has opted to remain in Japan as a professor of art history, a calling ideally suited to his erudition, articulateness, and intellectual turn of mind. Gazing out the window while listening to Gisors wax eloquent about his anguish, May suddenly makes a simple wordless gesture that speaks volumes to Gisors, that tells him exactly why she, for her part, must carry on the struggle for justice and human dignity: "Sans rien dire, elle lui montra du doigt l'un des coteaux proches: attachés par l'épaule, une centaine de coolies y tiraient quelque poids très lourd et qu'on ne voyait pas, avec le geste millénaire des esclaves. 'Oui,' dit-il, 'oui' " (429). Obviously, perfect communication has taken place without recourse to speech, which obliquely raises the whole question of the adequacy of conventional language as an instrument for social intercourse. The capacity of verbal expression to provide a nexus of understanding among individuals is in fact as vital an issue in *La Condition humaine* as the plight of women; both themes merge in the novel's culminating confrontation between its still fluent but now defeated patriarchal figure and its laconic but stalwart woman warrior (Kyo, it will be recalled, thinks of May as his "chère guerrière" [212]). In this perspective, the novel's concluding pages cast a retrospective light across the entire text.

Not a work of self-conscious fiction, *La Condition humaine* never flaunts its artifice as discourse, its status as verbal construct.[10] On

10. For a lucid discussion of self-conscious fiction (what it is, what it is not), see Robert Alter, *Partial Magic: The Novel as a Self-Conscious Genre* (Berkeley and Los Angeles: Univer-

the thematic level, however, a certain calling attention to language occurs throughout the novel. Some of this metalinguistic material works in concert with the periodic indications of date and time to create an aura of documentary authenticity for both the "historic" events chronicled and the exotic setting. After all, what better way to show that we are in turbulent, intrigue-riddled Shanghai in 1927 than to register the various languages used by the novel's characters, and even the various accents and dialects in which the languages are spoken? And what does it matter if the amount of detail included concerning language, accent, and verbal tics and idiosyncrasies seems finally excessive, quantitatively greater than would be required just to fix the novel's locale and to establish separate identities for its polyphony of voices? Indeed, none of this would matter were it not that the perceived surplus of information here, especially when added to the other metalinguistic data present in the text, has a particular, cumulative effect on the novel. In order to specify this impact, let us consider some of the ways in which speech acts per se are foregrounded in *La Condition humaine*.

The first conversation (if it can be called that) in the novel takes place in a hotel elevator. Tchen, a terrorist, has just killed an arms merchant staying at the hotel so as to secure papers that will enable the insurrectionists in Shanghai to steal a desperately needed shipment of guns. Trying to flee the scene of the crime as quickly and unobtrusively as possible, he finds himself in the hotel elevator being addressed by a complete stranger:

> "La dancing-girl en rouge est épatante!" lui dit en anglais son voisin, Birman ou Siamois un peu saoul. . . . Il bafouilla au lieu de répondre; l'autre lui tapa sur l'épaule d'un air complice. . . . Mais l'interlocuteur ouvrait de nouveau la bouche. "J'ignore les langues étrangères," dit Tchen en pékinois. L'autre se tut. . . . (185–86)

Thus an opening gambit in English—with phallocratically complicitous, sexually exploitative overtones—is rebuffed in a conclusive remark uttered in a North Chinese dialect. By a kind of reverse iconicity, Tchen's response enacts precisely what it says, inasmuch as the Burmese (or Siamese) drunk, it may be assumed, neither speaks nor understands the Pekinese in which Tchen has couched his terse declaration of linguistic incompetence. The novel's dual preoccupation with the plight of women and the problematics of verbal communication is effectively adumbrated in this initiatory, sexist, emphatically foreclosed conversation.

From this point forward in the narrative, frequent allusion to the material and conventional nature of speech makes the problematics of verbal communication increasingly palpable. These reminders usually take such direct form as the phonetic transcription of accents or of idiosyncratic habits of speech. Tchen, for example, pronounces the word "non" as if it were written "nong." This spelling of the word first occurs not long after the murder of the arms merchant, when Tchen is paying a visit to his former professor and present mentor, Gisors ("un peu moins que son père, plus que sa mère" [221]). The occasion is marked by the following observation: "Il parlait français avec une accentuation de gorge sur les mots d'une seule syllabe nasale, dont le mélange avec certains idiotismes qu'il tenait de Kyo surprenait" (221). This concise summary of Tchen's manner of speaking French serves at least two distinct purposes. First, it helps to individualize the fictional character in question. It also, however, underscores the fraternal bonds that link Tchen with Kyo and, in doing so, reinforces the simulacrum of a father-son relationship that exists between Gisors and Tchen. The latter relationship contributes significantly to the novel's themes (and is reprised, in a minor key, in Tchen's relationship with the missionary Smithson) in that it ratifies Gisors in his role as the novel's wise patriarch. We have already seen that Gisors serves in just this capacity as one of the novel's polar figures, his antipode being his other "child," his daughter-in-law May, one of whose functions, ironically, is to call into question the whole value system implicit in the notion of patriarchy.

Katow, the Russian revolutionary whose manner of speaking French is also commented upon and rendered orthographically, "parlait français presque sans accent, mais en avalant un certain nombre de voyelles, comme s'il eût voulu compenser ainsi la nécessité d'articuler rigoureusesment lorsqu'il parlait chinois" (189). The Russian's pronunciation of his "signature" word (" 'Absolument' passait dans toutes les langues que parlait Katow" [203]) typifies his compensatory swallowing of vowel sounds. For example, when he and several other insurrectionists board the vessel carrying the much-coveted supply of guns, Katow mocks and then threatens the ship's captain (who is quickly relieved of his single weapon) in characteristic enunciation:

> "Absolument pas la peine d'avoir tant de revolvers à bord pour n'en porter qu'un sur soi," dit-il en anglais.... "Si vous êtes trop pressé de descendre à terre, je vous préviens que vous serez 'bsolument d'scendu au premier tournant de rue."
> (233–34)

Announcing that Katow speaks English here highlights his impressive linguistic competence—he operates in Russian, French, English, and Chinese, depending on the requirements of the situation. Ironically, however, Katow alone harbors doubts about the capacity of ordinary language to ensure communication at life's most critical moments. After his arrest, he encounters Tchen's friend Souen with another detainee in the prison's holding area for revolutionaries. The youths are terrified at the prospect of being burned alive, the method of execution awaiting them all. Katow tries to console them, but he knows that in the present circumstances, "Y a pas grand-chose à faire avec la parole" (408). Earlier in the narrative, well before his arrest, he had sought to comfort the Belgian shopkeeper Hemmelrich, who was overwhelmed by feelings of rage toward his family and guilt toward Tchen because he had refused, out of fear of compromising the security of his abjectly dutiful wife and sickly child, to allow the terrorist to take refuge in his record shop. Katow seeks to convince the Belgian that he has done right to think first of protecting those most dependent upon and devoted to him. As in a parable from the Gospels, Katow tells a story from which he hopes Hemmelrich can draw the strength to accept his moral choice without bitterness. Katow's anecdote, clearly about himself, concerns a couple, a totally devoted woman and a man who reacts sadistically to the woman's constancy. According to Katow, if the woman can somehow transcend the man's verbal abuse, he (and the relationship) will be changed, remade. In order for this to happen, however, "on est obligé de croire aux qualités du coeur quand on les rencontre, ça va de soi" (333–34). For a brief moment Katow places his hope in non-verbal communication: "Par des paroles, il ne pouvait presque rien; mais au-delà des paroles, il y avait ce qu'expriment des gestes, des regards, la seule présence" (335). Eventually the Russian stops talking altogether, realizing that "peu de mots sont moins connus des hommes que ceux de leurs douleurs profondes," and he concludes by simply saying to Hemmelrich, "Il faut que tu comprennes sans que je dise rien. . . . Il n'y a rien à dire" (335). The episode draws to a close with no clear indication of the possible effect on Hemmelrich of Katow's words or mere presence.

At the same time, however, the conversation between the two men lays bare Katow's deep distrust of language, his apparent belief that words must be bypassed by those who would make contact with, and be guided by, "qualities of the heart." The conversation also implies a valorization of genuinely connected couples like Hemmelrich and his wife, Katow and his, and in their way, Kyo and May (with Kyo struggling to understand his anger and confusion when May tells him of a casual infidelity with a medical colleague, painfully probing his rage until he realizes that, given "la misogynie fondamentale de presque tous les hommes," May's one-tryst lover will now think of her as "cette petite poule" and believe he owns her [216]), as opposed to such empty pairings as Ferral and Valérie and, on another level, Gisors and his deceased wife. Recalling the transformation wrought in him back in revolutionary Russia by the bottomless love of his long-suffering, illiterate wife, Katow remembers "continuant par habitude l'action révolutionnaire, mais y emportant l'obsession de la tendresse sans limites cachée au coeur de cette vague idiote" (334). This view of the couple, redemptive and (first impressions to the contrary notwithstanding) fundamentally egalitarian, perhaps reflects the same ethos that informs the poetry of Paul Eluard and André Breton in the late 1920s and early 1930s.[11] Whether influenced by surrealism or not, however, Malraux's conception of the couple in *La Condition humaine* validates only those males who, like Katow and Kyo, and possibly Hemmelrich, are ready

11. Any number of poems from Eluard's 1926 collection *Capitale de la douleur* (e.g., "L'Egalité des sexes" and "L'Amoureuse"), as well as Breton's 1931 text "L'Union libre," reflect this ethos; see *Capitale de la douleur* (Paris: Gallimard, 1966), 51, 56; and André Breton, *Clair de terre* (Paris: Gallimard, 1966), 93–95. Malraux's relations with the surrealists at this time were complex and ambivalent, but he was well aware of what they were doing and writing, and of the extent to which they represented a break with traditional values in a variety of realms; see Lacouture, *André Malraux,* 124–26.

to work through the concrete, sometimes contradictory, conditions of human love beyond the bounds of discourse.

The art and antique dealer Clappique, Katow's moral opposite in this respect, has no interest whatever in communicating with another human being, perhaps least of all with women. The quintessence of logorrhea, of self-inflating tale-spinning and fraudulent declamation, his nonstop mythifying cuts him off irrevocably from those around him. He completely lacks Katow's dialogic orientation, a desire for meaningful exchange with others. And yet, it is precisely *because* of his prolixity, in combination with his failure as a communicator, that Clappique deserves our attention.

In his classic study of Malraux, W. M. Frohock argues that "in writing the novel, Malraux became so fascinated with his Clappique that the latter threatened to run away with the story";[12] indeed, it is impossible to ignore Clappique's flamboyant presence in the novel. No other figure in *La Condition humaine*, for example, foregrounds speech so steadily and systematically as Clappique. His seemingly possessed way of talking is attention-getting in the extreme, but there are also numerous explicit references in the text to his "mythomanie," his compulsion to invent the most outlandish tall stories. In addition, his pet phrase "pas un mot," which he liberally sprinkles throughout his monologues, giving them a tone of mock conspiracy, on the literal level suggests a categorical rejection of ordinary language. Clappique's use of this phrase points directly to what he may embody for Malraux, the living denial of words as a universally reliable means of communication.

An episode in part four of the novel seems to identify Clappique with just such a symbolic function. He has gone to Gisors's home in order to warn Kyo that, because of his suspected involvement in the robbery of the gun shipment, he may soon be arrested. Since Kyo has not yet returned home, Clappique joins in the conversation involving Gisors, his brother-in-law Kama, who is a Japanese painter, and two of Kama's disciples. In preliminary small talk, Clappique compliments Gisors on a newly acquired cactus plant. From the Chinese inscription on the plant's support stake, Clappique learns that it is a gift from Tchen. Though he reads Chinese, Clappique does not know

12. W. M. Frohock, *André Malraux and the Tragic Imagination* (Stanford: Stanford University Press, 1952), 74.

Japanese; hence he must rely on Gisors or on one of Kama's followers to translate the painter's replies to his queries. The subjects taken up in the ensuing conversation are among the most fundamental: art, love, language, death. From Kama's contributions to the discussion, it is soon apparent that his convictions form a seamless web. His every utterance, moreover, is thrown into relief by the "slowing down" effect produced by accompanying statements, such as "Le disciple laissa le croquis, traduisit"; "Kama répondit. Gisors traduisait lui-même"; "Clappique... écoutait avec attention... tandis que Gisors traduisait" (319–20).

In response to Clappique's initial question ("Pourquoi peignez-vous, Kama-San?"), the painter answers through one of his interpreters, "d'abord, pour ma femme, parce que je l'aime." When Clappique objects that he did not ask for whom but rather why, Kama, by way of rejoinder, deplores what he sees as the narcissism of Western art: "Plus vos peintres font des pommes... plus ils parlent d'eux. Pour moi, c'est le monde qui compte." This part of the conversation then concludes, "Le maître dit: 'La peinture, chez nous, ce serait, chez vous, la charité'" (319). For Kama, art, quite obviously, is a giving, loving, bonding activity. It is his language, his mode of sharing his decipherment and revelation of the world.

Clappique's final question for Kama—what would the painter do if his wife were to die—elicits this response: "On peut communier même avec la mort.... C'est le plus difficile, mais peut-être est-ce le sens de la vie" (320). Communication with the living, Kama ultimately seems to be suggesting, prepares one for communing with the dead. Because of the increasingly metaphysical, if not to say mystical, tenor of Kama's remarks; because of Clappique's surprising attentiveness to them (mythomaniacs, after all, usually listen only to themselves); and because of the retarding effect of formal translation, the conversation enjoys a special status and serves a special purpose in the novel. Played out as if in slow motion, it pits the character who is at once the most talkative and the least communicative (Clappique) against the one who is the most sensitive to the need for communication, solidarity, and even communion with others (Kama).

The shocking extent of Clappique's detachment from his fellow humans, however, comes fully to the fore later. He has just betrayed Kyo by not warning him of an impending police roundup of Communist leaders. Seeking oblivion from the pangs of guilt unleashed by his treacherous inaction, Clappique plunges headlong into a conversation with a prostitute whose sexual services he is about to purchase. In a complete fabrication, a stream of verbiage wholly disconnected from reality and truth, he casts himself in the sordidly glamorous part of a former gangster about to commit suicide. This time, the cozy, unreal world he has created with his words is a conscious, deliberate piece of fiction, perhaps especially the life-buttressing "lien qu'établit toute pitié humaine devant la mort" (364), the specious solidarity he has temporarily forged with the duped prostitute. With this tissue of lies, Clappique has made, and more outrageously than ever before, a mockery of the value of connectedness that Kama has articulated and Katow embodied (along with Kyo and May), and that functions as a kind of moral compass for the entire novel.

The essential connection in *La Condition humaine* exists or occurs between the "communicating vessels" of the loving couple. The man-woman relationship is thus primary, despite the novel's stress on male friendship. In fact, the former act of bonding allows the latter to come into being; beyond that, it allows human solidarity to develop on a broader scale. Kyo and Katow (and even Hemmelrich) can reach out to each other and, eventually, to the oppressed masses around them precisely because at some point they ceased to look upon the women in their lives as objects and as instances of an eternally foreign Other. The love that Kyo and May share, for example— intersubjective, virtually interpenetrating—precludes even the possibility of such alien otherness. At a critical juncture in the story—when Kyo has told May of his decision to go alone to an emergency meeting of Shanghai's Communist cadre, an act he suspects may be his last as a free man—May, trying to persuade her husband to let her accompany him on this dangerous outing, asks simply, and rhetorically, "Suis-je 'un autre,' Kyo?" (326). Later, after Kyo's death, May retrieves his body. Preparing it for burial, she speaks lovingly to the corpse: " 'Mon amour,' murmurait-elle, comme elle eût dit 'ma chair,' sachant bien que c'était quelque chose d'elle-même, non d'étranger, qui lui était arraché" (412). Where does she stop and Kyo begin, she could once wonder. But now the flesh of her flesh has been torn from her forever. Death has sundered the couple and in the process reasserted solitary suffering as May's fate. What lingers in the mind, however, is the couple's solidarity in life, their total, unconditional acceptance of each other, their common refusal to view alterity as something menacing, and the meliorative impact of that expansive refusal on their conduct as socially responsible beings.

Even the admirable Katow is spiritually enhanced by his contact (albeit at a remove) with such connectedness, as is suggested in the novel's climactic pages, those devoted, first, to Kyo's and, then, to Katow's death. Having decided to commit suicide rather than permit himself to be executed, Kyo performs a secular ritual of recollection to ready himself for the moment of truth. In the course of his meditation, he draws special strength from thoughts of May: "Depuis plus d'un an, May l'avait délivré de toute solitude" (405). Then, at the very instant of his passing, he hears and feels Katow, sprawled beside him among the other prisoners condemned to death, "l'intérroger avec angoisse et le toucher" (407). In context, this terminal act of touching—replicated moments later when Katow hands his suicide pill over to young Souen and his companion—resembles a mythic last rite, the transference of moral force at death. It is as if through this concrete, gestural affirmation of connectedness Katow were taking on his fallen comrade's fortitude and adding it to his own, thus rising to a hitherto unknown level of bravery, a plane of action and solidarity where he could choose to give away his cyanide capsule—not just once, but twice—and face up to the horror of execution by fire. Katow's extraordinary generosity in this situation appears to result directly from his absorbing the dying Kyo's spiritual strength. Kyo, for his part, seems to have found the courage to cleave to his choice of suicide by reflecting upon the solitude-canceling love he had found earlier with May. Thus both courageous deaths can be traced back to the values of connectedness and communication that inform the relationship between May and Kyo, with May assuming the role of ultimate enabler or catalyst in this scheme.

But if May occupies a dramatically (and socially) privileged position in the novel, she is no less a woman for all that, no less subject to the scorn, invisibility, and humiliation reserved for her sex generally in *La Condition humaine*. Accordingly, the sober, balanced argument she makes for talking seriously about improving the legal situation of abused wives in China falls on deaf ears, even in the case of Kyo (323). We have already noted Gisors's mistrust and antipathy toward her. Nevertheless, against the background in the novel of the limitations imposed on women as a class, the circumstances of May's life seem almost idyllic.

A number of passages scattered throughout the text reveal the hold of these demeaning limitations on women, reducing them, in one way or another, to the role of the threatening and/or contemptible Other. In one such passage, Kyo, momentarily bewildered if not exasperated by May, thinks of her as "une femme. Pas une espèce d'homme. Autre chose" (216). But a short while later, when an old Mandarin visiting Gisors extols the virtues of a social order in which "la femme est soumise à l'homme comme l'homme est soumis à l'Etat" (219), the latter privately muses, "La soumission des femmes? Chaque soir, May rapportait des suicides des fiancées" (220). When, following the Mandarin's departure, Gisors asks Tchen what he felt after he had murdered the arms merchant, Tchen replies, "De l'orgueil." Pressed by his interlocutor to expand on his answer, he adds, "De ne pas être une femme" (222). As for Hemmelrich's wife, we learn that during the time before she came to live with him, she had once been sold into concubinage for the sum of twelve dollars (312). In a conversation with Ferral, Gisors contends, "Il faut toujours s'intoxiquer: ce pays a l'opium, l'Islam le haschisch, l'Occident la femme." Ferral, for his part, asserts that "l'homme peut et doit nier la femme" (349). Alone a short while later, reflecting on his conversation with Gisors and recalling Valérie's claim that women too are human beings, Ferral scoffingly mutters, "Une femme, un être humain! C'est un repos, un voyage, un ennemi" (351). Ferral thus not only instrumentalizes women but also considers them hostile creatures to be crushed. When König, Chiang Kai-shek's chief of police, confides to Clappique the details of his torture at the hands of the Communists during the Bolshevik revolution, he bitterly confesses his humiliation—"J'ai pleuré comme une femme, comme un veau" (378)—and justifies his own use of torture by implying an implacable need to expunge this humiliation. In Kyo's first conversation in prison after his arrest, his cellmate tells him quite nonchalantly that he was arrested because he sells women for a living and that he gets thrown into jail whenever he neglects to pay off the police (388). In a host of other passages, women are viewed by men as sources of resentment and hatred, or as chattel to be dealt with according to male whim, running the gamut of negative responses from absolute avoidance or shunning to sexual violation.

Misogyny in its harshest form issues, not surprisingly, from Ferral. If Gisors's intoxication is opium, Tchen's terrorism, and Clappique's myth-making, Ferral's is control over others, especially women. A connoisseur of erotic art, in sexual relations he is essentially a voyeur; he prefers watching to touching, a not insignificant predilection in light of the novel's valorization of connectedness. Above all, his will must prevail over his partner's. As a consequence, the shadow of exploitation and contempt falls across all of his encounters with women.

But in Valérie, who is a prosperous dress designer, Ferral has met his match, and his nemesis. Successful in business, hence economically independent, emancipated in all of her attitudes, a disabused pragmatist in the conduct of her love life, she has what is for Ferral the unsettling knack of talking as if she has just stepped out of *Les Liaisons dangereuses*. With a smile, she can drop the most jaded comment into the middle of an intimate conversation with her lover. Furthermore, her sense of moral autonomy is easily as strong as Ferral's. If she loses one battle of wills with him, she wins the war between the sexes in which they are engaged. To avenge her humiliation by Ferral when, against her manifest wishes and efforts to the contrary, he kept switching the lights back on during their lovemaking so as to watch the transformation of her features during orgasm (267), Valérie arranges a stunning scenario of retaliation in which she wounds Ferral in his pride far more deeply than she was shamed by his fit of domination over her. The "coup de grâce" in her elaborate settling of accounts is a witty, disdainful farewell letter which concludes with the flippant admonition: "Et tout de même, la prochaine fois laissez donc les interrupteurs d'éléctricité tranquilles" (340).

The debonair, casually insulting tone of Valérie's letter makes its pithy message all the more vibrant. She is clearly preaching to Ferral while at the same time letting him know that she knows he is beyond the reach of her words. Her arch, superior tone also lets him know that she is not in the least interested in persuading him of anything. She argues her case (on behalf of women's liberation) brilliantly but, like a legal dandy, does not deign to show any concern for the possible effect of her brief on her adversary. Her letter has, therefore, something gratuitous about it. Patently indigestible to its addressee, it also goes against the grain of the smooth narratorial *style indirect libre* that dominates the novel as a whole.[13] A verbal jewel, it sits there on the page unassimilable to its textual surroundings.

And yet, both structurally and stylistically, Valérie's letter-manifesto (which contains such tart, lapidary formulations as "Je me refuse autant à être un corps que vous un carnet de chèques" [340]) is entirely justified within the novel, not only in thematic terms where its usefulness and perhaps even its necessity are obvious, but also in its polished style where it recalls Clappique's lush inventions. Both characters treat discourse as something to be fashioned with care and brio,[14] but Valérie moves in a direction diametrically opposed to Clappique's, toward reality and truth. On the other hand, by his speech, whether paraphrased or directly reported, Clappique sensitizes us to the phenomenon of empty or dissembling rhetorical flourish, thereby preparing us for the genuine article, for truth-bearing eloquence, when we encounter it. Paradoxically, his tall tales lend Valérie's epistle a degree of conviction and appropriateness it might otherwise not possess. In the perspective of the whole novel, Clappique's baroque deceptions call out to and almost call for Valérie's elegant argument.

The presence of Valérie's letter in the narrative is further justified by its immediate context. Though an eminently persuasive document, it does not, as we have noted, attempt to convince its recipient

13. In terms of the categories for the presentation of consciousness in fiction that Dorrit Cohn has so persuasively developed in *Transparent Minds: Narrative Modes for Presenting Consciousness in Fiction* (Princeton: Princeton University Press, 1978), it would be more precise to state that in *La Condition humaine*, a third-person narrative, Malraux, although relying most heavily on one particular narrative mode, moves freely among: "1. psycho-narration: the narrator's discourse about a character's consciousness; 2. quoted monologue: a character's mental discourse; 3. narrated monologue: a character's mental discourse in the guise of the narrator's discourse" (14). Of the three types, "narrated monologue" is closest to *style indirect libre*, and to a considerable degree overlaps with it. Nevertheless, I prefer the French expression when referring to the dominant narrative mode of Malraux's text. First of all, the term *style indirect libre* suggests quite explicitly that the blended voices can on some occasions favor the narrator and on others the protagonist. In addition, as Cohn makes clear in her comparative discussion of "narrated monologue" on the one hand and *style indirect libre* and *erlebte Rede* on the other (109–11), the French expression has a less restrictive range of application than the English one, the French connoting a *vision avec* while the English is more akin to a *pensée avec.* The somewhat broader scope of the French phrase in this regard and the varying emphases between narrator and protagonist accommodate make it especially apt for characterizing the dominant narrative mode of *La Condition humaine.*

14. Interestingly enough, Valérie finds Clappique's fanciful imagination ("sa fantaisie") enchanting (265).

of its validity. So presented, it hangs suspended in a rhetorical void. But analogous circumstances obtain whenever May speaks of the same subject, the plight of women. Both female characters make statements on behalf of their sex that are met with silence (at best) on the part of the novel's male characters. The rhetorical situation of Valérie's letter makes that silence explicit and active, if not altogether deafening. It is thus a fitting ironic twist that Ferral's greatest humiliation, prefigured in the whole episode involving Valérie's letter, should take the form of the repeated silences with which his pleas for financial support are greeted by bankers and government officials on his return to Paris near the novel's close (419, 422).

Essentially, the plot of *La Condition humaine* follows the unfolding events of the Shanghai uprising; yet the narrative's propulsive energy derives not from any chronicle but rather from certain recurrent, interlocking antitheses, and from our awakened and then sustained desire to reach a resolution of these conflicts.[15] The most fundamental of these is the ongoing dialectic between dignity and humiliation, a conflict that motivates characters as diverse as Kyo, König, and Ferral. At one point Kyo goes so far as to define the notions in terms of each other, as each other's opposites (394). Significantly, if Kyo (along with May and Katow) is committed to introducing a measure of dignity into the lives of the most oppressed members of Chinese society by lifting the burden of injustice and humiliation from their shoulders, Ferral and König, by contrast, are concerned only with their own sense of humiliation and lost dignity. Once again we see the novel's major figures dividing into antinomous groups of altruists and egoists.

For egoists, self must always take precedence over other, as must male over female. Similarly, the abstract will always win out over the concrete, as will death over life, fantasy over reality, book knowledge over the wisdom gained from living, and essentially narcissistic cogitation over a continuing dialogue between logic and experience. Tchen typifies these biases. His university-acquired Marxism fuels his thoroughly private addiction to terrorism, in dramatic opposition to the hunger for social justice that has animated his friend Souen

15. For an exploration of the "totalizing function" of desire in our experience of reading narrative, see Peter Brooks, *Reading for the Plot: Design and Intention in Narrative* (New York: Knopf, 1984), especially the chapters "Narrative Desire" (37–61) and "Freud's Masterplot: A Model for Narrative" (90–112).

ever since the latter witnessed his father's torture and subsequent murder by political thugs. Souen pointedly remarks to Tchen, "C'est pour les nôtres que je combats, pas pour moi" (316). In order to convey to Gisors his scorn for men who have not yet killed, Tchen derisively refers to them as "puceaux" (222), or male virgins, a term that inevitably recalls—and in its context here disparages—the more frequently seen and traditionally honorific feminine (singular) form of the word "pucelle"; thus does Tchen once again denigrate women. He is an isolate and a fantast unconnected to his fellow combatants (254) and, for want of memory, to the anchor of his past life (289). In attempting to explain to Kyo his fascination with his own death, Tchen enters a self-created verbal labyrinth that begins, "Je cherche un mot plus fort que joie. Il n'y a pas de mot. Même en chinois. Un... apaisement total. Une sorte de... comment dites-vous? de... je ne sais pas" (289).

Tchen's groping on this occasion for words adequate to his intoxication, besides revealing still another facet of the character's life-denying disconnectedness, reminds us of the centrality of the problematics of speech to the novel. Thematically, language is foregrounded and its reliability questioned virtually throughout the novel. On the other hand, definitions and glosses of all sorts abound, even turning up in footnotes (195, 207, 322, 336, 393). Mythomania, intoxication, intelligence, eroticism, the human condition, for example, are all discussed and explained at length. Terms still quite new to fiction, like "geisha" and "sadique" and "paranoïque," are used with ease and aptness. Dialects and accents are identified and commented upon (and with even greater frequency than the instances cited above might indicate). Taken together, the novel's manifold metalinguistic allusions at first give the impression that the verbal tools necessary for uncovering its secrets are, so to speak, handed to us on a silver platter. In fact, however, *La condition humaine* resists facile penetration via the terms, definitions, explanations, and commentaries it offers us so freely. Words alone, abstracted from their sociohistorical contexts and circumstances, can only deceive—or so Malraux's text seems to be signaling to us from somewhere beneath its surface. The novel's great users of speech are also its blatant abusers of speech—the glib explainers (Gisors), manipulators (Ferral), rationalizers (König), liars (Clappique), and nihilists (Tchen)—all of whom are possessed by their bloodless utterances rather than the other way around.

Communist homily and propaganda are directly associated with such lifeless, mechanized palaver in part three of the novel. Kyo and Tchen have gone to the city of Han-Kéou to convince Vologuine, a high Party functionary, that it would be suicidal for the Shanghai insurgents to obey the Party's latest directive and surrender their weapons to Chiang Kai-shek. For the long-range good of the Revolution, Vologuine turns down their manifestly valid request to have the directive rescinded. He does so at considerable length and with great patience, drawing inspiration from "les discours de Lénine, ces spirales opiniâtres par lesquelles il revenait six fois sur le même point, un étage plus haut chaque fois" (280). Following their fruitless meeting with Communist officialdom, Kyo and Tchen stand disconsolately for a moment on the sidewalk outside Vologuine's offices. Suddenly Tchen invites his friend to listen:

> "Ecoute . . . " dit Tchen. Transmis par la terre, le frémissement des machines de l'imprimerie, régulier, maîtrisé comme celui d'un moteur de navire, les pénétrait des pieds à la tête. . . . Kyo ne pouvait se délivrer de cet ébranlement de machines transmis à ses muscles par le sol—comme si ces machines à fabriquer la vérité eussent rejoint en lui les hésitations et les affirmations de Vologuine. (287)

In the steady vibration of the earth beneath his feet, Kyo under-stands that his life, as well as that of Tchen and their comrades back in Shanghai, is even now being sacrificed to "ces machines à fabriquer la vérité," the thundering maw of the Party's printing presses, a grotesque echo of Vologuine's labored but cool assertions.

May, for her part, explicitly rejects talk spun out of speakers in self-encasing cocoons. She contrasts the chilling anecdote of a young bride's failed suicide, and the dismaying regret of the bride's mother, with "nos discours sur l'état des femmes ici," with feminist addresses that are detached from life as it is actually lived. In May, evidently, a devotion to feminist principle (and to political liberation generally) does not exclude a basic skepticism with regard to language, including that of feminist discourse.

At the same time, however, inarticulateness hardly characterizes her verbal style, not even at the novel's close. Although Gisors would have much preferred a daughter-in-law who embodied the rhyming dictum "sage comme une image," May's quasi-muteness by the conclusion of the narrative in no way signifies that she has at last reconciled herself to decorous, self-effacing silence as her preordained lot. On the contrary, in the end she represents, more starkly than ever before, the inexorable rise of someone who will finally be heard, of that traditionally most censored Other, that ideal and yet real alternate subjectivity, the self-liberated woman. Ultimately in this perspective, the title of Micheline Herz's schematic but heuristic study, translated back into French, perhaps best epitomizes the novel, at least metonymically. As the text amply demonstrates, humanity's at once wretched and noble destiny attains its most compelling (if also its most occulted) form in woman's fate. What better way, then, to read *La Condition humaine* than as a palimpsest, with the last word of its title written over a blanked-out "féminine"?[16]

16. At least two other Malraux texts would indirectly support the "feminist" reading of *La Condition humaine* proposed here. The first of these texts appeared early in Malraux's career; the second, very late. In *Les Conquérants* (1928), for example, we soon learn that as a young man back in his native Switzerland, Garine, the novel's hero, was once arrested and brought to trial for complicity in financially aiding and abetting abortions for impoverished young women. The episode (*Romans*, 44–46) is clearly designed to establish the young anarchist's generosity and idealism, to provide him with the "correct" political credentials. But to illustrate these qualities via the cause of free, elective abortion in a novel of revolution in Asia seems far-fetched and gratuitous. On the other hand, critics have often thought of *Les Conquérants* as a kind of "dry run" for *La Condition humaine* (e.g., Frohock, *André Malraux*, 37), which would perhaps explain the protofeminist nature of Garine's early political commitment.

The second text is the funeral oration that the dying Malraux delivered at Chartres on 10 May 1975 on the occasion of the thirtieth anniversary of the Allied liberation of the deportation camps. The exclusive focus of his remarks is the camp at Ravensbruck in northern Germany where 8,000 French women Resistance members and sympathizers had been put to death or had simply died from the bestial treatment they were made to endure. The oration amounts to a paean, completely free of condescension, to the specifically "female" nature of the women's courage and posture of refusal in the face of Nazi brutality and oppression. The text occupies the closing pages of *Les Miroir des limbes* (Paris: Gallimard, 1976), 1006–11, the last book Malraux published in his life.

For a contrary approach to the question of Malraux and feminism, see Suleiman, "Malraux's Women."

Five

Fluency, Muteness, and Commitment in Camus's *La Peste*

Without question, *La Condition humaine* and *La Peste* are among twentieth-century French fiction's most successful realizations, deliberate or otherwise, of the ideal of commitment in literature. If we are to appreciate the achievement of these novels, however, we must understand what the notion of commitment in literature entails. To do that, certain distinctions must be drawn, such as the one between thesis fiction and the fiction of commitment. Accordingly, before analyzing the interplay of moralism and metalanguage in *La Peste*, I shall review, very briefly, the concept of commitment in literature, particularly as that concept or goal was developed by Sartre, and as it diverges from the authoritarian model for literature.

In the previous chapter, we saw how a privileging of human solidarity conjoins with a problematizing of human speech in *La Condition humaine*. An analogous conjunction of forces occurs in *La Peste*. This double convergence may be accounted for, at least in part, by what distinguishes thesis fiction from the fiction of commitment. Neither novel, for example, would meet the criteria for ideological or authoritarian fiction that Susan Rubin Suleiman has proposed in her stimulating study of that genre.[1] Suleiman defines the ideological novel, or the *roman à thèse*, as follows: "a novel written in the realistic mode (that is, based on an aesthetic of verisimilitude and representation), which signals itself to the reader as primarily didactic in intent, seeking to demonstrate the validity of a political, philosophical, or religious doctrine" (7). Judged in terms of this brief but cogent definition, *La Condition humaine* and *La Peste* would seem far too reticent in their affirmation of a single, absolute truth to be deemed authoritarian or thesis-bearing fictions. Suleiman continues: "the [exemplary] story must give rise not only to 'meaning' (a lesson) but also to a rule of action: its aim, in other words, is not only to teach something but also to influence the receiver's actions in a particular way" (46). Thus, the wish to impose a specific ideology on its readers characterizes authoritarian fiction. But such a dominant, coercive teleology hardly motivates either Malraux's novel or Camus's, in both of which, among other counterauthoritarian factors, the desire to please clearly holds its own with the need to instruct.

One could also argue that their very divergence from the exemplary or authoritarian model has kept *La Condition humaine* and *La Peste* alive, enabled them to speak to readers far removed, in time and culture, from their original publication. Susan Suleiman again sheds light on the subject: "Written in and for a specific historical and social circumstance, the *roman à thèse* is not easily exported. And even in its native land, it becomes 'ancient history' as soon as the circumstance that founded it no longer holds"(147). The continuing vitality of *La Condition humaine* and *La Peste* down to our own day and place therefore suggests, among other things, that these works transcend the sociopolitical conditions attending their birth and inspiring many of their themes. Somehow, with these novels of commitment, message and spectacle never compromise their interdependence, the mutuality ensuring them permanent life.

At the heart of the ideological or authoritarian novel lie fundamentally unproblematic notions of human language and human nature, neither of which, apparently, requires much thought. Also, doctrinal intertexts function in such works as a kind of ground bass

1. Susan Rubin Suleiman, *Authoritarian Fictions: The Ideological Novel as a Literary Genre* (New York: Columbia University Press, 1983). Subsequent page references to this work are in the body of the study, in parentheses.

for their salient sociopolitical melodic line. By their very prominence, moreover, the rules of action preached in these narratives
simply eclipse or overwhelm whatever doubts readers may harbor
about the soundness of the verbal vehicles carrying the lessons. On
the other hand, fictions of commitment like *La Condition humaine*
and *La Peste* treat words and, by extension, their users as uncertain,
potentially changeable entities. May's proud, heroic laconism in the
polarized final section of Malraux's novel, and Rieux's steady, equally
heroic taciturnity throughout Camus's text, for example, raise questions in readers' minds about the power and reliability of language.
Adding to our misgivings in this regard is the apparently unthinking
glibness of the least admirable figures in both narratives, where, sporadically, still other expressions of anxiety about the efficacy of
speech and writing reinforce our mounting suspicions. Ultimately,
our everyday trust in words as faithful reflectors or conveyors of reality, inner and outer, is shaken, although not destroyed, by these fictions. The instrument still works, but its flaws are beginning to show.

Eventually, inadequacies glimpsed in the instrument diminish our
confidence in its users, the fictional presences populating *La Condition humaine* and *La Peste,* instances of the generality called human nature. Sartre, in his quasi-official manifesto of *engagement,* the
"Présentation" that he published in the inaugural issue of *Les Temps
modernes* (October 1945),[2] condemns Proust precisely because
"son oeuvre contribue à répandre le mythe de la nature humaine"
(20). But is not the conception of human nature implicit in the Malraux and Camus novels also basically essentialist? Probably so. Yet
the question of whether essence precedes existence, fact is prior to
act, or vice versa, cannot be reduced to an either/or approach. To
restrict human nature to these alternatives would constitute a significant misrepresentation of human nature, whose sign, no doubt, is
contradiction itself.

Nonetheless, an overall harmony of concerns obtains among Sartre's manifesto and the Malraux and Camus novels. Sartre's text, for
example, contains the essential ingredients of his philosophy of *engagement:* freedom of choice as the defining characteristic and purpose of human existence; the assumption of responsibility as the

2. The "Présentation des *Temps Modernes*" has been reprinted in Jean-Paul Sartre, *Situations* (Paris: Gallimard, 1948), 2:9–30. Subsequent page references to this text are in the body
of the study, in parentheses.

writer's duty; the obligation of writers to act, through their writings, for the collectivity; the conviction that writers are situated in a certain time and place out of which they must write. Basically, according to his "Présentation," Sartre aspires to "changer à la fois la condition sociale de l'homme et la conception qu'il a de lui-même" (16). In broad terms, *La Condition humaine* and *La Peste* embody precisely these values.

With their novelistic practice, in fact, Malraux and Camus may outstrip, even as they illustrate, Sartre's theory of commitment. *La Condition humaine* and *La Peste* presuppose, it would seem, a universal, inherently flawed human nature. Both titles, for example, echo phrases drawn from Western civilization's consecrated literary tradition—Montaigne, Pascal, the Bible, Defoe. Entirely on their own, that is, without the (literally) book-length texts that follow them, both titles thus evoke timeless human dramas and eternal moral dilemmas. Also, the concluding sections of both novels dramatize the endless or cyclical (and thus foredoomed) quality of all ethical quests. On the other hand, the daily experience of freely choosing for or against human solidarity occupies center stage in both narratives, whose protagonists create themselves, forge their essence, out of the ongoing series of choices making up their existence. In this wider perspective, Malraux and Camus represent something quite remarkable, the grafting of existentialist tales onto the essentialist trunk of French letters. In a sense, therefore, an invigorating *conception synthétique* of human beings (as opposed to the destructive *esprit analytique* that for Sartre typifies the bourgeois class), which the founder of *Les Temps modernes* so passionately commends to fellow writers in his "Présentation," may already be achieved with *La Condition humaine* and *La Peste*.

The absence of specificity in the sociopolitical messages of *La Condition humaine* and *La Peste* correlates with the foregrounding of language that periodically interrupts the flow of the two texts. Where authoritarian fiction rides a sleek verbal vehicle to categorical edification, novels of commitment follow no comparably swift road in their struggle for the liberation of humanity. The humane visions sketched in these works never elide the halting, approximate mediation of the words that body forth the visions. On the contrary, in these complex narratives, a long, twilight struggle for justice and solidarity has its counterpart in an intermittent, crepuscular groping for genuine communication.

These gallant endeavors in tandem, moreover, seem destined from the start to settle for only partial successes and provisional victories. In both novels silence shadows the action, beckoning the protagonists to an alluring but solitary, hence fatal, stillness. "Only connect," these fictions finally murmur, but without authority. Yet what else can one expect? After all, the tattoo rarely sounds more certain than its trumpet, though its echo may outlast more strident calls to arms. It is against this background that we shall now examine the collaborative roles of fluency, muteness, and commitment in *La Peste*.

Moralistic analysis and metalinguistic commentary interpenetrate completely in *La Peste*. In Camus's long second novel, a pervasive skepticism regarding the usual forms of discourse, combined with an equally pervasive honoring of silence,[3] effectively devalues idiosyncratic, self-inflating acts of bravery in favor of self-effacing, socially binding, ethical attitudes. A bold thematic fugue, moreover, the interplay of verbal facility grown suspect, muteness as a necessary step toward the only saintliness man can aspire to, and group survival idealized at the expense of individual salvation, so marks *La Peste* as to constitute its most specific and perhaps most appealing feature as a work of fiction.

On the other hand, if *La Peste* is the longest and possibly the most ambitious of Camus's three novels, it has "le moins retenu l'attention des critiques."[4] This state of affairs may be attributed, largely, to the alacrity with which the novel was pigeonholed, at the time of its publication in 1947, as an allegory of France under the Nazi occupation. Also, Camus's participation in the Resistance during the occupation, followed by his editorial and journalistic work for *Combat* from 1944 to 1947, no doubt predisposed critics to find *La Peste* too intimately tied to recent history and too didactic in intent to merit sustained consideration as a novel.[5] Finally, there is the contrary indictment of critics, like Roland Barthes, who adjudged the work

---

3. Bethany Ladimer, in "Camus Chenoua Landscape," *Yale French Studies* 57 (1979): 109–23, heads her list of "the antinomies constantly present throughout Camus's work" with positively valorized silence and negatively valorized speech (113). See also in this connection Hiroshi Mino, *Le Silence dans l'oeuvre de Camus* (Paris: José Corti, 1987).

4. Brian T. Fitch, "Camus romancier: *La Peste*," *La Revue des Lettres Modernes*, nos. 477–83 (1976): 5.

5. See, for example, Germaine Brée's discussion of this matter in *Camus* (New Brunswick: Rutgers University Press, 1961), 89–90.

inappropriately removed from history, insufficiently cognizant of the concrete, human face of evil—in this case, Nazi Germany.[6] Whatever the reasons for the relative neglect of *La Peste* through the years, I contend that it is the most richly textured, complexly structured of Camus's longer fictions, and at the same time his most convincing effort in sociocultural criticism. While it is hardly my purpose to denigrate either *L'Etranger* (1942) or *La Chute* (1956), I believe *La Peste* to be unique within the author's canon, primarily as a remarkable fusion of metalinguistic commentary and moralistic analysis, but also as a brilliant amalgam of theory of literature and imaginative literature long before such combinations were as widely attempted as they are today.

Already between the novel's epigraph, drawn from Defoe's *Journal of the Plague Year,* and the concluding paragraph of its brief first chapter, the stage of *La Peste* is set, its central conflict delineated. What is immediately dramatized is the enormous difficulty that confronts the individual participant-observer who would recount his experiences objectively and in the process reveal truths that are valid for others, perhaps for an entire people or even all people. From the beginning, the sentences in *La Peste* periodically call attention to themselves as constituting the chronicle of one fictional character's struggle to reach perfect linguistic objectivity and hence reliability. At the same time, the events recounted, including the characters who participate in them, emerge as facets of a symbolic moral universe rather than true-to-life entities. *La Peste* is then not realistic in the usual sense.

On the other hand, it is not metafictional either; its "story" and "lesson" are too urgently felt by the reader for that. Also, in querying itself, the text of Camus's novel questions not so much language in general (*la langue*) as the language of an individual speaker or writer (*la parole*), and it does so explicitly. In the elaborately self-conscious close to the first chapter, the narrator refers to himself several times as "le narrateur," to his "chronique" (i.e., what we are reading), to the "dépositions," "documents," and "textes" he has consulted, and in general to the great effort he has made to keep his

---

6. Roland Barthes, *"La Peste,* annales d'une épidémie ou roman de la solitude," *Club* (February 1955), 6. See also Camus's reply to Barthes, "Lettre à Roland Barthes," in Albert Camus, *Théâtre, Récits, Nouvelles,* ed. Roger Quilliot (Paris: Gallimard, 1962), 1965–67.

"récit" as accurate as possible.[7] We must bear in mind that what is exposed here is not *La Peste*'s status as a verbal construct, but the compositional and ethical problems that are encountered by the novel's narrator when carrying out the task he has set for himself. The illusion of conventionally realistic fiction is still intact. *La Peste* would thus scarcely conform to the criteria for self-conscious fiction proposed by Robert Alter, who speaks of "a novel that systematically flaunts its own condition of artifice . . . and probes into the problematic relationship between real-seeming artifice and reality." On the contrary, to use Alter's characterization of the other great fictional mode, Camus's novel would seem to embody "an intent, verisimilar representation of moral situations in their social contexts."[8]

We must go one step further, however, in this effort to circumscribe, albeit roughly, the generic nature of *La Peste*. If precisely observed details lend a naturalistic flavor to whole sections of the novel, the dominant impulse is away from painstaking description toward a visionary, Manichaean approach to characters and situations. Moreover, the question of language and its limits is inextricably bound up with the schematizations and oppositions of character and theme that inform *La Peste*. Every important character, for example, reflects a position, positive or negative, on the question of language's capacity for true expression. Also, every character forms with every other character a compatible or an incompatible pair. Harmony or dissonance within each couple so formed turns on two specific issues, whether or not a given character "believes" implicitly in language and whether or not that character transcends egoism.

Rieux and his mother, for example, equally laconic, equally mistrustful of words and equally committed to struggling, in concert with others, against the plague, follow parallel if not convergent paths. The starkest antithesis in the novel involves Joseph Grand, the dedicated, nearly mute municipal employee, identified in the narrative as its hero (*TRN,* 1329), and Cottard, the voluble, suicidal black-marketeer, by far the novel's most villainous presence. The binary nature of the opposition between Cottard and Grand is obvious from their entering the narrative at the same moment (on the

7. Camus, *Théâtre, Récits, Nouvelles,* 1219–20. Subsequent page references to this work are in the body of the text, preceded by *TRN.*

8. Robert Alter, *Partial Magic: The Novel as a Self-Conscious Genre* (Berkeley and Los Angeles: University of California Press, 1975), ix–x.

occasion of Cottard's suicide attempt, foiled by Grand), their living in the same apartment house and the fact that both are or become patients of Dr. Rieux, the novel's main character and, we eventually learn, its narrator, the "author" of the "chronicle" we are reading. That Cottard is as destructive and self-dramatizing as Grand is discreet and concerned for others points to their essential polarity. When Rieux arrives at the former's apartment, having been called there by Grand, the doctor reads on Cottard's door, scrawled in red chalk, "Entrez, je suis pendu" (*TRN,* 1229). When Grand volunteers to spend the night watching over Cottard, a neighbor whom by his own admission he scarcely knows, he says to Rieux simply, as if to justify his solicitude, "Il faut bien s'entraider" (*TRN,* 1230). Here and throughout the novel, the prolix, greedy underside of Romantic heroism marks Cottard's conduct, in contrast to the verbal minimalism and anonymous good works that characterize Grand's.

The most fundamental if least immediately perceptible binary opposition in *La Peste* is that which obtains between its two major figures, Dr. Bernard Rieux and Jean Tarrou. Although starting at different points in time, both work steadfastly to combat the devastating effects of the scourge afflicting Oran, and both attempt to keep a record of the struggle, Rieux by means of his "chronique" and Tarrou with his "carnets." We of course read the former *in extenso* (presumably), but have access to Tarrou's notebooks only through those passages from them that Rieux elects to quote, summarize or otherwise describe in his chronicle. Nevertheless, by comparing the two figures through their respective "texts" and by taking additional note of Tarrou's words and actions merely referred to in Rieux's chronicle, we can discern profound differences between the two historians of the plague.

Let us consider the chronicle's author first. As we have seen, Rieux is virtually possessed by the idea of transcribing the events he has witnessed in the most objective manner possible, of blocking in advance, as it were, any personal, biased, or eccentric influence upon his depiction of the plague at its most typical. So obsessed is he with maintaining a neutral, detached attitude in his task that even after he has identified himself as the author of the chronicle (at the beginning of the book's closing chapter), he persists in using third-person narrative to the very end; that is, through the book's last sentence, despite the reader's full knowledge now of Rieux's central role in the dramatic events he is recounting. The cumulative effect of such un-relenting and finally ostentatious modesty is to foreground the entire notion of point of view in fiction and particularly the confessional mode, with its ubiquitous self-accusing, self-excusing, ultimately self-displaying "moi-je-me." (It is this aspect of *La Peste* that prefigures the basic premise of *La Chute.*)

First-person narration is thematized and undermined in various other ways in *La Peste,* all of which serve to echo what Rieux as third-person narrator stands for: a rejection of the inevitable self-validating, even self-promoting, hence basically unreliable, recounting "I." Grand's inability to verbalize his feelings, to express his love in words, may have cost him his marriage, for example, and his end-less reworking of the first sentence in his projected novel may keep him from ever writing the novel, but his diffidence in this area, a hes-itancy bordering on total inarticulateness, may bespeak the very quality that permits him to subordinate the needs of his private self to those of the collectivity. Grand's case in fact leads us to suspect that within the moral economy of *La Peste* glibness must give way to silence before human solidarity can be achieved; fluency must grav-itate toward its opposite, laconism, for commitment to the common-weal to replace egoism. Confirming our suspicions in this regard is the behavior of Rieux's mother, especially as registered by Tarrou, who marvels at her ability "de tout exprimer en phrases simples" (*TRN,* 1444).

Early in the narrative the same preference for quiet, salutary ac-tion over verbal dazzle is expressed. At Rieux's insistence, a public health commission has been convened at the prefecture. A debate ensues on how to formulate an official reaction to the fatal sickness affecting a growing number of Oranais. Exasperated by the inaction of the group and its haggling over words, Rieux asserts: "Ce n'est pas une question de vocabulaire, c'est une question de temps." Moments later, just before walking out of the meeting, he adds: "La formule m'est indifférente.... Disons seulement que nous ne devons pas agir comme si la moitié de la ville ne risquait pas d'être tuée, car alors elle le serait" (*TRN,* 1256–57).

An important distinction must be made here, however. Language is rejected in *La Peste* only under very particular circumstances: when it is showy, dilatory self-indulgence, a substitute for appropriate action—when doctors, for example, bicker over words instead of acting decisively to stop the scourge from spreading any further, when a preacher (Father Paneloux) employs his eloquence not to move people to action but in order to make the faithful accept the plague as just punishment for their sins, when an examining magistrate (Othon) merely continues in his role of posing questions and proffering judgments as if the plague would somehow go away by itself. As regards their use of language, all of the above lack critical self-consciousness, all are verbose instrumentalists, skilled but unreflective rhetoricians. On the other hand, when language in *La Peste* is not taken for granted, when it is deliberately renounced in favor of responsible gesture (Rieux), puzzled over as an engrossing occupation (Grand's constantly rewriting his novel's first sentence and reviewing his Latin "pour mieux connaître le sens des mots français" [*TRN*, 1240]), or stifled by forces beyond one's control (the journalist Rambert cut off from his Paris newspaper by the plague), the entire problematics of discourse is thrown into relief and valorized.

As I have already suggested, Tarrou is Rieux's polar opposite in the novel, especially with regard to the whole question of the use and awareness of language. When and why Tarrou has come to Oran remain unclear. He lives comfortably, apparently on the income from inherited wealth. "La seule habitude qu'on lui connût," notes Rieux, "était la fréquentation assidue des danseurs et des musiciens espagnols" (*TRN*, 1233–34). (This observation reminds us that Rieux first met Tarrou in the apartment of Spanish dancers living on the top floor of his building.) Tarrou's notebooks, according to Rieux, "constituent eux aussi une sorte de chronique de cette période difficile." But Rieux hastens to point out that the focus of Tarrou's record of the plague differs fundamentally from his own: "Il s'agit d'une chronique très particulière qui semble obéir à un parti pris d'insignifiance" (*TRN*, 1234). Rieux goes on to illustrate "la bizarrerie" (his term) of Tarrou's notebooks with a summary of those passages in them that concern a sadistic little old man living across the way from Tarrou. The old man would entice cats into the little street below by dropping bits of paper from his balcony. He would then spit on the cats vigorously and laugh when his spittle would hit one (*TRN*, 1235). On the next page Rieux simply quotes from Tarrou's notebooks without injecting any commentary of his own:

> A l'hôtel, le veilleur de nuit, qui est un homme digne de foi, m'a dit qu'il s'attendait à un malheur avec tous ces rats. . . . il

n'aurait pas été étonné qu'un tremblement de terre fît l'af-
faire. J'ai reconnu que c'était possible et il m'a demandé si ça
ne m'inquiétait pas.

—La seule chose qui m'intéresse, lui ai-je dit, c'est de trouver
la paix intérieure. (*TRN*, 1236)

In having Tarrou confess to his search for inner peace, Camus affixes
the final, identifying seal to the profile he has been sketching at two
removes from his subject. Through Rieux's reading of Tarrou's writings, the novelist portrays the lone, mysterious sojourner, the aristocratic individualist, the exoticist (here the Hispanophile), the
connoisseur of the bizarre, the exceptional, the cruel, the seeker of
surcease from spiritual unquiet. In short, Camus redraws Chateaubri-
and's René. Like his prototype, Tarrou is a pilgrim of the absolute
consumed by "une flamme future": in his case, by the dream of a
saintliness without God. He thus differs radically from Rieux who, as
we shall learn, has no taste at all "pour l'héroïsme et la saintété" and
aspires only "d'être un homme" (*TRN*, 1425).

The central binary opposition that links while it contrasts Tarrou
to Rieux is mirrored, extended, and clarified through other cou-
plings in the novel: Cottard and Grand; Paneloux and Rambert; even
such minor figures as the sadistic old man who spits on the cats and
the old asthmatic who methodically transfers chick-peas from one
container to another, the pair that Germaine Brée has called, most
appropriately, "crude replicas of Tarrou and Rieux."[9] By means of interlocking antitheses of character and theme reminiscent of Balzac,
Camus juxtaposes in order to oppose: restlessness and steadiness, lo-
quacity and taciturnity, narcissism and concern for others, morbidity
and the affirmation of life. Exactly which characters make up the polarities and which the replications, moreover, is never in doubt. Tarrou, for example, is our chief source of information about figures
who apparently strike a responsive chord in him, the old man with
the cats and Cottard, while Rieux is our prime informant regarding
Grand and Rambert. Also, life-affirming characters survive, while
the plague either kills the death-obsessed (Tarrou and Paneloux)
or leaves their fate seriously in doubt (the old man with the cats
and Cottard).

9. Brée, *Camus,* 123.

As the foregoing schematizations might suggest, a far-reaching thematic symmetry structures *La Peste*, to such an extent that it would be a radical misinterpretation to read it as sociopolitical history in the guise of naturalistic, thesis-bearing fiction. In no sense, for example, are we given an even remotely authentic picture of the caste-ridden French colonial scene, a lack that appears all the more glaring against the background of the Algerian War, which was to break out within seven short years of the publication of *La Peste*. Nowhere in news accounts of the violence in Algerian cities from 1954 to 1962, of the urban warfare between *pied noir* and Arab, does one recognize the essentially homogeneous, thoroughly European Oran of Camus's novel. In the final analysis, however, this case against *La Peste*, which has been brilliantly argued by Conor Cruise O'Brien,[10] seems beside the point. For the novel's intentions are clearly more visionary than documentary. By dramatizing various facets of the "final-solution" mentality, from the seemingly anodyne (the dreamers of innocence) to the patently lethal (the defenders of death), Camus seeks to expose the insidious, all-pervasive nature of a human evil. By opposing religion and medicine, absolutism and relativism, obscurantist verbiage and enlightened deeds, and by punishing death's loud collaborators and rewarding those who quietly but systematically resisted, he is condemning totalitarianism in all its forms.

Diametrical opposition between babbling egomania and wordless generosity carries through to the end of the novel in the form of a closing contrast between Cottard and Grand. As already noted, the last chapter of *La Peste* opens with Rieux's admission that he is in fact the author of the chronicle we are reading. Then, after resuming the theme of his self-assigned duty to speak for all in his account of the plague, the narrator observes that there is one citizen of Oran for whom Dr. Rieux cannot speak and that "il est juste que cette chronique se termine sur lui qui avait un coeur ignorant, c'est-à-dire solitaire" (*TRN,* 1467). The narrator goes on to recount that on leaving the section of Oran where the plague's demise is being celebrated and "au moment de tourner dans la rue de Grand et de Cottard" (*TRN,* 1467), he is stopped by the police and informed that a madman is firing into the crowd. At this point Grand walks up to Rieux,

10. Conor Cruise O'Brien, *Albert Camus of Europe and Africa* (New York: Viking, 1970), 51–59.

but he knows no more about the situation than the doctor. Suddenly Grand says: "C'est la fenêtre de Cottard" (*TRN*, 1468), which, among other things, identifies the "coeur ignorant, c'est-à-dire solitaire" just referred to by Rieux. After further exchanges of gunfire, the police storm the building and are soon dragging Cottard outside. Twice within five lines the latter is described as shouting continuously: "... qui criait sans discontinuer.... Il criait" (*TRN*, 1469).

This detail reminds us that in his most recent previous appearance in the text Cottard was described as "parlant de la peste avec abondance" and "gesticulant de façon désordonnée, parlant vite et haut" (*TRN*, 1446). Cottard's raving on that occasion is thus simply renewed at a higher pitch of intensity here, where it is immediately followed by Grand's telling Rieux that he has resumed work on his novel's first sentence and has dropped all the adjectives from it: "J'ai supprimé, dit-it, tous les adjectifs" (*TRN*, 1470). The epitome of quasi-mute commitment to others is therefore associated one last, crucial time with the rejection of language, and this immediately after Cottard's exit in a torrent of words. So as the narrative draws to a close, Cottard and Grand are shown to be moving farther and farther apart, the former spinning out of control beyond human contact on an ever-expanding balloon of volubility, the latter steadily approaching, or so it would seem, the silent communion of perfect human solidarity.

La Peste, we now realize, builds toward the very same contrastive juxtaposition of *solitaire* and *solidaire* that will later conclude (literally, textually) Camus's short story entitled "Jonas ou l'Artiste au Travail" (*TRN*, 1652). Malraux's influence, readily acknowledged by Camus,[11] seems strongest at just this point, inasmuch as the recurring conflict between human solitude and human solidarity, which thematically grounds *La Condition humaine*, performs an analogous function in Camus's novel and story. Malraux's impact on Camus, however, stops short of shaping the latter's conception of heroism. In this matter, as with other key aspects of *La Peste*, a comparison of Tarrou and Rieux may prove instructive.

11. For direct testimony from Camus concerning Malraux's impact on him, see the interview entitled "Réponses à Jean-Claude Brisville," in Albert Camus, *Essais*, ed. R. Quilliot and L. Faucon (Paris: Gallimard, 1965), 1923. Subsequent page references to this work are in the body of the text, preceded by *Essais*.

The sixth chapter in part four of the novel paves the way for the *solitaire/solidaire* antithesis at the novel's end. It consists primarily of the conversation between the two principals toward the close of which, in response to Tarrou's saying "Peut-on être un saint sans Dieu, c'est le seul problème concret que je connaisse aujourd'hui" (*TRN,* 1425), Rieux replies that he desires only to be a man, not a hero or a saint. The conversation ends shortly after this exchange, following Tarrou's suggestion that the two go for a swim in the ocean. The chapter then concludes with a detailed description of the swim and the men's reaction to it, a climactic passage in the novel (*TRN,* 1426–27). The immediate context of the passage is the preceding discussion between hubristic Tarrou and modest Rieux, the verbal clash of extraordinary heroism with ordinary humanity. The debate continues, by eloquent gesture now instead of crude word, during the swim; in transposed, telescoped fashion the entire narrative up to this point is mutely recapitulated. Rieux dives into the sea (of trouble) first. He swims (struggles against the plague) regularly, systematically, adjusting his rhythm to the exigencies of the situation. Tarrou then joins him loudly, dramatically, and at his own self-willed pace. Here as always before, the two men are the same and yet different. (An analogy would be that although both walk, one struts and the other marches.) Throughout the experience perfect communication has taken place without a word having passed between them. Like the unspoken "amour viril" (to quote Malraux) that suffuses the climactic pages of *La Condition humaine,* those devoted to the magnificent deaths of first Kyo and then Katow,[12] a wordless pact of coordinated acts gives Rieux and Tarrou the courage to "recommencer." But the successive crescendos that form the climax of *La Condition humaine* are lacking here; of Camus's two principals, only Tarrou, manifestly not the hero of *La Peste,* would have enough panache to achieve a hero's death à la Malraux, which of course he does not do. The announced hero of *La Peste,* it will be recalled, is its least melodramatic, least Malraux-like character, faceless, almost inarticulate Joseph Grand who, moreover, does not die.

As has already been noted, that staple of Romantic literature, the confessional mode, with its verbose, self-aggrandizing recounting "I," is rejected in Camus's novel in favor of a quiet, detached, third-person narrative. Now a novelist who in and by his fiction extols the

---

12. André Malraux, *Romans* (Paris: Gallimard, 1947), 405–11.

virtues of a thoroughly unassuming, almost voiceless voice, is on the verge of equating silence with innocence, and certainly the character of Joseph Grand suggests that such an equation may constitute the generative nucleus of *La Peste.*(It will doubtless be recalled that Rousseau, that fountainhead of confessional writing for the modern era, also equates silence with innocence. But it is precisely in their capacity as one of Romanticism's prime sourcebooks that the *Confessions,* although only obliquely evoked in *La Peste*—via Tarrou's *carnets*—stand for everything Camus would seem to be deploring in his novel.)

On closer inspection, moreover, Camus's handling of the silence-innocence equation reveals his respect for the classical ideal of *mesure.* If parts of the *Discours sur l'origine de l'inégalité* and *La Nouvelle Héloïse* virtually throb with regret for the preverbal innocence that, according to Rousseau, attended the earliest, purest moments of human history, as well as Julie and Saint-Preux's nascent love,[13] no such *nostalgie d'absolu* can be found in *La Peste.* Perfect silence and perfect innocence are never presented here as attainable or even desirable goals. Tarrou's extreme, obsessive cult of innocence, for example, is continually undercut by his association with the moderate, restrained, more admirable Rieux, while laconic Grand never falls totally silent. Although paired in *La Peste* in ways generally reminiscent of Rousseau, in the actual circumstances of Camus's novel, silence and innocence function as unreachable summits inspiring, at most, a kind of perpetual ascesis, an inner purification to be undertaken repeatedly and always *ab ovo.*

Repetition or cyclicity as a positive, anti-Romantic value is dramatized in a variety of ways throughout Camus's novel. For example, just as the climax of *La Peste* ends with the word "recommencer," so the novel as a whole culminates in a lyric restatement of the classical motif of the eternal return, of cyclicity—the expected resuscitation one day of the plague bacillus with all its consequences, including, by implication, the need to struggle against it. Thus another value of Romantic literature, uniqueness for its own sake, whether of character or of event, is repudiated at the novel's close by the affirmation of repetition's rule over human destiny.

13. See Timothy M. Scanlan, "Jean-Jacques Rousseau and Silence," *Modern Language Studies* 7 (Fall 1977): 59–76.

Throughout his life Camus was drawn to Mediterranean culture, to classical (and neoclassical) literature, particularly that of ancient Greece,[14] and to practicing his writer's craft in the most disciplined manner possible. To please and to instruct were his constant goals, and nowhere more so than in *La Peste*. If, as Valéry has proposed, a classical writer is simply one who "porte un critique en soi-même, et qui l'associe intimement à ses travaux,"[15] Camus is clearly such a writer. The signs of such an aesthetically self-conscious turn of mind in this classical or Valéryan sense are everywhere in *La Peste*, but perhaps especially in the treatment of the theme of separation which Camus himself called "le grand thème du roman."[16] All the "good" characters are bereft in some sense, in relation to some previous condition of greater human contact: Rieux is separated from his wife, Rambert from his mistress, Oran (certainly a character in an allegorical sense) from the rest of the world; even Madame Rieux's widowhood and Grand's status as an abandoned husband suggest permanent separation.

Two-thirds of the way into the novel Camus artfully replicates his "grand thème" with an astonishing *mise en abyme*. Cottard and Tarrou (together here as elsewhere) are attending a performance of Gluck's *Orphée*, the only opera still being performed, week after week, in the plague-sequestered city. Suddenly, during his grand duet with Eurydice in act 3, the singer playing Orpheus lurches toward the footlights and drops to the floor, dead (*TRN*, 1380). Beyond the stark personification in Tarrou's account of the incident ("la peste sur la scène sous l'aspect d'un histrion désarticulé") lies the deeper symbolism of an archetypal story of separation, that of Orpheus and Eurydice. Underlining the myth's point in the present circumstances is Orpheus's real-life death on stage; he is torn from Eurydice liter-

14. See in this connection (for example) the thesis that Camus wrote for his Diplôme d'Etudes Supérieures, "Métaphysique chrétienne et néoplatonisme," which may be read, along with an informative commentary on it by R. Quilliot, in *Essais*, 1220–1313. See also "Politique et culture méditerranéennes" and "Mesure et démesure" (from *L'Homme révolté*) in *Essais*, 1314–31, 697–704. Finally, there is this avowal by Camus in a 1945 interview: "Je n'aime, et profondément, que la grande littérature classique française" (*Essais*, 1427). For further discussion of Camus's "Mediterraneanism," as well as his "Hellenism," see Herbert R. Lottman, *Albert Camus: A Biography* (Garden City, N.Y.: Doubleday, 1979), passim.

15. Paul Valéry, *Oeuvres*, ed. Jean Hytier (Paris: Gallimard, 1957), 1:604. It seems worth recalling here that the very same quotation from Pindar serves as the epigraph to Valéry's "Le Cimetière marin" and Camus's *Le Mythe de Sisyphe*.

16. Albert Camus, *Carnets: Janvier 1942–Mars 1951* (Paris: Gallimard, 1962), 80.

ally, definitively, before she can be separated from him ritually, provisionally, until next week's performance.

The Orpheus episode in *La Peste* has other functions, as well. It calls up the entire universe of classical antiquity and in the process reminds us of the formative impact of its ethos on Camus. The figure of Orpheus is also of course that of the primordial singer-poet: as such, it embodies the purely verbal concerns and emphases of *La Peste*, the recurrent metalinguistic commentary. Camus's novel, moreover, has its own Orpheus in the character of Joseph Grand, who continually longs to be reunited with his Eurydice, his wife Jeanne, and who, like Orpheus, whiles away his time, mitigates his suffering, by singing—that is, in Grand's case, by writing and rewriting his novel's first sentence.

The mere mention of Grand's name, however, calls to mind quite another set of associations at the very heart of *La Peste*. As we have seen, Grand especially, but also Rieux, Mme Rieux, and Rambert, suggest by their behavior that fluency must bow to muteness for social commitment to make its appearance. A generalized sense of restraint, combined with the surrender of individual self-interest for the benefit of the group, informs the spare utterances and exemplary conduct of these characters. Through them, the strident, imperial ego of Romantic literature is mocked in a variety of ways, large and small. For example, Rieux's constant recourse to the simple phrase "nos concitoyens" in the end so merges his destiny with that of his fellows as to rule out any question of a special fate or a "separate peace" for him. Also, Rieux's choice of the label "chronicle" instead of "history" for his narrative effectively reduces his role as author to that of invisible recorder (a chronicle being a strict sequential recounting of events while a history attempts to explain or interpret the events it narrates). Furthermore, his very stance as chronicler rather than historian, even without the compounding avoidance of first-person singular, smacks of a programmatic and perhaps corrective discretion on Camus's part.

In *La Peste*, Camus obviously chose Greece, that is, moderation, decorum, and discretion over what he had long recognized as his Spanish or Romantic side, his "côté castillan,"[17] his tendency toward

17. See Roger Quilliot, "Genèse de *La Peste*," *Preuves*, no. 142 (December 1962): 34.

lyricism and excess.[18] Situated at opposite ends of the Mediterranean Sea, as well as of the millennia defining Western culture, "La Grèce Antique" and "Romantique Espagne," only slightly disguised, form the essential polarity of Camus's imagination in *La Peste*. (Tarrou, it will be recalled, seeks out the company of Spanish dancers and singers, while the subject of the eternally reworked first sentence of Grand's novel, "une svelte amazone," springs full-blown from Greek mythology.) It need hardly be stressed that these are, for Camus, countries of the mind, images with no necessary connection with what Greece really was or what Spain in fact is. They are, however, no less real to the reader for all that, and Camus presents his critique of totalitarianism, as well as of a plausible literary counterpart to that mentality, Romanticism, by manipulating stock notions set off in the minds of his readers through the invocation of these diametrically opposed images.

Thanks to Léon-François Hoffmann's *Romantique Espagne*,[19] we have a reasonably detailed picture of Spain's image in France between 1800 and 1850, an image that has lived on well into our century. It is a Spain of natural aristocrats in every social class, of brilliant color and startling contrasts, of fidelity to abstract values and ideals, of unflinching courage and faultless integrity. But it is also a Spain of grand heroics and beaux gestes, of arrogance and cruelty, the natural extension of *pundonor* (point of honor). It is toward this latter imagining of Spain, a Spain of dark Romanticism and lethal absolutes, that the figure of Tarrou is pointing. In this perspective, Camus's decision to set *L'Etat de siège*, his dramatic adaptation of *La Peste*, in Spain, site of totalitarianism under Franco, seems almost inevitable.[20]

But there is another Spain in Camus. Beneath the sound and fury of Romantic Spain throbs the steady pulse of quiet, clear-eyed Hispanic endurance, represented in Camus's life by his hard-working, speech-impaired, long-widowed Spanish mother, and in *La Peste* by Rieux's asthmatic patient, who is at times referred to as "le vieil

18. For commentary on the determinative impact of ancient Greek civilization on Camus, see Roger Quilliot, *La Mer et les prisons: essais sur Albert Camus* (Paris: Gallimard, 1956), 103–4; 250–52.

19. Léon-François Hoffmann, *Romantique Espagne: L'Image de l'Espagne en France entre 1800 et 1850* (Paris: Presses Universitaires de France, 1961).

20. For a discussion by Camus of his reasons for choosing Spain as the setting for *L'Etat de siège*, see "Pourquoi l'Espagne" in *Essais*, 391–96.

Espagnol." In the novel's last conversation, which takes place between Rieux and the Old Spaniard, the latter scoffs at those who do
not see that the plague is simply life itself, at the very people who
will soon be celebrating the plague's end with official speeches.
Thus on the novel's penultimate page verbal facility and true vision
are portrayed yet again as mutually exclusive capacities. All things
considered, Mme Rieux, Rieux, Grand, and the Old Spaniard may
simply be versions of the mother whose "admirable silence" Camus
once glimpsed at the very center of his oeuvre: "Rien ne m'empêche
[. . .] d'imaginer que je mettrai encore au centre de cette oeuvre
l'admirable silence d'une mère et l'effort d'un homme pour retrou-
ver une justice ou un amour qui équilibre ce silence" (*Essais*, 13).[21]
More persuasively than any other of his fictions, *La Peste*, with its
relentless quest for justice *and* love, shows how necessary quasi-
muteness is for righteous conduct to flourish in a context of human
solidarity, and how admirable a goal silence can be.

---

21. Louis Guilloux's first impressions of Camus's mother, recounted in Patrick McCarthy, *Camus* (New York: Random House, 1982), are suggestive of both her "admirable silence" and her
relationship with her son: "Guilloux's outstanding memory of the trip [to Algeria] is his meeting with Camus' mother. 'She had the nobility of a queen,' he recalls. She and Camus scarcely
spoke to each other but their silence contained an understanding which Guilloux could feel in
the room" (237).

Part Three

In the Wake of the *Nouveau Roman* (1960–1980)

Words for Love in Duras's *L'Après-midi de Monsieur Andesmas* and *Le Ravissement de Lol V. Stein*

I n its extremely subtle exploration of human emo-
tions, especially love, Marguerite Duras's fiction recalls *A la recherche du temps perdu.* To illustrate: traditionally, lyric poetry alone
can give articulate utterance, hence enduring existence, to inter-
stices of the heart, those fleeting, in-between, half-enfolded feelings
that nearly everyone knows but almost no one can name. Likewise,
intermittences of the heart, those surges of normally repressed emotion that are unleashed by the smallest sensations, those affective
aftershocks that constitute irrefutable if unfathomable proof that obsession is not a steady-state affair but rather a string of sporadic inner
eruptions—this experience, too, usually only the lyric registers.
Proust and Duras, though novelists, track just such mysterious
rhythms and recesses of the heart in their writings and in this sense
(at least) are poets, and similar poets as well.

Reading Duras, however, one is continually reminded not only of
Proust but also of René Char, specifically of his lapidary, paradoxical
definition: "Le poème est l'amour réalisé du désir demeuré désir."[1]

---

1. René Char, *Fureur et mystère* (Paris: Gallimard, 1967), 73.

Duras's narratives deal constantly, relentlessly with love, but with love as both consummation, condition realized, and as desire forever deferred, hence never gratified. Love in Duras is at one and the same time experienced and anticipated. Her stories tell of incredibly sustained desire, of passion both fulfilled and postponed. The phrase "l'amour réalisé du désir demeuré désir" could stand as an epigraph for her entire corpus, whose essential equations would seem these: to live is to love, to love is to wait, and to wait is to exult and to despair simultaneously.

Even more significant than her affinities with Proust and Char, however, have been Duras's parallels and ties since the late 1950s with the mutually overlapping worlds of "New Wave" cinema and the *nouveau roman*. For example, just as Agnès Varda combines techniques of the documentary with those of the fiction film in her motion pictures, Duras blends fiction and autobiography in her novels, tales, and screenplays. In this regard, Duras's and Varda's contemporary respective achievements are exemplary, the novelist's in *La Douleur* (1985) and the director's in *Sans toit ni loi* (1985). Further, the well-known filmmaker, Alain Resnais, has collaborated with both Duras and Varda, as well as with the *chef de file* of the New Novelists, Alain Robbe-Grillet, while Varda dedicated her 1985 film to Nathalie Sarraute, another pioneering practitioner of the *nouveau roman*. These and other interconnections suggest that over the last three decades Duras has shared, at least in a general way, the aspirations of avant-garde French novelists and cinéastes. Scrutiny of two of her narratives, *L'Après-midi de Monsieur Andesmas* (1962) and *Le Ravissement de Lol V. Stein* (1964),[2] may thus shed light on her indebtedness, however limited or tangential, to the then-new ambient aesthetic, as well as on her subsequent evolution as a writer.

L'Après-midi de Monsieur Andesmas and *Le Ravissement de Lol V. Stein*, however, represent noteworthy texts of transition in Duras's oeuvre for more reasons than the fact that they were written shortly after, and possibly to some degree under the influence of, the rather boisterous arrival of the *nouveau roman*. Chronologically they were among the last prose narratives to which Duras would affix the generic labels of, respectively, "récit" and "roman." After *Le Vice-*

---

2. Marguerite Duras, *L'Après-midi de Monsieur Andesmas* (Paris: Gallimard, 1962) and *Le Ravissement de Lol V. Stein* (Paris: Gallimard, 1964). Subsequent page references to these works are in the body of the study, in parentheses.

Consul (1965) and *L'Amante anglaise* (1967), Duras would almost never again inscribe such rubrics on her books' covers, and would henceforth produce hybrid genres or "textes éclatés."[3]

Along with this fast-approaching change in form and nomenclature, another, more substantive development began to affect Duras's fiction writing in the early to mid-1960s, starting with *Le Ravissement*: the erosion of the autonomy of her prose narratives as self-contained, sharply delimited and, consequently, inviolable textual wholes. Although relying not so much on the device of reappearing characters (à la Balzac or Zola) to achieve this end, from the early sixties onward Duras has, in effect, been recounting one long, complex, but ultimately single story: a "family romance" in which basically the same finite set of characters, situations, and concerns (parent, nubile daughter, and some combination of sibling, friend, and/or lover) interweave from book to book, in only superficially different guises and settings. Some two decades after publishing her first novel (*Les Impudents,* 1943), and a dozen years after the appearance of the first book to bring her a measure of fame (*Un Barrage contre le Pacifique,* 1950), Duras began to see herself, it would seem, as developing an infinitely expandable collection of texts. It is as if she now understood that the divisions in her work, occasioned by the practical necessity of writing and publishing individual books, would henceforth have little or no bearing on the fundamental continuity and integrity of her larger enterprise.[4] Before examining *L'Après-midi* and *Le Ravissement,* which mark the beginnings of this transformation in the novelist, however, we must consider that henceforth Duras's "exploded texts" mix metalanguage and moralism, hyper-self-consciousness regarding words and ethical fervor regarding love, in ways peculiar to her alone.

Several of Duras's titles refer explicitly to love: *Hiroshima mon amour* (1960), *L'Amante anglaise* (1967), *L'Amour* (1971), and *L'Amant* (1984). Virtually all of her writings, moreover, whether prose narrative, film scenario, or play script, engage the subject of

3. See Carol J. Murphy, *Alienation and Absence in the Novels of Marguerite Duras* (Lexington, Ky.: French Forum, 1982), 121.

4. As Sharon Willis has observed in *Marguerite Duras: Writing on the Body* (Urbana: University of Illinois Press, 1987): "The texts from the 1960s to the present resemble more one long narrative than a series. They constitute a sort of inverted *A la recherche du temps perdu,* substituting dispersal for recollection" (3).

love in an obsessive if usually oblique manner. In an interview published in 1977, Duras alluded to the probable source and rationale of her preoccupation. From her responses to the interviewer's questions, it becomes clear that Duras strongly identifies with her female protagonists, all of whom are love-struck, and that she equates woman with desire: "La femme, c'est le désir." She goes on to contend that women writers do not write "au même endroit que les hommes. Et quand les femmes n'écrivent pas dans le lieu du désir, elles n'écrivent pas, elles sont dans le plagiat."[5] In another interview, this one published in English two years earlier, Duras had expatiated on the dual question of male versus female writing and female plagiarism:

> I think "feminine literature" is an organic, translated writing . . . translated from blackness, from darkness. Women have been in darkness for centuries. They don't know themselves. Or only poorly. And when women write, they translate this darkness. . . . Men don't translate. They begin from a theoretical platform that is already in place, already elaborated. The writing of women is really translated from the unknown, like a new way of communicating rather than an already formed language. But to achieve that, we have to turn away from plagiarism. . . . I think feminine literature is a violent, direct literature.[6]

Duras's diction throughout this interview betrays a nostalgia for a kind of female Eden, a pre-verbal, pre-theorized time-place of unmediated experience. Her choice of words reveals a longing for a direct rendering of *le vécu* through an "organic," specifically woman's "translation" of the as yet unformulated, that amorphous "blackness" left unexpressed by men. For her, this realm of praxis preexists and eludes the grasp of received, cerebral, male discourse. Only a truly "feminine literature," according to Duras, can "translate" the "darkness" of such heretofore unspoken, "violent" passions.

---

5. Marguerite Duras and Michelle Porte, *Les Lieux de Marguerite Duras* (Paris: Editions de Minuit, 1977), 102.

6. From an interview conducted by Susan Husserl-Kapit for the journal *Signs* (Winter 1975), reprinted in *New French Feminisms: An Anthology*, ed. Elaine Marks and Isabelle de Courtivron (New York: Schocken Books, 1981), 174.

Whether or not one accepts at face value Duras's claims for a "feminine literature," at the very least they serve as a useful introduction to her own writing, particularly as that writing attempts to account for the extraordinarily complex, scarcely expressible crosscurrents of the most ordinary human attachments. In her fictional universe, the lures of desire, the ties that bind, both positively and negatively, assume supreme importance. The task Duras seems to have assigned herself is to give voice to that affective enslavement-cum-liberation, to find the right words for love, thus to negotiate an adequate exchange between "texte" and "hors-texte."

One of the most stunning instances of such a negotiation in Duras's writings occurs in a brief autobiographical text that she first published in the feminist review *Sorcières* in 1976 and later (in 1984) reprinted in a volume of collected journalistic pieces. The piece in question, entitled "L'Horreur d'un pareil amour," which occupies only slightly more than two of the volume's pages, is divided into two paragraphs, the first of which is rather long, the second quite short, with, very noticeably, a larger than usual amount of white space obtruding between the two paragraphs. The first paragraph describes, in predominately simple but cumulatively moving declarative sentences, the events and circumstances immediately following Duras's being delivered of a baby boy, who died shortly after birth, in late May 1942. Despite her repeated requests to those around her at the maternity clinic, she is not allowed to hold or even to touch her dead baby. The paragraph concludes as follows:

> La peau de mon ventre me collait au dos tellement j'étais vide. L'enfant était sorti. Nous n'étions plus ensemble. Il était mort d'une mort séparée. Il y avait une heure, un jour, huit jours; mort à part, mort à une vie que nous avons vécue neuf mois ensemble et qu'il venait de quitter séparément. Mon ventre était retombé lourdement sur lui-même, un chiffon usé, une loque, un drap mortuaire, une dalle, une porte, un néant que ce ventre. Il avait porté cet enfant pourtant, et c'était dans la chaleur glaireuse et veloutée de sa chair que ce fruit marin avait poussé. Le jour l'avait tué. Il avait été frappé à mort par sa solitude dans l'espace. Les gens disaient: "Ce n'était pas si terrible à la naissance, il vaut mieux ça." Etait-ce terrible? Je le crois. Précisément ça: cette coïncidence entre

sa venue au monde et sa mort. Rien. Il ne me restait rien. Ce
vide était terrible. Je n'avais pas eu d'enfant, même pendant
une heure. Obligée de tout imaginer. Immobile, j'imaginais.

Here now, in its entirety, is the second—and last—paragraph:

Celui qui est là maintenant et qui dort, celui-ci tout à l'heure,
a ri. Il a ri à une girafe qu'on venait de lui donner. Il a ri et ça
a fait un bruit de rire. Il y avait du vent et une petite partie du
bruit de ce rire m'est parvenue. Alors j'ai relevé un peu la capote de sa voiture, je lui ai redonné sa girafe pour qu'il rie de
nouveau et j'ai engouffré ma tête dans la capote pour capter
tout le bruit de rire. Du rire de mon enfant. J'ai mis l'oreille
contre le coquillage et j'ai entendu le bruit de la mer. L'idée
que ce rire était dispersé dans le vent, c'était insupportable.
Je l'ai pris. C'est moi qui l'ai eu. Parfois quand il bâille, je re-
spire sa bouche, l'air de son bâillement. "S'il meurt, j'aurai eu
ce rire." Je sais que ça peut mourir. Je mesure toute l'horreur
d'un pareil amour.[7]

The transitionless succession of the paragraphs, with only the enlarged white space between them to reflect the radical shift in perspective, speaks volumes to the reader, giving vibrant life, ironically,
to the concrete, ever-threatening presence of death. The cliché that
holds that children are hostages to fortune, suddenly gains fresh, urgent vitality. The joy and fear and pain and need of a mother who
would suck in the laughter and even yawn of a beloved infant, come
insistently alive in all their raw, unspeakable power, even though—
or possibly because—the key word, "amour," appears for the first
time only at the text's end.

What is perhaps most remarkable about this text is that its emo-
tional pulse throbs in a void, a place of no writing, the conspicuous
space between the paragraphs, whose obtrusive whiteness evokes
that oppressive darkness Duras speaks of in her 1975 interview, the
pre-verbal inky sea that only women writers (according to Duras)
can navigate, translate, and embody in words. All that separates the

7. Marguerite Duras, *Outside: papiers d'un jour* (Paris: P.O.L., 1984), 281–82.

"rien" of the dead child from the "rire" of the living one is the mother/writer's will as she traverses the breach, the blank abyss, tracing black on white, as she thrusts her head/pen into the now hooded baby carriage in a primal act that would reverse the scattering force of the wind with its entropic fall into undifferentiation. Here, indeed, Duras's "texte"—her words and pauses, her script and white space—seems equal ("pareil") to the task of conveying the horror of such love, of this "hors-texte."

The collection of reprinted essays that includes "L'Horreur d'un pareil amour" bears, curiously enough, the English title *Outside*. Duras explains her choice of title in an "Avant-Propos" in which she distinguishes between writing books, which she considers an intimate, private activity turned away from the public sphere, and writing articles, which she claims is always provoked by something foreign to her private self, by something "outside, dans la rue" (11), be it a perceived social injustice or some quite banal occurrence. Her distinction between "inside" (book) writing and "outside" (article) writing, however, will hardly convince readers who have followed her career since the early sixties. Although she wrote the "Avant-Propos" for *Outside* in late 1980, thus at an opportune moment to take stock of her production of nearly forty years, Duras alludes not once in her foreword to the increasing convergence of her writings, across the decades, toward a unitary scriptural mode not readily divisible into traditional categories of genre or function. And certainly a piece like "L'Horreur d'un pareil amour" strikes one as no less intimate, no less private, no less "inside," than, say, the largely autobiographical *L'Amant* (1984) or *La Douleur* (1985). By the same token, if it is taken seriously, the brief prefatory text to *L'Après-midi de Monsieur Andesmas,* a preface identified at its close as the transcription of a patently "outside" occurrence, a "propos entendu dans l'été 1960," muddies the taxonomic waters considerably for Duras's 1962 *récit,* presumably one of her "inside" texts par excellence.

It seems all the more appropriate to note this apparent blind spot in Duras's retrospective glance at her corpus up to 1980 because she begins her "Avant-Propos" for *Outside* with a series of peremptory utterances that could conceivably introduce all of her writings, not just her journalistic pieces:

Il n'y a pas de journalisme sans morale. Tout journaliste est un moraliste. C'est absolument inévitable. Un journaliste c'est quelqu'un qui regarde le monde, son fonctionnement, qui le surveille de très près chaque jour, qui le donne à voir, qui donne à revoir le monde, l'événement. Et il ne peut pas à la fois faire ce travail et ne pas juger ce qu'il voit. C'est impossible. (11)

For what, after all, is Duras doing in *L'Après-midi de Monsieur Andesmas* if not playing her *moraliste* scriptural card, holding up for inspection, and judging, the little world of Monsieur Andesmas? What could she be undertaking in her 1962 novella if not coordinating the activities of twins, the comparably imperious demands of writing and judging, the similarly exigent, problematic requirements of metalanguage and moralism?

In this haunting narrative of barely 120 pages, everything seems to flow from uncertainties and confusions produced by failed attempts at verbal communication. At the same time, everything seems to flow from obsessive love—of a doting old father for his spoiled grown daughter, of a long-suffering wife for a husband she knows to be unfaithful to her, of a middle-aged married man for a capricious young woman of dazzling blond beauty. And yet nothing really happens. An overweight old man, Monsieur Andesmas, drowses in the sun on a wicker chair outside a hilltop house, waiting in vain an entire afternoon for Michel Arc, an architect with whom he has an appointment, a man expected to arrive at the house with the old man's daughter, Valérie. Monsieur Andesmas's solitary waiting is interrupted first by a wandering dog with whom he establishes no contact; then by the daughter of the man he is waiting for, a strange child whose bizarre behavior repeatedly derails meaningful conversation; and finally by the wife of the architect the old man is waiting for, a woman with whom the old man cannot communicate because of their similar but ultimately divergent obsessions.

The narrative's tone is vaguely Proustian throughout, thanks to a kind of pervasive sensuality, and to the repetition of expressions which, although commonplace, carry forward an acute if indirect analysis of a soul in torment, Monsieur Andesmas. The latter is manifestly in the grip of extreme spiritual and physical lassitude, a precipitous decline in his moral and verbal capacities. Monsieur

Andesmas's afternoon—not unlike his life and his ability to speak and to listen—is drawing to a close in a place and a state of utterly empty warmth. What lingers in the reader's mind beyond the tale's end is the dubious reliability of speech, Monsieur Andesmas's growing abulia yet willful ignorance, his pointless waiting for death and, by extension, the pathetic egoism and bad faith of all human beings. Thus, first impressions to the contrary notwithstanding, we seem not to have progressed very far beyond the mind-set of a Chamfort or a La Bruyère, or even a La Rochefoucauld.

The foregoing synopsis/description of *L'Après-midi de Monsieur Andesmas,* of course, says little about what might be called the poetic dimension of Duras's tale. Particularly notable in this regard is that certain recurrent themes and images pair off among themselves in overlapping polarities that form a sturdy textual chain binding the tale together. This web of interwoven parallels and contrasts constitutes nothing less than the armature, as well as the texture, of *L'Après-midi,* and therefore must be elucidated.

As in *La Peste,* a basic structuring device in *L'Après-midi* is that of binary opposition, each character having his or her antipode in the text: the contrary figure is linked to the original by both similarities and dissimilarities. Monsieur Andesmas and Michel Arc illustrate this continual crisscrossing of sameness and difference perfectly. The old man is angry with the younger one ostensibly because Michel Arc is late for his appointment with Monsieur Andesmas. Actually, however—even if the old man is loath to admit this—he is jealous of Michel Arc; the architect has apparently alienated his daughter's affections, and that is the root cause of Monsieur Andesmas's hostility toward Michel Arc. But the men converge in their common obsession with Valérie, both are fathers of daughters of roughly the same age, and Monsieur Andesmas would *like* to transfer his obsessive love for his own daughter to Michel Arc's when the latter pays him a visit. Moreover, if Monsieur Andesmas is about to be deserted by Valérie, Michel Arc is about to desert his family for Valérie, thus abandoning *his* daughter. One could continue to enumerate areas of contact and divergence between Monsieur Andesmas and Michel Arc (e.g., their initials versus their names) almost indefinitely. *L'Après-midi* is an intricate series of *pas de deux,* where virtually every figure merges with every other figure, if only to pull away an instant later: mother with daughter, wife with mistress, Valérie's father with Valérie's lover. Even Monsieur Andesmas and Madame Arc draw together in their respective abandonments and then apart in their respective reactions to their fate, with Monsieur Andesmas taking refuge in somnolent, foolish withdrawal and denial, while Madame Arc accepts her grief lucidly, anticipating the full weight of her suffering to come, but also the new loves she will encounter in the more remote future.

Implicit in the preceding is the enabling role of repetition. Like *En attendant Godot*, which Duras's narrative in many respects recalls, *L'Après-midi de Monsieur Andesmas* is divided into two nearly equal parts (or "acts"), with no change of setting and, apparently, very little development, other than the passage of time, differentiating part one from part two. In both works, part two, in a sense, simply repeats part one. (Needless to say, the foregrounding of waiting as such, combined with the problematizing of verbal communication, also links *Godot* and *L'Après-midi*.) If anything, however, repetition may be even more central to Duras's text than it is to Beckett's. Part two, for example, reprises and thickens the interconnected imagery and thematics of part one. Evocations of Monsieur Andesmas's dark bulk silhouetted against the whitewashed wall of the hilltop house alternate throughout with references to Valérie's black automobile parked on the sunlit square in the valley below the house. The *plate-forme* in front of the hilltop house, the flat stretch of ground on which Monsieur Andesmas wants Michel Arc to build a terrace for Valérie, noted again and again, serves as a foil for the repeated mentions of the *gouffre de lumière* that the valley containing the village square represents for Monsieur Andesmas. Reassuring dull surface (the *plate-forme*) and menacing bright abyss (the *gouffre de lumière*), subtly echoed in reverse by periodic glimpses of the sea (glistening surface, dark depths), take turns impinging on Monsieur Andesmas's consciousness. Forgetfulness alternates with remembering, sleep with wakefulness, dancing with stillness, desire with indifference, waning light with lengthening shadow, lucidity and sanity with self-deception and madness. Perhaps the most striking repetition involves the snatch of song that regularly wafts up to the hilltop house from the square below:

> Quand le lilas fleurira mon amour
> Quand le lilas fleurira pour toujours
> (15)

The rhyming words (here *amour, toujours,* elsewhere *jour, toujours*), suggesting as they do naive trust in the permanence of love and light (*jour*), are an ironic counterpoint to the increasing obviousness of the transience of just these elements in Monsieur Andesmas's life on this fateful afternoon.

Repetition thus collaborates with opposition in *L'Après-midi* to create an effect of constant oscillation in the text. The back-and-forth movement, eventually concentrated in the mismatch of Monsieur Andesmas and Madame Arc, swings between perfect repose, the condition Monsieur Andesmas yearns to achieve, and passionate intensity, the state Madame Arc has come to accept. What Micheline Tison-Braun claims for Duras's characters in general applies to the polar figures in *L'Après-midi de Monsieur Andesmas:* "Les personnages de Duras donnent le sentiment de vivre entre deux mondes... la vie intense, la vie tranquille."[8]

The oscillation between the demands of *la vie intense* and those of *la vie tranquille* gathers momentum in part two of *L'Après-midi* and reaches a climax in the novella's concluding pages, at which point Michel Arc and Valérie's arrival is imminently expected. The two waiting figures, Madame Arc and Monsieur Andesmas, behave in a manner characteristic of each, as well as of their relationship, that is, of *la vie intense* pitted against *la vie tranquille* (126). To the bitter end, Monsieur Andesmas refuses to admit or even to believe that he hears his daughter's voice drawing near. Madame Arc, equally tenacious, insists that Valérie and her husband will be there very soon (127–28). The intensity/tranquillity oscillation continues through the tale's last sentence: "Elle parla cependant, sa main sur la sienne, la secouant ou la caressant tour à tour, pendant les quelques minutes qui restèrent avant l'arrivée éblouie des autres devant le gouffre rempli d'une lumière uniformément décolorée" (127–28). The text's final words hint at the impending arrival not only of two human beings but also of uniformly fading light (significantly, "décolorée" can also refer to bleached blond hair), more invasive and all-encompassing than dusk. The disturbing premonitions that Madame Arc experienced exactly one year earlier, when she saw beautiful blond Valérie arriving in the village for the first time, in another moment or two will come true on this, the anniversary, the repetition of that earlier "arrivée éblouie."

---

8. Micheline Tison-Braun, *Marguerite Duras* (Amsterdam: Rodopi, 1985), 74.

But Madame Arc, quite obviously, is not destroyed by her husband's betrayal, even though, to her great sorrow, she knows she is about to witness its final confirmation. On the contrary, she never doubts the value of love, intense life distilled, which for her is worth all the pain it leaves in its wake. Accordingly, she finds Monsieur Andesmas, who refuses to acknowledge this pain, not worth talking to about anything:

> —Ah, quelle difficulté, raconte-t-elle, quelle difficulté il y a à décrire cette douleur si simple, une douleur d'amour. Quel délicieux soulagement ç'aurait été que de rencontrer quelqu'un à qui pouvoir le raconter! Comment décrire quoi que ce soit à ce vieillard qui est sorti de toutes les difficultés excepté celle d'avoir à mourir, seulement? (122)

Madame Arc only regrets not meeting, at this critical juncture in her life, someone other than Monsieur Andesmas. What a comfort it would have been for her to have been able to tell her story, that is, if she were able to resolve the difficulties involved in rendering "cette douleur si simple, une douleur d'amour." Her regret seems to arise as much from frustrations of expression as from frustrations of emotion, perhaps the novella's most blatant twinning of metalanguage and moralism.

Unlike Swann in *Un Amour de Swann,* Madame Arc does not consider "une douleur d'amour" an irretrievable loss, as wasting the best years of her life on someone (in her case a straying husband) "qui n'était pas [son] genre."[9] And this is where Proust and Duras part company, on the question of love's capacity to confound and still vivify. By all rights, Swann's love for Odette should have been just another one of his many flings, but it wasn't. Similarly, Madame Arc's love for her husband, now unrequited, even betrayed, should have ruined her life, but, as merely another "douleur d'amour," it didn't. In Proust, love is a catastrophic illusion, while in Duras it is a compound of pain and joy as unavoidable as it is ineffable. In both novelists, love is obsessive, but only in Proust are its principal ingredients consuming possessiveness and jealousy, with the onset of

---

9. Marcel Proust, *A la recherche du temps perdu,* ed. Pierre Clarac and André Ferré (Paris: Gallimard, 1954), 1:382.

indifference the inevitable and sole cure. In Duras, by contrast, great expectations never fully yield to love's unutterable mix. And if love is always a lure, it is never a decoy; it promises only what it can deliver, a heightening of everything through "la vie intense" for a season or two.

As has already been suggested, Duras assiduously avoids attempting to formulate love's horror directly, which in itself reflects her sense of the inherently "unsayable" nature of the subject. In *L'Après-midi*, she is at her most tellingly oblique on the matter in her treatment of its central character, Monsieur Andesmas. With an "objective" style reminiscent of both New Wave cinema and the *nouveau roman*, her narrative remains "outside" Monsieur Andesmas much of the time, tracking his slow movements, his dozing, shifting bulk, recording his words without analyzing them. And when the narrative does penetrate Monsieur Andesmas's mind, it registers only his conscious thoughts; it does not reach down into deeper layers of motivation or unconscious drives in order to unmask the character's self-deception. Paradoxically, however, the very absence of an explicitly omniscient dimension to the narrative contributes in no small measure to its exposure of Monsieur Andesmas's bad faith. As Tison-Braun has aptly pointed out, Monsieur Andesmas's interior monologue "est censuré ... par le personnage lui-même. On voit seulement ce que M. Andesmas pense consciemment. Au lecteur de faire les recoupements nécessaires" (44). Thus, love's horror as experienced by Monsieur Andesmas is never presented as such, but must be inferred from a text made up almost entirely of evasions, hence blanks, as far as the subject in question is concerned.

In its preference for description over analysis, as well as in its sporadic shifts from third- to first-person singular, *L'Après-midi*'s narrative resembles *nouveau roman* writing. In other respects, however, Duras's fiction, including *L'Après-midi*, seems to proceed from assumptions not generally held by *nouveaux romanciers*. These assumptions indicate that Duras retains a more traditional notion of both human nature and fiction writing than do the novelists of the *école du regard* persuasion. For example, she has, as we have seen, a special predilection for exploring the myriad byways and frailties of the human heart. Fundamental to such a project is, in some form or other, the belief in a universal, and universally flawed, human core. That Duras's convictions in this regard might replicate those of the classical French moralists seems unlikely. More probably, she shares with them a broad belief in an irreducible entity that all humans possess, and by virtue of which each individual existence transcends day-to-day contingencies. In Aristotelian terminology, a Duras character carries within itself an invariant *substance* to which all *accidents* adhere, a dynamic quality of soul that persists through incident, that perdures through change. In *L'Après-midi*, Madame Arc harbors this inner spark. In her, the enduring element, the spiritualizing force, the vitalizing dose of being, is called desire.

The role of desire—which elsewhere Duras explicitly equates with love[10]—is even greater in *Le Ravissement de Lol V. Stein* than it is in *L'Après-midi de Monsieur Andesmas*. Also, blank spots, sudden pauses in the speech of the novel's eponymous Lola Valérie Stein intrude upon the text even more startlingly than Monsieur Andesmas's brusque evasions punctuate the earlier narrative. In *Le Ravissement*, Lol's abrupt silences seem intimately tied to her quasi-perpetual "ravissement," her grotesque (in Victor Hugo's sense of that term) enactment of rapture—hence desire actualized—wedded to self-dispossession. Thus, as the title suggests, irresolvable ambiguity attends Lol's conduct; she is simultaneously *carried off*, abducted, so to speak, from herself, and *carried away*, lost to ecstasy.

The process of self-dissolution, of becoming absent to oneself through a ravishment that is both annihilating and enthralling, in fact defines the central figure's fate in *Le Ravissement*. To a lesser degree, the same process marks the destiny of the novel's other characters. Tatiana Karl, for example, Lol's best friend, is as fascinated by Lol as she is frightened of her. Tatiana, moreover, lives her internal conflict so completely that she, too, seems to abandon all sense of herself as separate from Lol. Similarly, the men in Lol's life—her husband, Jean Bedford, and especially her lover (and the text's narrator, we eventually learn), Jacques Hold—become so caught up in her obsession with her first, lost love that in their different ways they aspire, it would seem, to stand in for Michael Richardson, the faithless fiancé of Lol's youth. Finally, in *Le Ravissement*, dispossession also assumes the more banal thematic form of one woman's stealing another's fiancé or of one man's stealing another's wife.

10. Marguerite Duras and Xavière Gauthier, *Les Parleuses* (Paris: Editions de Minuit, 1974), 222.

Dispossession as flickering indeterminacy of character, event, and point of view pervades *Le Ravissement* Lol's very being, for example, has a hole, a gap, at its center. Long before Michael Richardson was stolen from her, something essential seemed missing in Lol's make-up. As Tatiana Karl puts it:

> Au collège, dit-elle, et elle n'était pas la seule à le penser, il manquait déjà quelque chose à Lol pour être—elle dit: là. . . . Etait-ce le coeur qui n'était pas là? Tatiana aurait tendance à croire que c'était peut-être en effet le coeur de Lol V. Stein qui n'était pas—elle dit: là—il allait venir sans doute, mais elle, elle ne l'avait pas connu. (12–13)

The lack noted by Tatiana Karl undermines the plausibility of any real love's ever having existed between Lol and her fiancé. Moreover, this subverting notion is introduced into the narrative at its virtual outset, and right before the passage recounting Michael Richardson's defection to Anne-Marie Stretter at the fateful Casino Ball in T. Beach outside S. Thala. Lol's need, years later, to return to S. Thala, the scene of her loss, and to reexperience that scene again and again, through substitutions of figure and locale, strikes the reader as both impenetrable and inevitable—impenetrable because of Lol's innate lack, her still undeveloped heart, yet inevitable because of the searing betrayal she suffered on the earlier occasion. The entire narrative, in a sense, flows out of Lol's all-consuming desire to replay the exact moment of her loss, a loss which, as we have seen, is foreshadowed by a specific prior deprivation, her inherent lack of desire, at least as perceived by others.

After its first chapter, *Le Ravissement de Lol V. Stein* tells, essentially, the story of Lol's return to S. Thala following a ten-year absence, now married and a mother herself, and of her repeated attempts to reenact the all-determining trauma of her youth, a trauma of loss that, as has been noted, revolves around a void, a previous or even primordial lack. Accordingly, much of what Christopher Prendergast, borrowing from Lacan, has observed about Nerval's *Sylvie,* can doubtless also be applied, mutatis mutandis, to Duras's *Ravissement:* "The 'original' object of desire is/was never there; it is primordially lost, the 'objet primordialement perdu.' Around that inaugural absence, desire circulates, forging its compensatory representations for what it can never know or have."[11] Just so, Lol's original object of desire—Michael Richardson—was never really hers to lose in the first place, because of the prior lack of an appropriate capacity on her part. All actions motivated by her desire will therefore be compensatory for what it, too, can never know or have.

For somewhat analogous reasons, *Le Ravissement* also recalls *L'Education sentimentale.* At the close of Flaubert's novel, it will be remembered, Frédéric Moreau, the novel's protagonist, and Deslauriers, Frédéric's boyhood friend, are reminiscing about their misspent youth. Eventually they remind each other of their first visit to a brothel, from which Frédéric fled in fright, with Deslauriers close behind, before either could engage the services of the establishment's vastly amused occupants. Chuckling together now over the event—more accurately the nonevent—they repeat to each other the unwittingly ironic claim: "C'est là ce que nous avons eu de meilleur."[12] Clearly unappreciated by Frédéric is what his anecdote reveals, that he ran away from his prospective *déniaisement* before it could occur. In retelling the incident to and with Deslauriers, he turns a nonoccurrence, a stereotypical *rite de passage* into male adulthood that never happened, into an originating fullness, a peak experience standing at the threshold of an entire life. The deeper irony here, of course, is that Frédéric's thwarted love life is prefigured, the reader belatedly learns, in an adventure whose essential, initiatory ingredient—desire expressed, actualized—is missing. It is in this sense that unaware Frédéric and somnambulistic Lol move through their otherwise quite different lives replaying a comparable inaugural lack.

The hole in Lol's very being, which anticipates the experience of loss that she later tries obsessively to recapture, has a second echo in the announced absence of the right word for rendering that loss. If Lol could only penetrate the mysterious instant of her loss, "ç'aurait été pour toujours, pour sa tête et pour son corps, leur plus grande

11. Christopher Prendergast, *The Order of Mimesis: Balzac, Stendhal, Nerval, Flaubert* (Cambridge: Cambridge University Press, 1986), 151. See also in this connection the chapter on "The Blanks" in Trista Selous, *The Other Woman: Feminism and Femininity in the Work of Marguerite Duras* (New Haven: Yale University Press, 1988), 87–137.

12. Gustave Flaubert, *L'Education sentimentale,* ed. Edouard Maynial (Paris: Editions Garnier Frères, 1961), 427.

douleur et leur plus grande joie confondues jusque dans leur définition devenue unique mais innommable faute d'un mot." The narrator's (Jacques Hold's) voice, usually merged, as here, with Lol's
consciousness in a kind of limited *style indirect libre*, then steps
back from that fusion, if only briefly, in order to speculate about Lol
almost objectively. In the course of the narrator's reflection, the desired but missing word suddenly becomes a freshly dug grave or a
black hole swallowing up all other words:

> J'aime à croire, comme je l'aime, que si Lol est silencieuse
> dans la vie c'est qu'elle a cru, l'espace d'un éclair, que ce mot
> pouvait exister. Faute de son existence, elle se tait. C'aurait
> été un mot-absence, un mot-trou, creusé en son centre d'un
> trou, de ce trou où tous les autres mots auraient été enterrés.
> (48)

The narrative, moving then still further away from both Lol's and
Jacques Hold's consciousness, is soon indistinguishable from a voice
we strongly sense to be Duras's own. Inevitably, we think of Flaubert's brief, celebrated lament in *Madame Bovary*, as it breaks
through Rodolphe's cynically pragmatic, cliché-seeking thought patterns to bemoan the fact that "la parole humaine est comme un
chaudron fêlé où nous battons des mélodies à faire danser les ours,
quand on voudrait attendrir les étoiles."[13] At this point *Le Ravissement*, too, turns into an unabashed lamentation on the subject of the
eternally elusive adequate word, the soul-piercing dilemma of all serious writers.

This dilemma, once noted, reminds us that the fusion (and confusion) of normally discrete, if not opposed, terms, notions, and entities, characterizes *Le Ravissement* from the beginning. Lol, "cette
dormeuse debout" (33), is both asleep and awake, dreaming her
life and living it. Also, "elle recommence le passé, elle l'ordonne, sa
véritable demeure, elle la range" (46) to counter the chaos of her
present existence. Furthermore, her exclusive, consuming project is
to impose order on her disordered present life through an elaborate

---

13. Gustave Flaubert, *Madame Bovary*, ed. Claudine Gothot-Mersch (Paris: Editions Garnier
Frères, 1971), 196.

mise en scène, an updated, controlled version of the triangular love relationship (Michael Richardson, Anne-Marie Stretter, Lol V. Stein) that excluded her and threw her into disarray during her youth.[14]

The most telling confusion in *Le Ravissement* concerns all of the novel's central figures, who, strangely enough, are both witnesses to and participants in their destiny. While the narrator, Jacques Hold, reveals his identity only about one-third of the way into the text (74–75), from a considerably earlier point it is clear that, as regards the events he is recounting, he is both actor and spectator. A similar oscillation between observer and observed is more marked still in the case of Lol who, as the "watcher in the rye," somehow manages to remain outside looking in on Jacques Hold's trysts with Tatiana Karl at the Hôtel des Bois even after she has replaced Tatiana Karl in Jacques Hold's arms. She becomes a principal player in the drama unfolding at the Hôtel des Bois without really renouncing her status as spectator. In this way, Lol stays herself even as she merges with Anne-Marie Stretter, who years before had seduced Michael Richardson away from her, and with Tatiana Karl, once her closest friend, now the betrayed, excluded third party. Lol is thus, by turn, *bourreau* and *victime,* stage director and actor, mesmerized (rapt) voyeur, treacherous (ravishing) friend and smitten (ravished) lover.

By the end of the narrative Lol has again taken up her lookout post in the field of rye behind the Hôtel des Bois. She has fallen asleep waiting for Jacques Hold and Tatiana Karl to arrive for their regular assignation, an assignation that Jacques Hold agreed to keep only at Lol's insistence: "Le soir tombait lorsque je suis arrivé à l'Hôtel des Bois. Lol nous avait précédés. Elle dormait dans le champ de seigle, fatiguée, fatiguée par notre voyage" (191). Lol's dream of perfect control is reflected in these closing sentences, with the ambiguous "notre" hinting that she has somehow inserted herself into the hotel room with Jacques Hold and Tatiana Karl as a disturbing yet oddly enabling "tierce," thus completing the triangle once again. But as this concluding passage also suggests, only in sleep can Lol, that eternal sleepwalker, find a stillness capable of matching her prematurely

14. For an analysis of *Le Ravissement* as a purifying dramatization of triangular love, see Michèle Druon, "Mise en scène et catharsis de l'amour dans *Le Ravissement de Lol V. Stein,* de Marguerite Duras," *French Review* 58 (February 1985): 382–90. It should perhaps be noted that Druon identifies her essay as a follow-up to Jacques Lacan, "Hommage fait à Marguerite Duras, du ravissement de Lol V. Stein," *Cahiers Renaud-Barrault* 52 (December 1965): 7–15.

arrested yet ever restless heart. Like the princesse de Clèves, Lol above all seeks respite from the tedious, stressful burden of living and loving, "elle souhaite une interruption dans la sempiternelle répétition de la vie" (145). And as with Madame de Lafayette's creation, obliqueness and evasion characterize Lol's conduct. Unlike the princesse, however, Lol knows that indirection and interruption provide only provisional relief from life's and love's ineluctable pain, from "la vieille algèbre des peines d'amour" (19).

If in Tatiana Karl's eyes Lol speaks of her life as if it were a book, a text (76), in reality Lol has little faith in words, least of all in their capacity to decipher the dolorous, arcane algebra of love. She says at one point to Jacques Hold: "Ce qui s'est passé dans cette chambre entre Tatiana et vous je n'ai pas les moyens de le connaître. Jamais je ne saurai. Lorsque vous me racontez il s'agit d'autre chose" (136). Particularly salient in this passage is Lol's admission that she does not possess the wherewithal ("les moyens") to know (about) love, an apparent allusion to her primordial lack. Even more significantly perhaps, Lol's avowal is interwoven here with her skepticism about equivalences made between sentence and event. For her, slow dancing at the Casino Ball and "playing house" at the Hôtel des Bois obviously say more about love than mere words ever can. Only gesture, at once performed and seen, partaken of, yet followed at a certain remove, can convey love's rapture.

If the expectation of love is inseparable from its consummation in Duras, likewise, watching love—a form of waiting for her anyway— merges with making love in her fiction. And only the dream, with its confusion—and fusion—of actor and spectator, its unexpected but smooth modulations, its uniform yet pregnant silence, can mime the force of love. Blank spaces on the printed page, sudden pauses in speech or conversation, entranced interruptions in the waking life—these and these alone can capture love's mystery.

Le Ravissement de Lol V. Stein is Duras's "book about nothing" in the sense that its abiding preoccupation, love, remains essentially unformulated throughout, lurking always in the text's hesitations. The central character's *ravissement,* her sudden absence to herself, is also a *saisissement,* a breathtaking hesitation, a gasp in the text as well as a gap, a swoon or a faint corresponding to the blank at the heart of Jacques Hold's account of Lol's life. For the narrator, as he frequently admits, invents, imagines what he records as much as he observes it, thereby calling our attention to the holes in his knowledge. As we have seen, moreover, Lol's primordial gap or lack, her heart-lessness, anticipates her loss of Michael Richardson, who was never hers to lose in the first place; it foreshadows her being eclipsed by Anne-Marie Stretter at the Casino Ball and her supplanting Tatiana Karl at the Hôtel des Bois; it prefigures the haunting presence-absence within the narrative of "un mot-absence, un mot-trou, creusé en son centre d'un trou"; finally, it prepares the way for the unexpected pauses in Lol's speech.

Julia Kristeva's general observations about Duras's fiction are particularly apt here: "It is a literature of limits . . . because it expresses the limits of the unnameable. The characters' elliptical discourse [and] the obsessive evocation of a 'nothing' that could sum up the malady of pain designate a wreckage of words in the face of the unnameable affect."[15] Implicit in Kristeva's remarks and consistently detectable in Duras's fiction, but especially so since *L'Après-midi de Monsieur Andesmas* and *Le Ravissement de Lol V. Stein,* is the novelist's constantly renewed effort to reach the "hors-texte" through a "texte," to make "a wreckage of words" in fact reflect "the unnameable affect."

What Duras's fiction demonstrates with ever-increasing urgency is that "the unnameable affect," the emotion that binds us, willy-nilly, to one another, specifies our nature, and that if words fail us when we attempt to define and thus master that emotion, the fault no doubt lies first in ourselves and only later in our instrument. Like Monsieur Andesmas and Lol V. Stein, we are flawed from the outset; some indispensable combination of lucidity and articulateness is missing in our makeup, a lack or defect leading us, it would seem, into a kind of guilty aphasia and ignorant neediness. And we suffer because we can no more help being drawn to one another than we can understand and verbalize our need.

For Duras, these thrilling, agonizing, unintelligible, above all unyielding attractions, the human networks to which we are fated to belong, begin and end in the family. All other relationships are but variants of that originating web. Our parents, moreover, if they could, would spare us the consequences of such entanglements. Lol's

15. Julia Kristeva, "The Pain of Sorrow in the Modern World: The Works of Marguerite Duras," *PMLA* 102 (March 1987): 151.

mother, for example, tries, unsuccessfully, to protect her daughter from Anne-Marie Stretter's plundering visit to the Casino Ball, while the old father in Duras's 1962 novella would keep his offspring free of sentimental attachment. But, forever absent to ourselves, we seek plenitude precisely in dialogue and human intercourse, in an almost literal exchange with another, in absorbing another's very breath. A specific Duras text springs to mind in this regard: the heart-stopping piece in which Duras describes how she gulped down her second baby's laughter, its *rire,* as if to fill the emptiness, the *rien,* created in her by her first baby's death. We think also of the white space on the page that, in the piece in question, perfectly mirrors the ineffable horror of such love. For if the eternally problematic mother-child bond is, for Duras, originary of "the unnameable affect," arresting white space on a page of print is her purest version of "a wreckage of words" thrown up in the face of that founding emotion.

As all of the foregoing implies, in *L'Après-midi de Monsieur Andesmas* and *Le Ravissement de Lol V. Stein,* Duras completely integrates the communicative and the poetic functions of literature. Her blending of message and spectacle in these narratives, however, is profoundly ironic in that a spectacle of absence, perceived at virtually every level of these texts, carries a message of presence. A sense of presence, of primal connection with another, before and outside the bounds of discourse, drives writer and reader on in these fictions. At the same time, Duras can only encircle, never call by its name, that primordial experience, thus the proliferation of the signs for absence in her writing. Accordingly, rather than with the imaginative universes of Proust and Char, or the innovative procedures of *le nouveau roman* and *la nouvelle vague,* Duras's deepest affinities seem to be with the practice of a great moralist-scriptor out of France's past. The novelist simply shows us once again, but in an entirely new way, what La Rochefoucauld's contemporary and confidante, Madame de Lafayette, showed us more than three centuries ago: that periphrasis alone has the requisite power to speak about (i.e., around) love.

Seven

Sarraute's *L'Usage de la parole,* or Re(en)trop(iz)ing *Tropismes*

Successive waves of fright, rage, and guilt assail the consciousness of Nathalie Sarraute's fictional creations. Like some latter-day Madame de Lafayette (if not quite the same Lafayette as the one who seems to have prefigured Duras), she portrays in her imaginative works the attacks of anxiety, surges of resentment, and pangs of remorse that afflict those who live in constant fear of others, suffer from bad faith regarding their own motives, and yet are cursed with intermittent lucidity. They see through everyone and everything, including, sporadically, their own rationalizations. Most of the time, however, their relations with their interlocutors assume the form of barely sublimated warfare, with the other perceived as an evil force to be defeated and the self as utterly blameless. But intimations of their complicity in the banal horror of everyday social intercourse wash over them from time to time, leaving unbearable self-disgust in their wake. Through it all, deceptively slight verbal exchanges and their heavy, convoluted underpinnings carry the burden of the action. Simple conversations and not so simple "subconversations" (to use Sarraute's celebrated term) tell the story, in which harmless-looking words change suddenly, without warning, into so many swords and shields.

These rapid, involuntary shifts from cold terror to righteous fury to paralyzing shame seem to arise out of an implicit belief on Sarraute's part in the irredeemable frailty of human nature. In this sense she recalls not only *La Princesse de Clèves* but also the great moralists of seventeenth-century France. For her, as for them, human nature is one and it is tainted; the writer's duty, it would seem, is to expose, whether in brief, highly concentrated texts or in longer, more elaborate works, humanity's basic flaw, its ineradicable egoism.

In other respects, however, Sarraute belongs fully to our century. For example, one could hardly accuse her of trying to achieve the paradoxical equilibrium of the *maxime*, the incisive observation of the *portrait* or the spiraling self-examinations of a princesse de Clèves. Sparkling wit, penetrating analysis, and psychological depth, staples of the neoclassical writer, interest Sarraute not at all. In her work, the turbulent to-and-fro of raw emotion bodies forth in a (seemingly) roiling mass of thrusts and parries. Her operating aesthetic would appear to be about as far removed from the decorous, confident, seventeenth century as that of her near coeval, Samuel Beckett, who summed up his artistic credo as follows: "To find a form that accommodates the mess, that is the task of the artist now."[1] For Sarraute, too, the "mess," particularly the confused spectacle of one ordinary psyche doing battle, alternately, with itself and another, is all, and to try to capture that frenzied drama in artistic form is today the writer's highest goal.

Despite her kinship with Beckett in this regard, Sarraute remains considerably closer than Beckett to the centuries-old moralistic strain in French literature. On the other hand, more consistently than they have Beckett, critics have linked her to that recent phenomenon, the *nouveau roman.*[2] In part because of her affinities with both tradition and the new in literature, her roots in French moralism and her ties to a self-consciously innovative, problematical approach to fiction-making, Sarraute has emerged as one of the most

1. Quoted in Deirdre Bair, *Samuel Beckett: A Biography* (New York: Harcourt Brace Jovanovich, 1978), 523.

2. Jean Ricardou, in *Le Nouveau Roman* (Paris: Editions du Seuil, 1973), no doubt typifies the approach of most of those who have studied this subject since 1970 in treating Sarraute but not Beckett.

authentic and compelling French writers of our time. Moreover, as each new book has appeared, her profoundly *moraliste* outlook, filtered through a genuinely postmodern artistic temperament, has become ever more arresting, to the point where *L'Usage de la parole*, published in 1980, may well represent the most remarkable and appealing fusion thus far of these two essential aspects of her work, her metalinguistic and moralistic preoccupations.

With *L'Usage de la parole* Sarraute returned to a form (or a format) for her fiction that she had not used since her first book, *Tropismes* (1939), that is, to a series of short, self-contained prose texts. During the four decades between *Tropismes* and *L'Usage* she had published no fewer than seven novels, an impressive collection of essays on the novel genre and her place in its evolution, and five plays which, perhaps inevitably, extend to the realm of theater her novelist's preoccupation with dialogue and its undercurrents. By the late 1950s or early 1960s, thanks to the power and originality of her writing, as well as to the plaudits it had received from such diverse figures as Sartre, Claude Mauriac, and Gaëtan Picon,[3] she was recognized as a major contributor to the novel's renewal and as one of the prime movers of the *nouveau roman*. Since that time, however, it has become increasingly evident that while Sarraute no doubt deserves credit for helping to revitalize the novel, grouping her with such writers as Michel Butor, Alain Robbe-Grillet, and Claude Simon in the "school" of the New Novelists obscures as much as it reveals about her fiction. Furthermore, of all the writers whose names have at one time or another been associated with the *école du regard,* in hindsight hers seems perhaps the least appropriate.

This is not to suggest that Sarraute shares nothing with Robbe-Grillet and company. On the contrary, like theirs, for example, her writing demands active participation, even sustained effort on the part of the reader. Also, virtually every figure who has ever been dubbed a "nouveau romancier," including Sarraute, rejects sociopolitical commitment as an aim of writing. For all, the text is its own justification and any involvement on the author's part in causes beyond it plays little or no role in the text's production. As regards

3. See Jean-Paul Sartre's "Préface" to Sarraute's *Portrait d'un inconnu,* first published in 1947 and reprinted in *Situations* (Paris: Gallimard, 1964), 4:9–16; Claude Mauriac, *L'Alitté-rature contemporaine* (Paris: Albin Michel, 1958), 242–59; Gaëtan Picon, "Le Planétarium" in *L'Usage de la lecture* (Paris: Mercure de France, 1961), 2:276–80.

technique, most of the so-called New Novelists—including, once again, Sarraute—have forsaken conventional plot, with its chronological recounting of past events, in favor of colloquies, situations, and incidents rendered more or less simultaneously in a kind of quasi-perpetual present. Further, in Sarraute and the others, sharply delineated fictional personae have disappeared: when characters do appear in a *nouveau roman* they are often blurred at the edges, devoid of stable identities, anonymous, interchangeable; from one passage to the next, "I" blends into "she" or "he" or "we" or even "you." Finally, a palpable self-consciousness pervades the writing generally in the *nouveau roman,* and perhaps especially the works of Sarraute, where refrainlike repetitions and recurring images (for example) bespeak a deliberateness in textual construction more characteristic of poetry than of prose.[4]

Certain recurrent expressions are in fact the "subject" of *L'Usage de la parole.* The repeated phrases, often clichés, always commonplace, function elsewhere in the French language as devices for concealing unpleasant truths. In *L'Usage,* however, they show their lethal underside. Each of the collection's ten prose pieces, moreover, has as its title the leitmotif words, which are then worried over, dismantled, or in some other fashion glossed in the body of the text. Where the individual pieces in *Tropismes,* all untitled, mock the hypocritical, self-deceiving behavior of easily recognizable bourgeois types, the texts in *L'Usage,* harsher still, lay bare the inherent unreliability of the very instrument of such critiques: habitual language.

Tropismes attempts to capture, within each of its twenty-four fluent, plainspoken, and yet oddly abortive vignettes, "une matière psychologique nouvelle ... une matière anonyme qui se trouve chez tous les hommes dans toutes les sociétés."[5] For Sarraute, this anonymous psychological material, swarming just below the surface of speech, possesses protean dimensions; it is "un foisonnement innombrable de sensations, d'images, de sentiments, de souvenirs, d'impulsions, de petits actes larvés qu'aucun langage intérieur n'exprime, qui se bousculent aux portes de la conscience, s'assemblent en

---

4. For further discussion of Sarraute's points of contact with *nouveau roman* values, assumptions, and techniques, see Gretchen Rous Besser, *Nathalie Sarraute* (Boston: Twayne, 1979), 158–68.

5. Nathalie Sarraute, "Conversation et sous-conversation" in *L'Ere du soupçon* (Paris: Gallimard, 1956), 112.

groupes compacts et surgissent tout à coup, se défont aussitôt, se combinent autrement et réapparaissent sous une nouvelle forme."[6] *L'Usage*, by contrast, obsessively explores some of the pet phrases with which speakers seek to hide these abrupt inner movements, these tropisms. Where the former work gives prominence to "la sous-conversation," the latter emphasizes discrete fragments of "la conversation" per se.

In *Tropismes* no. XI, for example, Sarraute offers a wicked caricature of the "culture vulture," female variety, stressing the rapacious, despoiling nature of this rather special category of *arriviste*. Throughout her text, the author hints at all the unuttered cries and whispers churning beneath *elle's* headlong, pathetic, shamelessly avid pursuit. The last three of the ten paragraphs making up the vignette epitomize its tone and thrust:

> Dans les recoins les plus secrets, dans les trésors les mieux dissimulés, elle fouillait de ses doigts avides. Toute "l'intellectualité." Il la lui fallait. Pour elle. Pour elle, car elle savait maintenant le véritable prix des choses. Il lui fallait l'intellectualité.
>
> Ils étaient ainsi un grand nombre comme elle, parasites assoiffés et sans merci, sangsues fixées sur les articles qui paraissaient, limaces collées partout et répandant leur suc sur les coins de Rimbaud, suçant du Mallarmé, se passant les uns aux autres et engluant de leur ignoble compréhension *Ulysse* ou les *Cahiers de Malte Laurids Brigge.*
>
> "C'est si beau," disait-elle, en ouvrant d'un air pur et inspiré ses yeux où elle allumait une "étincelle de divinité."[7]

It is such apparently harmless phrases as "c'est si beau" that Sarraute's 1980 volume of *récits* will expose for all their power to intimidate and even devastate.

The opening text in *L'Usage de la parole*, entitled "Ich sterbe," differs from the nine following it in at least two important ways. First, its title—hence its refrain as well—consists of a non-French expression. Second, throughout most of its length, the piece radiates

6. *L'Ere du soupçon*, 115.

7. Nathalie Sarraute, *Tropismes* (Paris: Editions de Minuit, 1957), 70–71.

compassion for the figure who utters the recurring remark. In the rest of this generally unforgiving collection, foreign phrases and feelings of sympathy are conspicuous primarily by their absence. Even so, as we shall see, "Ich sterbe" constitutes an ideal overture to *L'Usage de la parole*. The words "Ich sterbe," we are informed in the second line of the text, mean "I am dying" in German. They are the first and last words of the text, its title, and its refrain. Everything in "Ich sterbe" thus falls literally under the heading of the somber German phrase. Indeed, the whole piece may be construed as at once a meditation on the phrase and a dramatization of its sobering effect on one and all.

The point of departure for "Ich sterbe," its origin "outside" the text, rapidly but poignantly sketched in the opening paragraph, sets the tone for the piece. It seems that Anton Chekhov, shortly before his death, journeyed with his wife to a German spa, ostensibly in search of a cure for his tuberculosis. In reality—after all, he was a medical doctor quite familiar with the fatal effects of the disease— he had knowingly gone there to die. When his final moment approached, he sat bolt upright in his bed, his wife on one side, his German doctor on the other, and announced in a loud, clear voice: "Ich sterbe," after which he fell back, dead. In Sarraute's text, these simple words uttered by that humane writer in those extreme circumstances trigger a complex, sometimes contradictory series of reflections on life and language.

These reflections, which make up the remainder of "Ich sterbe," amount to a commentary on Chekhov's death that is also a commentary on the human condition. By choosing his host's language over his own to articulate the unutterable, Chekhov stayed true to his unassuming, undemanding self. But the choice of language, implying as it does the loss of the mother tongue, also works in concert with the Russian writer's imminent, ultimate deprivation: the soul departs when authentic speech leaves. At the same time, a certain formality and distance, if not actual mastery accompany the introduction of the sharply etched foreign words into this dire situation. Death is in a sense neutralized homeopathically by the use of the precise, alien, hence perfectly lifeless (for Chekhov) formula. Also, by *speaking* his end in the proper person and tense of the foreign tongue, in sturdy, reliable German, Chekhov addresses the Other, the doctor, rather than that variant of his Self, his wife, to whom "je meurs" (in its Russian equivalent), soft, familiar, intimate, could only evoke wordless rapture, the phrase having progressed by now too far down through time toward its ecstatic figurative sense to convey any longer its dreadful literal meaning.

Nevertheless, if in this particular context the phrases, "Ich sterbe" and "je meurs" prove to be antonymic and thus incommensurate, certain pronoun subjects take on, in the very same context, a rather elastic applicability. "Vous," for example, refers on some occasions to the German doctor and on others to the reader. The first-person singular, whether "Ich" or "je," applies in some instances to Chekhov, in others to a highly self-conscious narrator and in still others to both together, as in the following paragraph:

> Je vais, moi-même, opérer... ne suis-je pas médecin aussi?... la mise en mots.... Une opération qui va dans ce désordre sans bornes mettre de l'ordre. L'indicible sera dit. L'impensable sera pensé. Ce qui est insensé sera ramené à la raison. Ich sterbe.[8]

The last two words of the passage undercut everything preceding them. Chekhov's—and the narrator's—grandiose plans for "la mise en mots," for the creation of order and reason out of chaos, for giving tongue to the ineffable, are destroyed retroactively by the spare, devastating, terminal avowal.

What eventually emerges from this ambiguous, extremely suggestive text is that the grammatical subject of the key sentence implicates the reader, too. For in due course the terse declaration becomes the reluctant admission of our common dark destiny—even as it remains a desperate assertion of our dignity: "Avec ces mots affilés, avec cette lame d'excellente fabrication... je devance le moment et moi-même je tranche: Ich sterbe" (15). Our awareness of the coming night, combined with our capacity to verbalize that awareness, confers on us our specificity as human beings. "L'Usage de la parole" in extremis defines us in all our humble grandeur.

By the end of "Ich sterbe," however, the note of modest triumph that dominates these antepenultimate passages has disappeared. In

8. Nathalie Sarraute, *L'Usage de la parole* (Paris: Gallimard, 1980), 11–12. Subsequent page references to *L'Usage* appear in the body of the study, in parentheses.

the final paragraph, a detached narrative voice tells us that what we are seeing here are merely a few of the "légers remous" and "brèves ondulations" that the key words have set in motion. We are then invited to follow out any other patterns we may detect in and around the words, assured in advance that anything we shall spot is truly there, "en chacun de nous," rippling outward from the upheaval caused by "Ich sterbe."

The eerie, removed finality of this close has been subtly prepared by the transitional penultimate paragraph. In the paragraph immediately preceding the transition, a variation on the triumphant claim "je devance le moment et moi-même je tranche: Ich sterbe" was offered: "j'abaisse sur moi la dalle, la lourde pierre tombale" (15). Now, in the next-to-last paragraph, the proud "je" has become a weak "il" and the ability to rise above one's destiny through conscious formulation is no longer certain. More ominous, the vibrant present tense has given way to the remote past tense of the verb: "Mais peut-être... quand il soulevait la dalle, quand il la tenait au-dessus de lui à bout de bras et allait l'abaisser sur lui-même... peut-être y a-t-il eu comme une faible palpitation... Ich sterbe" (15–16). The heretofore sympathetic narrator-observer is then suddenly eclipsed, replaced by a doom-laden omniscient narrative voice: "Et si celui qui l'observait, et qui seul pouvait savoir, allait l'interposer, l'empoigner fortement, le retenir.... Mais non, plus personne, aucune voix.... C'est déjà le vide, le silence" (16).

In light of this downward modulation, the conclusion of "Ich sterbe" comes as no real surprise. Cumulatively, its closing paragraphs make its "lesson" finally quite unambiguous. Humanity, though wittingly and grievously impaired in its spiritual autonomy, is nevertheless prone to self-deception, to looking for ways of denying its awful knowledge. It will even venture into alien linguistic territory in the vain search for some semblance of control over its fate. Such a quest is itself of course only further proof of humanity's immutable bad faith, its eternal dependency on cozy illusions. For the expression "Ich sterbe," too, is an illusion, an empty collocation of words, used up, worn out. In the end, ironically, it can mean just what it says, but no more than that. And so death has, literally and inevitably, the last word. Speech, even foreign speech, is thus not the sign of our nobility, but merely another mask for our frailty, one more stopgap defense of the imagination.

As the foregoing discussion indicates, the opening text of *L'Usage de la parole* judges the spoken word harshly, unmasking its hubris, the overweening pride of its reach and the feebleness of its grasp. The nine pieces that come after "Ich sterbe" in a sense merely ring the changes on this lament. Most take as their subject (and hence title) some trite French expression that can be heard (or overheard) virtually every day in the most banal conversations. Like Flaubert in *Madame Bovary*, about whom she has tellingly written in this regard,[9] Sarraute in *L'Usage* makes platitudes themselves the stuff of her fiction. Both novelists foreground clichés to call attention to the basic dilemma posed by language: its endless fascination and at the same time its frustrating inadequacy as an instrument for true expression. What is specifically stressed in Sarraute's work, however, is the oral origin and function of language, its rootedness not in solitude or in writing but in speech and in society. In *L'Usage*, the spoken work always occurs "in situation," in the dynamic "twoness" of dialogue, not the static "oneness" of monologue.

The second piece in *L'Usage*, entitled "A très bientôt," illustrates the crucial role of "twoness" in the collection. Once again, the descriptive and the meditative are fused in an oblique but searching prose narrative. The narrator, standing at a discreet distance from the unfolding action, begins by gently posing a question and then just as gently issuing a command: "Où va-t-il, celui-là, plein d'ardeur et d'allant? Voyez-le traversant en tout hâte la chaussée sans prendre garde aux signaux, il est tellement pressé, il déteste tant faire attendre... surtout un ami, et un ami pareil, toujours si délicat, si prévenant" (19). This beginning introduces some of the main concerns of the piece, the most obvious of which is the theme of friendship (about which more below). Another concern is the far subtler idea of friendship's vitalizing pull, its life-giving power of attraction. Friend No. 1 is drawn to Friend No. 2 as to an irresistible, inspiriting magnetic force. Friend No. 2 infuses Friend No. 1 with eagerness, recklessness, the desire to please, and a great appreciation of Friend No. 2's qualities. Friend No. 1 literally leaps to life on the page in his heedless, headlong rush toward Friend No. 2, in the tropistic lurch itself. Already in the first two sentences of "A très bientôt" we

---

9. Nathalie Sarraute, "Flaubert, le précurseur," *Preuves*, no. 168 (February 1965): 3–11. Reprinted in Nathalie Sarraute, *Paul Valéry et l'Enfant d'Eléphant; Flaubert le précurseur* (Paris: Gallimard, 1986), 59–89.

suspect that Friend No. 1 exists only in this valence, in his blind need
to unite with Friend No. 2.

As the "story" develops beyond this fast-paced starting point, we
realize that Sarraute has used the in medias res conventional beginning against itself, so to speak. She has plunged us into the middle of
an action that has neither an earlier preparatory phase nor any subsequent resolution in the traditional sense. Everything is held constant, all is in Friend No. 1's keyed-up anticipation of the spate of
words that he will deliver to Friend No. 2, whether today or "à très
bientôt" at the next of their fortnightly luncheon meetings. It is not
the substance of what is said but the enormous flow itself, particularly in prospect, that spurs Friend No. 1 on and that defines him.

Then suddenly, barely four pages under way, the "story"—such as
it is—is halted, *its* flow is interrupted: "Ici il faut nous arrêter" (23),
to be resumed four pages later: "Après cette brève interruption, le
flot de paroles reprend son cours" (27). The explicitness of these
framing sentences advertises the parenthetical status of this section
of the text. The radical self-reflexiveness of the digression sets it off
dramatically from what precedes it and follows, and thus serves to
enact within the text, iconically and by antiphrasis, its thematic concern with speech as an inexorably advancing flood of words. The
text's self-consciousness at this juncture as a pause in the story's
progress makes us keenly aware of our role as readers, as "creators"
of the tide on which we are moving forward. Just as Friend No. 1 is
led on willy-nilly by his ever-pressing need to expatiate on any and
every subject to Friend No. 2, just so have we been caught up in the
spasmodic processes of reading, in its fits and starts, its spurts and
pauses and new spurts. A subliminal message accompanies this realization, telling us that this text, this ebb and flow of words, engages
our destiny, too.

The digression directly addresses a topic alluded to in the text's
first two sentences: friendship. It does so in a manner reminiscent
not of Montaigne, or anyone else who has treated this "sacred" topic
in the past, but rather of Sarraute's contemporary, Sartre. The latter,
of course, ever alert to the taboos of existentialism, never wrote formally on such a patently "essentialist" notion as friendship. In fact,
he systematically opposed the idea of trafficking in such abstract
concepts, on the grounds that they had no valid ontological status.
For Sartre, Friendship—like Love or Wisdom—can have a hyposta-

tized reality only. It can be only a myth, an invention, one of the convenient labels humanity has devised for disguising the darker impulses that interpersonal relations can unleash.[10]

It is in this realm, especially, that Sartre's affinities with Sarraute come to the fore, affinities of which he was quite conscious. As early as 1947 he saw in her a kindred spirit. In his preface to the novel that she published that year, *Portrait d'un inconnu*, he refers glowingly to her depiction of "le règne de l'inauthenticité" in *Tropismes*.[11] According to Sartre, thanks to Sarraute's work we catch a glimpse of the human psyche for what it is, that is, not as a well of admirable sentiments, but rather as a tangle of conflicting evasions: "Si nous jetons un coup d'oeil, comme l'auteur nous y invite, à l'intérieur des gens, nous entrevoyons un grouillement de fuites molles et tentaculaires."[12] An even more relevant Sartre text in the present circumstances is *La Nausée*, in which abstract concepts of the type mentioned above are consistently associated with the Autodidact, the character who is portrayed in Sartre's 1938 novel as smug, ridiculously naive, and thoroughly self-deceiving. He believes unquestioningly in all the reassuring rubrics that the novel's protagonist, Antoine Roquentin, caught in the vise of *l'innomable*, has come to distrust and even despise. Indeed, the muted "debate" in *La Nausée* between Roquentin and the Autodidact, on the validity of hypostatizing terms like Experience, Learning, and Travel, paves the way for Sarraute's treatment of Friendship in "A très bientôt."

Both Sartre and Sarraute mock society's apparent need to reify complacent abstractions. In the case of *La Nausée*, one thinks of the long visit that Roquentin pays to Bouville's municipal museum where the heroes of the city's past are memorialized in works of art. His tour ended, he is filled with disgust for the pompous display of History, Order, and Duty that he has just witnessed. Roquentin then turns to the assembled statuary and canvases and says: "Adieu Salauds."[13] In the digression section of "A très bientôt," Sarraute makes similar sport of society's tendency to institutionalize the values it holds dear, although in her text there is no figure like Roquentin

10. See especially the section entitled "Les relations concrètes avec autrui," in Jean-Paul Sartre, *L'Etre et le néant* (Paris: Gallimard, 1943), 428–503.

11. See *Situations*, 4:12.

12. See *Situations*, 4:13.

13. Jean-Paul Sartre, *La Nausée* (Paris: Gallimard, 1938), 135.

with whom readers can comfortably identify while passing judgment. After the pause in the text has been duly noted, the digression begins in earnest with a question—really two questions—and an answer:

> Où sont-ils, ces amis? Où sommes-nous avec eux? Nous nous trouvons à l'intérieur de ce monument qui porte gravé sur son fronton . . . disons "en lettres d'or" pour souligner son caractère éminemment respectable, imposant . . . qui porte donc gravé en lettres d'or au-dessus de l'entrée son nom: Amitié. C'est, vous le savez, une institution. . . . (23)

The digression continues with a leisurely but devastating dissecting of this friendship in particular, and of friendship generally, in a discussion that effectively eviscerates the idea—and the ideal—altogether. Friendship is revealed as merely a nervous tic of shallow, insecure, compulsive babblers more in need of a sounding board, "un autre moi-même" (26) in the literal sense, than of a genuine other. As if to confirm the hollowness of the relationship between the two friends, as well as the emptiness of the "institution" that enshrines it, a casual slur uttered one day by a mutual acquaintance tolls a distant death knell for the relationship. When the acquaintance says to Friend No. 1 that he has never been able to stomach Friend No. 2—"Je fuis toujours les gens comme lui, les orgueilleux" (26)—the seeds of the friendship's dissolution are sown, seeds that will bear fruit in the section following the digression.

The "story" resumes with a chance encounter between Friend No. 1 and another mutual acquaintance, this one a person who, unknown to him, has frequently been the object of disparaging comments by the two friends at their fortnightly meetings. The mutual acquaintance tells Friend No. 1 in confidence of the peculiar impact that his (i.e., the mutual acquaintance's) affection for Friend No. 2 has on his comportment. He speaks of the eagerness with which he looks forward to their meetings, of his obliviousness to the world around him when he hurries to them, of the uncontrollable urge he feels to talk about everything to Friend No. 2, and of his need always at the end of a meeting to set a date for the next one: "J'ai envie, j'ai besoin que bientôt tout recommence" (29). Needless to say, Friend No. 1, dumbstruck by what he has heard, recognizes his own behavior in his acquaintance's account. Completely undone by this mirror image of himself, he shouts: "Je suis comme vous, exactement comme vous, et vous savez ce que je découvre, vous savez ce que je crois: notre ami que nous aimons tant, il ne ... eh bien, c'est clair, il ne m'aime pas" (30). Before long, the acquaintance in turn shouts triumphantly: "Moi aussi j'ai trouvé, tout est clair pour moi aussi, la vérité est qu'il ne nous aime pas!" (31).

This shocking double treachery announces the birth of a new twosome, a new alliance, an event consecrated in the text by the substitution of the phrase "deux parleurs" for "deux amis." The "discovery" made by the two talkers, we are then informed, has a special meaning for us: "Cette découverte ... pour nous a l'intérêt de nous faire voir tout à coup ce flot de paroles qui nous fascine, sous d'assez curieux et imprévisibles aspects. ... " (31). A penultimate section of the text immediately follows, consisting in a rising litany of seven brief paragraphs, each of which begins with the phrase "Des paroles" and goes on to explore "this wave of words" in such a way as to shed light on one of its more frightening aspects. The final paragraph in the series typifies and climaxes the entire litany: "Des paroles porteuses d'offrandes, de richesses ramenées de la terre entière et déposées sur l'autel devant un dieu de la mort assis au fond du temple, dans la chambre secrète, la dernière chambre ... " (32). Words, at once our main weapon and our principal armor in the long war of life, prove ultimately to be ineffective on both counts. The basic components of human existence are anxiety and fear: fear of others and anxiety about ourselves and our destiny. For a time the floodtide of utterance can protect us from that knowledge, but not forever. Betrayal is inevitable because our need for permanent reassurance, for perfectly comforting words, exceeds our capacity as humans to provide such security to one another. We make haste to talk in order not to hear the deadly murmur of the heart's most secret chamber.

But this is not the end of "A très bientôt." As was true of "Ich sterbe," a concluding paragraph undercuts the nihilism of the penultimate passages and closes the text on a note of detached control. If anything, however, the tonal shift from night to day marking the text's culminating portions is starker still in "A très bientôt." The narrative voice at the close of this text, figuratively speaking, retreats from the horror of what has gone before to assume a post of Olympian skepticism and imperturbability: "Mais où peut-on parfois être entraîné, porté par le cours d'une conversation familière, toute banale, à la table d'un restaurant où se retrouvent régulièrement pour déjeuner ensemble deux amis" (32). After reading this serene, composed conclusion, however, we find ourselves still haunted by a gnawing question: exactly who got carried away here? Friend No. 1? The talkative acquaintance? The narrator? The reader? All of the above? In the final analysis, "A très bientôt" is just as disturbing, just as malaise-provoking as "Ich sterbe" ever was. Perhaps even more so, for it concentrates even more unrelievedly on the drama of elemental fear (Heidegger's *Sorge,* Camus's *souci*) and its palliatives, on the existential anguish of living. Sartre, in his 1947 essay on Sarraute, observed in reference to her earliest works: "Les livres de Nathalie Sarraute sont remplis de ces terreurs: on parle, quelque chose va éclater, illuminer soudain le fond glauque d'une âme et chacun sentira les bourbes mouvantes de la sienne."[14] He could have been speaking, prophetically, of "A très bientôt."

Quite obviously, Sartre and Sarraute share a number of assumptions, even more than those already indicated. In both, for example, fear is life's basic given, and its denial leads to *mauvaise foi,* self-deception in all its forms. For both writers, the inauthentic will manifest itself in cliché-ridden or stereotypical patterns of speech, or in recourse to a kind of verbal pigeonholing that forecloses on the inherently intractable quality of lived experience. An even more striking similarity may be found in the texture of their respective works. Both Sartre and Sarraute seem to gravitate to images of viscosity, of invasive oozing and stickiness, when seeking to convey the unspeakable horror of brute existence.[15]

It would be a mistake, however, and a disservice to both writers, to see a complete overlapping of views between them. Indeed, on certain fundamental questions they could hardly be more different. Sartre, for example, is first, last, and always a thinker, an intellectual who is at some moments interested in matters of aesthetics, at others in philosophy, and at still others in sociopolitical issues, with the last eventually claiming most of his attention. In her writing, by contrast, Sarraute exhibits a profoundly artistic temperament and, to the degree that such distinctions are valid, appears to respond to both life and art primarily as a sensibility and only secondarily as an intellect.

14. *Situations,* 4:14.
15. See, for example, *L'Etre et le néant,* 695–708, and *Tropismes,* 17.

Her fiction and drama thus operate in eloquent if no doubt purely fortuitous support of Camus's contention in *Le Mythe de Sisyphe* that the work of art "naît du renoncement de l'intelligence à raisonner le concret."[16] Her critical essays, moreover, including those collected in *L'Ere du soupçon* plus the fugitive pieces—a mixture of articles and interviews appearing over the years in a scattering of periodicals and magazines[17]—contain in their aggregate no systematic approach to art and literature, and are more practical than theoretical in orientation. Also, unlike Sartre's trilogy, *Les Chemins de la liberté,* or the bulk of his writings for the theater, Sarraute's imaginative works carry no weighty sociopolitical message or ideology. Although the deeply troubled world of the French upper bourgeoisie occupies center stage in her writings, her characters (using that term loosely) reflect not the foibles of a class but rather the defects of a species, of humanity itself.

This brings us back to the matter of Sarraute's roots in traditional *moralisme.* As is true of La Rochefoucauld, the assumption of a universal (flawed) human nature informs her writings. In "Ich sterbe" and "A très bientôt," for example, the same phrase, "chacun de nous," strategically placed, serves to put all the "characters," fictional and real, on an equal footing. Author, narrator, protagonist, antagonist, implied reader, actual reader are all down in the arena struggling; no one merely watches, safe and serene, from a vantage point on higher ground. We are all wounded, disadvantaged from the start, and yet are somehow responsible for our destiny. Once again, we are confronting a profound divergence between Sarraute and Sartre; for as the latter makes clear in *L'Existentialisme est un humanisme,* he rejects out of hand the classical moralist's belief that humanity always and everywhere partakes of an unchanging and permanently crippled nature.[18]

The most important difference, however, between Sartre and Sarraute concerns their respective attitudes toward language, a difference that has become particularly salient with the publication of *L'Usage de la parole.* At several points in his autobiographical work, *Les Mots,* Sartre refers to the great effort he had to sustain over many

---

16. Albert Camus, *Le Mythe de Sisyphe* (Paris: Gallimard, 1942), 132.

17. For a list of Sarraute's uncollected articles and interviews through 1976, see Besser, *Nathalie Sarraute,* 185–86.

18. *L'Existentialisme est un humanisme* (Paris: Gallimard, 1946), passim.

years in order to free himself finally of language's sway over him, of what he called the "piège de la nomination."[19] Somewhat ironically, Sartre's increasing mistrust of language almost exactly parallels Sarraute's growing fascination with it as the key to humanity's deepest nature. Between *Tropismes* and *L'Usage,* across the intervening novels and plays, Sarraute concentrates more and more exclusively on words themselves, as if trying to make them yield up their innermost secrets. The gathering dominance of this focus in her writing becomes completely overt in 1970, surfacing in the very title of her radio play of that year, *Isma.* G. R. Besser's characterization of the play speaks directly to this issue:

> In *Isma,* the provocation for the drama is... nothing more tangible than a disagreeable sound. "Isma" refers to the infinitesimal accentuation of words ending in "isme," like *capitalisme, structuralisme, syndicalisme...* labels... that serve to categorize and define. But it is not their content or meaning that matters here, only their pronunciation.... Words are emptied of their meaning; their hollow shell alone remains.[20]

(Is *tropisme* then but another "isma" thrown on the rubbish heap by Sarraute's 1970 play? Such a question must at least be entertained.)

The radical foregrounding of the words in a text continues in Sarraute's 1976 novel, "disent les imbéciles." The novel's title, in quotation marks and lowercased on the title page, is repeated in this form at irregular intervals throughout the novel in such a way as to undermine virtually every thought adumbrated within it. (In this sense the title of the novel is the novel's literal "subject," which is also the case, as has been noted, with the various texts that make up *L'Usage de la parole.*) The novel's drama consists in the struggle the "characters" engage in while attempting to protect their ideas and opinions from savagely dismissive remarks like "disent les imbéciles."

Sarraute's scrutiny of totalitarianism in language finds its most concentrated expression in *L'Usage de la parole,* particularly in the texts entitled: "Ton père. Ta soeur," "Mon petit," "Eh bien quoi, c'est

19. *Les Mots* (Paris: Gallimard, 1964), 117. See also 39, 151, and 209.
20. G. R. Besser, *Nathalie Sarraute,* 126.

un dingue" and "Ne me parlez pas de ça." The first of these texts explores the language of threat and menace used by parents trying to manipulate children. The title, as we learn with the first sentence of the piece, is simply an abbreviated, telegraphic version of "Si tu continues, Armand, ton père va préférer ta soeur" (49). Jealousy, sibling rivalry, extortion, invidious comparison, all evoked by the four words of the title, are exploited by the would-be controlling elder. The text entitled "Mon petit," an indirect, low-key, and yet dazzling study of everyday cowardice and its rationalizations, presents the disheartening drama of condescension unleashed when a presumably offhand, affectionate mode of address, "mon petit," is dropped into the middle of a quiet conversation between friends. As the "story" progresses, we discover that the title remark is but a half-step away, in its power to belittle, from the phrase "le pauvre petit" (110). The text of "Eh bien quoi, c'est un dingue" erects a metaphoric wall of refusal and rejection around one of the two interlocutors, while reducing the other to the role of crackpot, the fool to be brushed aside with the back of the hand. The dismissive gesture par excellence, ideally formulated in the title/leitmotif phrase, is always accomplished in the name of superior wisdom and sophistication. Unfortunately, however, no superior being possessing these qualities survives the gesture's grand destructive sweep. The now familiar format of a dialogue of two friends reappears in "Ne me parlez pas de ça." Once again, the "little murders" of quotidian life occur, implicating everyone, reader included. The brutally conclusory thrust of the title phrase is examined from every conceivable angle. It is even compared to the seemingly synonymous expression "Ne m'en parlez pas," but only so as to demonstrate how this latter wording has in fact an exactly opposite meaning, suggesting as it does "un acquiescement, un accord, une parfaite entente" (133), while "Ne me parlez pas de ça" expresses only—and categorically—a loud, commanding No.

The closing text in *L'Usage de la parole*, entitled "Je ne comprends pas," brings out, more forcefully than those preceding it, the full extent of Sarraute's indictment of totalitarian patterns of speech. It also bears witness to the distance the author has traveled since *Tropismes*. Once again a conversation between two friends, overheard, or perhaps just imagined, is recounted by a discreet narrative voice. Again it appears that one of the two interlocutors in the "story" has spoken while the other has merely listened. After quickly establishing the setting ("Deux personnes assises sur un banc de jardin dans la pénombre d'un soir d'été paraissaient converser" [147]), the narrator admits that while all the words he overheard (or dreamed he overheard) were intelligible, he could not grasp their overall meaning. Anticipating our objection that he may simply have been eavesdropping on "un poème longuement élaboré, puis récité, ou jailli sous la poussée de l'inspiration" (148), he hastens to assure us that such a misunderstanding on his part is not even remotely possible, that persuasion, in the most prosaic, conventional sense of the word, was the unmistakable object of the utterance in question (149).

At precisely this point in the text the locus of the discourse abruptly changes. The present tense of the verb replaces the past and the listener in the "story" becomes indistinguishable from the narrator and, eventually, from the reader. For the next several pages (149–52), the two-phased experience of active incomprehension countered by an unavailing effort to overcome it, gives rise to a series of simple but telling metaphors: e.g., "Sans cesse de nouvelles paroles arrivent et aussitôt s'étiolent.... Celui en qui elles se déposent a l'impression que son esprit est devenu une terre ingrate d'où des émanations asphyxiantes se dégagent, un champ jonché de parole sans vie ... " (151–52).

Immediately following this passage the discourse undergoes another transformation. Over the next several pages (152–56) the title phrase, "Je ne comprends pas," always in quotation marks, occurs no fewer than eight times, serving as a refrain in this climactic section of a text whose drama at last emerges with undisguised directness. The listener's plight is explicitly identified with that of both narrator and reader (152). We are then asked whether we have ever dared say to a friend assaulting us with opaque jargon, "Je ne comprends pas" (154). The narrator, for his part, in effect confesses that he has never had the courage to do so. Suddenly, miraculously, the listener breaks his silence and utters the magic words: "Je ne comprends pas" (154). By his avowal, the listener has taken upon himself, on behalf of us all, so we are informed, the enormous risk of showing himself to be unworthy of the verbal pearls that the speaker was casting before him. On the other hand (and the discourse now becomes tentative and speculative), should the speaker per chance be the one who is re-

duced to silence by his interlocutor's courageous admission, should
he be obliged to reflect on the abuses he has wrought upon speech,
to acknowledge that he has used words "pour pervertir, pour escro-
quer, terroriser, soumettre, opprimer" (155). (It is here that the
book's title, sufficiently transposed to suggest "l'abus de la parole" as
much as "l'usage de la parole," is inscribed in the body of the text.)
What in fact transpires is more surprising still, to the point where
one might even be tempted to believe "que tout cela décidément
n'était qu'un rêve" (155). In yet another stunning reversal of expected behavior, the speaker, overcome with the joy of relief, thanks
the listener warmly for his candor and congratulates him for refusing
to accept "les absurdités" (156). In a flash, the fog heretofore blot-
ting out understanding has lifted and the happiness of clarity shines
down on everyone.

The penultimate paragraph of "Je ne comprends pas" raises the
text's cycle of peripeteias to a new level of refinement. For this reason, it is worth quoting in its entirety:

> La menace est écartée. Tout est en paix. En ordre, l'ennemi
> s'est métamorphosé en allié. Ce lieu de séquestration, de tor-
> ture, est devenu un flot de résistance. Au milieu des océans
> d'obscurantisme, de charlatanisme, de terrorisme, de con-
> formisme, de lâcheté qui l'entourent, il est un lieu où la pa-
> role est en sécurité. (156)

Once again, the tone or locus of the discourse has shifted, but in
more subtle fashion now than previously. The forces of iniquity, of
linguistic oppression—of *isma*—have been routed while "la parole"
has been restored to all its power and glory. The wicked lose out and
the righteous triumph. In light of what has gone before, however, can
we have faith in this solution? Does not everything seem just a little
bit too pat, a shade too good to be true? Sunny, simplistic generalities
have crept into the piece at virtually the last moment, inspiring
doubt rather than belief in the rapidly approaching, stereotypically
happy ending. The brief, sentence-long concluding paragraph con-
firms our mounting suspicions: "Mais vraiment c'est à croire que
toute cette belle, trop belle histoire n'était finalement rien d'autre
qu'un conte de fées" (157). A final reversal thus upsets the artificial
equilibrium of the text's penultimate paragraph. Here, too, as in

earlier texts of *L'Usage de la parole,* the detached tone of the closing passage retroactively neutralizes the entire text, this time through the mask of an omniscient parent-narrator, perched high above it all, recounting a harmless fairy tale to his children-listeners.

By now in our reading of *L'Usage de la parole* we of course know better than to trust such a poised, superior, narrative voice. Though wittily oblique in its charge that faddism, chicanery, and intellectual terrorism often characterize the conversations of friends, "Je ne comprends pas" nonetheless lacks neither passion nor the capacity to convince. Paradoxically, in fact, its dispassionate, bemused close serves to remind us that no privileged status exists in *L'Usage,* no higher ground puts judges beyond the reach of judgment. The constant shifting of levels and tones, the perpetual crisscrossing of divergent voices, which continues up to the very end, enriches the text immeasurably and at the same time destroys the very possibility of any hierarchy's structuring its various discourses. Indeed, what we are encountering here is truly "une poésie des discours" (to borrow A. S. Newman's lapidary definition of Sarraute's style as a novelist),[21] a playful imbrication of voices, which is a form of "literariness" that, irony of all ironies, makes the bleak "lesson" of "Je ne comprends pas" all the more imposing and credible. The text's intersecting verbal planes constitute both a remarkable display of "poetry" and concrete, incontrovertible proof that no one lives "en sécurité," safe from sullying contact with evil—least of all users of "la parole."

Evidence of a strictly "literary" side to "Je ne comprends pas" crops up in the text's opening sentences:

> Je ne l'ai pas fait moi-même, du reste si je l'avais fait, la modestie ne devrait-elle pas me retenir de me targuer d'un tel exploit? J'ai seulement eu la chance d'en être le témoin, ou peut-être l'ai-je rêvé, mais alors c'était un de ces rêves que nous parvenons difficilement à distinguer de ce qui nous est "vraiment" arrivé, de ce que nous avons vu "pour de bon."
> (147)

In a blatant but amusing subversion of the hoary convention which presents the narrator of a story establishing his credibility at the out-

---

21. A. S. Newman, *Une poésie des discours: essai sur les romans de Nathalie Sarraute* (Geneva: Libraire Droz, 1976), esp. 196–97.

set by identifying an authoritative source for his tale, Sarraute's narrator launches his "story" in a cloud of ambiguity concerning its
origins. He in effect both claims and disclaims for himself the events
he is about to recount. To compound our confusion, he then suggests that he either witnessed the events or dreamed them, all the
while implying (like Nerval's narrator in *Aurélia*, so much admired
by Proust and André Breton) that no particular importance is to be
attached to distinctions made between dream and waking reality.
The text's third sentence, quoted earlier in its entirety ("Deux personnes assises sur un banc de jardin dans la pénombre... "), evokes
Verlaine's "Colloque sentimental" ("Dans le vieux parc solitaire et
glacé / Deux formes ont tout à l'heure passé"), especially because of
the role played by colloquy throughout *L'Usage de la parole*. Upon
entering "Je ne comprends pas," we are thus immediately confronted
by the highly visible traces of its roots and antecedents not in life but
in literature.

In view of what follows in the body of the text, its beginning could
scarcely be more fitting. The series of peripeteias that we have seen
punctuating the piece, for example, in their capacity as the primary
engine or main propulsive mechanism for comedy, come straight out
of Molière and his countless imitators. The flaunting of this device in
"Je ne comprends pas" effectively waves the banner of literariness
across its length and breadth. The question of poetry versus prose is
of course explicitly raised near the beginning of the piece in connection with the speaker's impenetrable monologue. It will also be
recalled that at its close the text is "formally" assigned to the genre
of the fairy tale. But no doubt the most patently "literary" dimension
of "Je ne comprends pas" relates to its covert satire of the cultism
and obscurantism that sometimes pass for innovative thinking
among those most snobbishly sophisticated users of words, writers
and critics. Sarraute has treated the subjects of literary creation and
literary celebrity before, with varying emphases, in *Le Planétarium*
(1959), *Les Fruits d'or* (1963), and *Entre la vie et la mort* (1968). In
"Je ne comprends pas" these themes turn up again, this time in a text
that is more rigorous, less forgiving, and more conspicuously "literary" than any previous Sarraute work touching on these matters. As
the closing text in *L'Usage de la parole*, "Je ne comprends pas" thus
caps a process begun much earlier by Sarraute, the gradual annex-
ation of writing itself, in its most sacrosanct form, the writing of

"literature," to the territory mined by the moralist. Spanning the decades from *Tropismes* to *L'Usage de la parole,* a single, increasingly voracious *examen de conscience* directs her steadily expanding vision.

Nevertheless, despite the essential continuity of Sarraute's production, the texts of *L'Usage de la parole* differ in at least one fundamental respect from those in her first book. Where the early work contests (if not to say condemns) everything in its world but its own instrument, its monochrome lexical palette, nothing, not even (especially not even) "la parole," is spared in the later work. Where *Tropismes* nos. X and XIII, for example, offer devastating portraits of the superficial, deceitful, gossipy, shopping-filled days of upper-middle-class matrons, "Ich sterbe" and "Je ne comprends pas" broaden the scope of Sarraute's merciless critique considerably, not only to include all classes, ages and sexes, but also to put words themselves on trial. The moralist's pitiless gaze, having survived the long years intact, now examines its own medium, language, in order to lay bare the unavowedly oppressive nature of our most cherished clichés. If *Tropismes* captures the slight, involuntary, and yet somehow shameful responses or hidden inner movements that accompany the menacing stimuli of ordinary social intercourse, *L'Usage de la parole,* while recapitulating elements of what Sarraute wrote between 1939 and 1980, in a sense reprises the writer's similarly constructed earliest work so as to enlarge its critical sweep, to bring the whole literary enterprise, that supreme use of the word, within the purview of the moralist. The basic trope in *Tropismes*—that of an abrupt, automatic turning of the consciousness toward an awesome external force as epitomizing human interaction—folds back on itself, so to speak, in *L'Usage de la parole,* setting off a convulsion, an internal upheaval. The miniscule explosions of the former work give way to the tiny entropic implosions of the latter, in which the commonplace expression "l'usage de la parole" ends up a searing, transparent trope for "l'abus de la parole." Roland Barthes has shown in his essay on La Rochefoucauld that the demystifying moralist must eventually self-destruct.[22] The same may be true for Nathalie Sar-

22. Roland Barthes, "La Rochefoucauld: 'Reflections or Sentences and Maxims,'" in *New Critical Essays,* trans. Richard Howard (New York: Hill and Wang, 1980), 3–22, esp. 20–22.

raute, who, in a sense, must demolish her own project by displaying in its verbal spectacle the harsh but essential truth that tragic discourse and ludic discourse in the end converge to annihilate the subject of all discourse. *Ich sterbe,* then? Precisely.

Conclusion

Just Words:
From Gide to Sarraute

I t is time to take a closer look at the points of contact that exist among the narratives and novelists discussed in the preceding chapters. Although we have already observed how a comparable ideal of commitment, linked to misgivings about language, animates Malraux and Camus, more must be said on that subject. Colloquy or dialogue tied to moral vision in both Duras and Sarraute, as well as the interplay of quotation and judgment in Gide and Proust alike, also deserve more attention. Similarly, feminist concerns, cutting across period, gender, and style to bond Flaubert and Malraux with Duras, would benefit from fresh examination. Most significant, all of these novelists, from Gide (or even Flaubert) to Sarraute, have a like propensity to scrutinize both instrument and self simultaneously, and to find both wanting. This, too, merits review.

Let us begin our reconsideration of these writers and texts in their interconnections by again exploring how ethical and aesthetic parity in *La Condition humaine* and *La Peste* relates to distinctions one can draw between the fiction of commitment and that of ideology. This time, however, we shall bring Sartre more directly into the discussion. Interestingly, Sartre dismissed out of hand, without saying what it was, "littérature . . . à thèse."[1] By contrast—although here, too, he provides no stable, concise definition of the concept—the idea (and ideal) of commitment in literature never lost its urgent appeal for him. The author of *Les Chemins de la liberté* never tired of stressing the value of *engagement,* as is attested time after time in his writings and utterances, from the *prière d'insérer* that he wrote for *Les Mouches* in 1943 to the interview he gave in Prague a quarter of a century later.

The notion of commitment, as was pointed out above in the chapter on *La Peste,* pervades the "Présentation" that Sartre wrote for the first number of *Les Temps modernes* in October 1945. Significantly, he concludes his manifesto in a manner that, as regards the newly minted phrase "littérature engagée," assigns at least as much weight to the first term as to the second: "Je rappelle . . . que dans la 'littérature engagée,' *l'engagement* ne doit, en aucun cas, faire oublier la *littérature* et que notre préoccupation doit être de servir la littérature en lui infusant un sang nouveau, tout autant que de servir la collectivité en essayant de lui donner la littérature qui lui convient."[2] But even before this elegantly balanced conclusion to his "Présentation," Sartre had made it pellucidly clear to readers that he envisioned his review "comme un organe de recherches," baldly announcing that "nous n'avons pas de programme politique ou social," and that "nous recourrons à tous les genres littéraires pour familiariser le lecteur avec nos conceptions: un poème, un roman d'imagination, s'ils s'en inspirent, pourront, plus qu'un écrit théorique, créer le climat favorable à leur développement" (28). With these blunt penultimate avowals, Sartre had shown (at least in principle) that ethical considerations would not induce him to propound a particular sociopolitical thesis or to neglect the role of the aesthetic in his project.

Thus, if he rejects the notion of an unvarying, universal human nature, and if he will devote *Les Temps modernes* to "l'étude des problèmes concrets de l'actualité" (28) in the hope of increasing, for all members of society but especially for workers, the number of available choices in their lives, Sartre's project as both a writer and a mag-

1. Jean-Paul Sartre, *Situations* (Paris: Gallimard, 1948), 2:238.
2. The "Présentation des *Temps modernes*" has been reprinted in *Situations,* 2:9–30. The quoted passage appears on page 30. Subsequent page references to this volume are in the body of the study, in parentheses.

azine editor will not be narrowly ideological. No single rule of social or political action will enjoy his automatic, unswerving support. He is after bigger game; he is seeking to bring about deeper changes in individuals and in society than could possibly ensue from his advancing a particular program or policy. Marx may receive more favorable mention than Proust in these pages, but the former's writings would no more constitute a doctrinal intertext for Sartrean *engagement* than the latter's.

More than two decades after the "Présentation" to *Les Temps modernes* first appeared, confirmation of Sartre's nonprogrammatic approach to literary commitment turns up yet again, in the 1968 interview that he gave in Prague:

> L'engagement pour l'intellectuel, c'est raconter ce qu'il sent, le raconter du seul point de vue humain possible, ça veut dire qu'il doit réclamer pour lui-même et pour le monde cette liberté concrète qui n'est pas tout simplement la liberté que les bourgeois nous donnent, mais qui n'est pas, non plus, la suppression de cette liberté. Ça veut dire donner à la liberté un contenu concret, la transformer en une liberté en même temps matérielle et formelle. Il n'est donc pas possible, aujourd'hui plus que jamais, de ne pas s'engager. La seule chose qu'un écrivain et romancier puisse faire en tant que romancier et écrivain, c'est de montrer de ce point de vue la lutte pour la libération de l'homme, la situation dans laquelle il vit, les dangers qu'il court et les possibilités de changement.[3]

On the basis of these remarks, it is obvious that key aspects of Sartre's conception of *engagement* have remained unaltered through the years: it is literary, it is individual, it enhances freedom in concrete ways and supports positive sociopolitical change. Still absent are precisely those concepts and attributes that would assimilate the literature of commitment to that of any one ideology. For Sartre, too, human solidarity and ethical enlightenment—the very values that

---

3. Taken from *Les Ecrits de Sartre: chronologie, bibliographie commentée*, ed. Michel Contat and Michel Rybalka (Paris: Gallimard, 1970), 478. This indispensable critical bibliography of works by Sartre (up to 1969) comprises, among many other invaluable features, a veritable anthology of Sartre's pronouncements on the subject of *engagement.*

inform *La Condition humaine* and *La Peste*—take precedence over articulatable rules of action and identifiable doctrinal intertexts.

Particularly noteworthy in the pervasive valorization of human solidarity and connectedness in *La Condition humaine* and *La Peste*, is that in these novels verbal isolates—figures who avoid meaningful exchange with others—are precisely those for whom language remains an unproblematical given and those who directly or indirectly choose death over life. On the other hand, colloquy is both a crushing burden and an indispensable enabler in these texts, in which genuine dialogue emerges as the agonizing sine qua non of authentic existence. Malraux especially, but Camus as well, would thus seem to illustrate "Bakhtin's concept of language as essentially dialogic,"[4] with all that such a concept implies regarding the profoundly social, interactive nature of humans speaking and humans being, regarding the moral and historical indebtedness (and embeddedness) of words and their users. We have seen the extent to which polyphony characterizes *La Condition humaine*, in spite of that novel's ultimately coherent (though far from monologic) vision. The same is true for *La Peste*, even if here the discordant voices are all quoted within (thus to a degree seemingly homogenized by) Dr. Rieux's conspicuously monotone chronicle. In both novels, a struggle to communicate with others, destined never to reach closure, overspreads an equally unclosed struggle to commit oneself to mutuality and interdependence with one's fellows. Joseph Grand's succinctly formulated credo in *La Peste*, "Mais il faut bien s'entraider," thus resonates far beyond its immediate context. In the end, a two-tiered drama, without prospect of resolution, involving on one level human conduct and on the other human language, defines both fictions.

Far more compellingly than either André Malraux or Albert Camus, however, Nathalie Sarraute demonstrates the unique capacities of dialogue for governing human affairs. In 1983, three years after bringing out *L'Usage de la parole*, a collection of tales undergirded entirely, as we have seen, by colloquy, Sarraute published *Enfance*,[5]

4. David Lodge, "The Novel Now: Theories and Practices," *Novel* 21 (Winter–Spring 1988): 135. For a discussion of Bakhtin's notion of the inherently dialogic nature of language, and of the heuristic potential of that notion for the study of fiction in particular, see David Lodge, *After Bakhtin: Essays on Fiction and Criticism* (London: Routledge, 1990).

5. Nathalie Sarraute, *Enfance* (Paris: Gallimard, 1983). Subsequent page references to this

an autobiographical volume in which mostly painful memories of childhood crystallize around literally unforgettable pieces of conversation raining down on her consciousness out of the past. Her stepmother Véra, it seems, had a special talent for wounding young Natacha with talk. One day, with a recklessness born of desperation, the child blurts out at her stepmother the perfectly logical but utterly taboo question: "Dis-moi, est-ce que tu me détestes" (252)? Between the question and its answer, and again after the answer, an elaborate commentary weaves in and out around the question's (and the answer's) key word, the verb "détester." When the answer is finally given, its detached tone and casual obliqueness chill the reader, as they must surely have chilled the writer seven decades before: "Comment peut-on détester un enfant" (253)? But readers of *Enfance* are distracted, distanced, saved from the horrific power of the stepmother's long-ago words by the writer's cool, almost seamless latter-day gloss of them.

Clearly there is a lesson to be learned from this interplay of text and gloss, a lesson that must somehow relate to the fact that we have now almost finished *Enfance,* that we have only one more three-page "chapter" to read. In fact, the final two "chapters" of *Enfance* collaborate very effectively to bring Sarraute's autobiography to a satisfying end, if for obvious reasons not to a conclusion. In the penultimate three-page chapter, commentary explains, extends, and speculates about—hence supersedes and displaces—the brief exchange between stepdaughter and stepmother. The last chapter, a straightforward narration of a past event, followed by an equally straightforward dialogue from time present, mimes and in that sense repeats the lesson articulated in the second-last chapter. Paired, the final chapters make the pedagogical thrust of the volume as a whole completely manifest, a thrust that culminates first in the climactic question-and-answer conversation (together with the analytical discussion around it) and then in the ending chapter's account of Natacha's going off for her first day of school at the lycée Fénelon. For the first time, she is allowed to take the tram by herself. Véra has accompanied her to the stop and helped her to board the tram: "Elle me dit encore une fois de faire bien attention, je la rassure d'un geste

---

work are in the body of the study, in parentheses. Interestingly enough, Sarraute's more recently published *Tu ne t'aimes pas* (Paris: Gallimard, 1989), a novel, is written entirely in dialogue form.

et je vais m'asseoir sur la banquette en bois sous les fenêtres, mon lourd cartable neuf bourré de cahiers neufs et de nouveaux livres, posé par terre entre mes jambes.... Je me retiens de bondir à chaque instant" (256). Everything in this passage, as throughout the final chapter, tells us that a whole new life is about to begin for Natacha. (Significantly, in the paragraph immediately preceding the one from which this passage is taken, we read the phrase "cette 'nouvelle vie' au lycée Fénelon.")

The lesson of *Enfance* may be summed up in a single word, freedom or, more precisely, self-emancipation. As its final chapters show, freedom draws nearer, paradoxically, when one renounces the false autonomy of mute isolation, when one joins the verbal nexus, when one enters into dialogue with another, as fraught with the possibility of dangerous entanglement as such a social act may seem ("Dis-moi, est-ce que tu me détestes?"). Independence approaches the day one leaves silence and passivity (i.e., childhood) behind, even if the occasion is marked not by words but by a single gesture ("je la rassure d'un geste"). Freedom is at hand when one ceases being merely the reader of one's life and starts being both its reader and its writer.

Freedom impends for Natacha the moment she stops being the forlorn little girl who was deserted by her biological mother and rejected by her stepmother, when she fuses these twin losses into one and transforms that double abandonment, by deliberate choice, into a single separation in which she can rejoice, her departure from childhood. Armed with the models and tools of her craft-to-be, brand new books and brand new notebooks, bursting with anticipation and enthusiasm for the new life on which she is about to embark, Natacha Tcherniak, former child, is at last on her way to becoming Nathalie Sarraute, future writer.

All of her earlier work points toward what *Enfance* makes unmistakably clear and extraordinarily vivid, that for Russian-born Sarraute freedom will come when, in the terms of Bakhtin scholars, we accept as our common fate "the architectonics of answerability."[6] In Sarraute, the drama of comportment disappears into the drama of speech, and human conduct and human language merge in one and the same interactive ritual. If her writing often folds back on itself in

---

6. See Katerina Clark and Michael Holquist, *Mikhail Bakhtin* (Cambridge: Harvard University Press, 1984), 63–94.

acts of self-scrutiny, the playfulness of frivolity has nothing to do with that habit; her scriptural game could hardly be more serious. Some of the most basic issues of social intercourse, consequently of human existence, are in fact at stake and brought to luminous life in Sarraute's writings. In the process, traditionally divergent strains of metafiction and expressive realism find common ground, behavorial and linguistic concerns combine; moral conscience and verbal self-consciousness interpenetrate to a degree scarcely imaginable before her arrival on the novelistic scene.

Dialogue and connectedness as recurrent novelistic elements and themes—what could be closer to the heart of Marguerite Duras? The differences between Sarraute and Duras, however, regarding the form and function of dialogue in their respective fictions, are no doubt greater than their similarities in this area. Likewise, the thematics of connectedness would appear to play a rather different role in Duras from the one it plays in Malraux or Camus. Unlike Sarraute, Duras in her dialogues deploys hesitation as skillfully as talk, awkward or even disturbing patches of silence as effectively as speech. For the author of *Le Ravissement de Lol V. Stein,* discomforting blanks in a conversation are often more eloquent than the actual words. Pause-marked dialogue, in fact, appears to be one of her favorite means of representing—if not directly presenting—the idea of absence or lack, a notion that occupies a privileged position, as we have seen, in both her panoply of techniques and her metaphysic (if one dare use such a term in reference to so antitheoretical a writer as she). A brief look at an autobiographical volume by Duras can shed light on the novelist's vision, as well as on her writerly procedures, including her use of dialogue.

First, however, we should recall a basic narratorial device that an autobiographer typically employs when recounting his or her earlier life. Most writers of autobiography try to bridge the abyss of time, often spanning decades, separating their past (younger) selves from their present (older) selves, by using (at least) two fairly distinct personae, one for then, the other for now: the former is innocent, naive; the latter, experienced, disabused. Thus in an important sense autobiography involves its author in a kind of dialogue between (at least) two quite different selves. Each author will of course stage the drama of these temporally (and in other ways) distant selves according to the dictates of his or her particular designs and purposes.

Sarraute, for example, anchors her remembering/transcribing self firmly in time present by opening *Enfance* with a querulous dialogue between a *je* and a *tu*, aspects of the present self that are debating and questioning the very idea of trying to " 'évoquer [s]es souvenirs' " (9–10). On the fourth page of the text, this self at war with itself, over the very validity of remembering/transcribing, simply takes the plunge ("tu m'y plonges" [12]) and the first of those stinging, unforgettable phrases out of the author's past, around which the bulk of *Enfance* is organized, appears (in quotation marks, of course): " 'Nein, das tust du nicht... Non, tu ne feras pas ça' " (12). Nodal phrases such as this one, together with the purely descriptive or narrative passages situating them, locate the author's younger self unambiguously in time past, the time of childhood. On the other hand, the more detached, analytical commentary accompanying these phrases (and their microcontexts) belongs *near*, but not entirely *in* time present. This latter time is always clearly marked in the text by the reappearance of the querulous dialogue of *je* and *tu*, which contests the legitimacy of the very autobiography we are in the midst of reading.

This dialogue within a dialogue inscribes, in the text of the autobiography itself, whatever doubts we as readers may have about the value of *Enfance* as a source of something approximating truth concerning the author's past. But just as, ironically, La Rochefoucauld's inclusion of mitigating qualifiers in his otherwise sweeping *Maximes* enhances rather than reduces their range of applicability, Sarraute's literally dramatic inscription of doubt *about* her project *in* her project, increases rather than diminishes its credibility. Announced, acted out, in a manner that is the opposite of pro forma, her text's flaunted unreliability disarms us, subverts our skepticism in advance. Thus, if we are ready to believe this autobiography, it is precisely because of its author's ingenious (and ingenuous) disclaimer of certainty for it.

With her handling of narratorial personae in *L'Amant*,[7] the autobiographical volume she published in 1984, Duras diverges considerably from Sarraute's manner of dealing with this problem in *Enfance*. The basic dichotomy between a self belonging to time

7. Marguerite Duras, *L'Amant* (Paris: Editions de Minuit, 1984). Subsequent page references to this work are in the body of the study, in parentheses.

present and one belonging to time past, of course, remains. In *L'Amant,* however, a special stylistic device underscores not, as in *Enfance,* the self-contesting immediacy of a present self, but rather the utter remoteness of a past self. The effect of this device on her text goes to the heart of Duras's scriptural enterprise, and therefore deserves careful attention.

Perhaps more than most autobiographers, Duras is fascinated by the unreal reality of now *versus* then. A note appearing at the end of *L'Amant,* "Neauphle-le-Château—Paris février—mai 1984," reveals that she wrote the book during the year in which she turned seventy. The book's opening paragraph shows that, from the instant she sat down to write it, she was extremely conscious of her advanced age and was eager to face up to the challenge of confronting the self of her youth with that of her mature years and beyond. But the links between this paragraph and the next one, the book's second, are not obvious:

> Je pense souvent à cette image que je suis seule à voir encore et dont je n'ai jamais parlé. Elle est toujours là dans le même silence, émerveillante. C'est entre toutes celle qui me plaît de moi-même, celle où je me reconnais, où je m'enchante. (9)

Especially puzzling for readers of this second paragraph is its paucity of information about a referent for "cette image," hence about the paragraph's main subject. To what image or picture is the author referring? How she appears now? What she looked like when she was young? Something else entirely? Or something not yet identified, but related in some fashion to the perceived (by others) beauty of her face when she was young versus its perceived beauty in old age, both of which are evoked in the first paragraph? This last possibility seems the most likely, and it gains plausibility as we read further in *L'Amant.*

The "image" referred to in *L'Amant* is finally explained on the eighth and ninth pages of text, where we find mention for the second time of the author's "quinze ans et demi" and "la traversée du fleuve." And then this paragraph:

> C'est au cours de ce voyage que l'image se serait détachée, qu'elle aurait été enlevée à la somme. Elle aurait pu exister,

> une photographie aurait pu être prise, comme une autre, ailleurs, dans d'autres circonstances. Mais elle ne l'a pas été. L'objet était trop mince pour la provoquer. Qui aurait pu penser à ça? Elle n'aurait pu être prise que si on avait pu préjuger de l'importance de cet événement dans ma vie, cette traversée du fleuve. Or, tandis que celle-ci s'opérait, on ignorait encore jusqu'à son existence. Dieu seul la connaissait. C'est pourquoi, cette image, et il ne pouvait en être autrement, elle n'existe pas. Elle a été omise. Elle a été oubliée. Elle n'a pas été détachée, enlevée à la somme. C'est à ce manque d'avoir été faite qu'elle doit sa vertu, celle de représenter un absolu, d'en être justement l'auteur. (16–17)

The image in *L'Amant* thus resembles a photograph that was not taken, a purely imaginary picture of the author at fifteen and a half, crossing the Mekong river on a ferry. (Later we shall discover that the crossing was pivotal in the author's life, since it delivered her literally into the arms of her first lover.) Like the story of her life, and the photograph never taken, the image does not exist outside the author's imagining. For the author, however, its nonexistence as a tangible object in no way affects either its status as something real or its potency. On the contrary, its nonexistence gives it absolute power, that of an originating lack. Within Duras's personal myth of herself, the image turns into an inaugural absence, the enabling black sun at the center of her obsessional system.[8]

For Duras, the image captures something unchanging about her, a diamond-hard quality of soul that transcends youth and old age and reconciles them. It is so materially real to her that it has its own *punctum*, to borrow Barthes's term, its striking, poignant detail in which the energy of the whole is somehow concentrated: "un chapeau d'homme aux bords plats, un feutre souple couleur bois de rose au large ruban noir. L'ambiguïté déterminante de l'image, elle est dans ce chapeau" (19).

---

8. It seems worth noting here that the original title of *L'Amant* was "L'Image absolue"; see Marguerite Duras and Hervé Masson, "L'Inconnue de la rue Catinat," *Nouvel Observateur* (28 September 1984): 52. For a discussion of the role of photographs in *L'Amant*, see Susan D. Cohen, "Fiction and Photographic Image in Duras' *The Lover*," *L'Esprit Créateur* 30 (Spring 1990): 56–68.

So stable and solid, so hypostatized, does the image become that it allows the narratorial self of time past in *L'Amant* to switch from first person to third person, from *je* to *elle,* almost without the reader's noticing it. Once this change in subject personal pronoun enters the text, the self of time past, of childhood or adolescence, will henceforth be rendered by either *je* or *elle.* The latter will be reserved for recounting incidents that verge on the exotic by virtue of their alien remoteness from the life and mood of the author's time present (where, not surprisingly, first-person narration is the rule). Nevertheless, the parts of *L'Amant* in which the narratorial self of time past is carried forward by *elle,* are precisely those in which the author appears to be the most overwhelmed by her "story," the most mesmerized by the spectacle of her younger self. Ironically, when she uses first-person narration for describing or commenting on events or situations from time past, the tone is more reflective, freer of incident's thrall, than it is when *elle* performs that function. That *elle* springs from *image* is patent, incontrovertible.

Where Sarraute, with her mutually contesting *je* and *tu,* dramatizes the dubious struggle that remembering/transcribing involves, Duras, with her *image* and her *elle,* enacts the equally uncertain combat that forgetting entails. Along the way, her nonexistent picture of herself at fifteen and a half, crossing a great river into adult life and love, turns truly indelible; she will never be able to erase it from her memory. Her *image* and her *elle,* moreover, root her self of time past so securely in that time that genuine dialogue between then and now almost seems possible for awhile. But, of course, her interlocutor from the past will always remain *sage comme une image,* as mute, if also as eloquent, as the most treasured snapshot in a family album or the most coveted specimen in a collection of period photography. Our childhood stays with us forever as an urgent, haunting presence, albeit as the silent partner, the perfect still picture, in the endless colloquy we hold with memory.

Despite its purely subjective status, the essential, radiant image in *L'Amant,* perfect still picture par excellence, takes on even greater significance when it is viewed in the context of Duras's writings as a whole. There it becomes an emblem of the feminine condition, suggesting as it does objectified silence and passivity, combined with alluring, latent eroticism. Be "as pretty as a picture," "as quiet as a mouse," be "sage comme une image"—injunctions such as these, though unspoken, figure prominently, Duras (and others) would maintain, among the subliminal commands issued regularly to women and children in patriarchal societies. Duras scholars have frequently pointed out that her scriptural production reprises, and by implication indicts, the age-old conflation of silence and womanhood. Certainly her lifelong preoccupation with blanks of every conceivable order includes female speechlessness, and possibly before any other category of lack or absence.[9]

In this perspective, *Le Ravissement de Lol V. Stein* recalls *La Condition humaine* and *Madame Bovary:* in all three novels, major female figures operate within the confines of a narrow linguistic dispensation, largely, it would appear, because they are women. For example, more than once Lol V. Stein, quintessentially female in her embodiment of lack, latency, and expectation, seems dispossessed primarily of her tongue. If Valérie Serge, in *La Condition humaine,* impresses with her throwaway irony and dazzling fluency, it should be remembered that she occupies a summit of emancipation toward which the novel's more important May Gisors is still climbing in her own laconic, almost tongue-tied way. Unlike the adult male characters in *Madame Bovary,* who can change codes when the need to do so presents itself, Emma serves out a life sentence in a prison made of the Romantic clichés she internalized in her youth. Despite enormous differences, all three novels show woman's fate, historically, as characterized by millennial muteness, a silence that in the end only women can break.

In *Madame Bovary,* chiefly through his depiction of the dilemma confronting the sexually indeterminate, Chérubin-like, virtually aphasic adolescent Justin, Flaubert demonstrates that when young males begin to speak as adults, they leave childhood innocence behind, to enter, wittingly or not, into the ancient fraternity of misogyny. If, like Justin, the budding male reaches out verbally to make genuine, caring contact with a woman, by that simple gesture he automatically forfeits his future position of privilege in the adult male clubhouse of controlling verbiage. He must then disappear, just as Justin disappears on the day after Emma's funeral. Thus, in Flaubert's novel, breaking silence connotes not self-liberation (at least not for

9. See, for example, in Trista Selous, *The Other Woman: Feminism and Femininity in the Work of Marguerite Duras* (New Haven: Yale University Press, 1988), the chapter entitled, appropriately enough, "The Blanks," 87–137.

women) but rather oppression of the other, that is, of women; when males speak (or write) in this novelistic universe, they forever renounce even the possibility of authentic, egalitarian connection with women.

In order to escape this oppression, women must stop babbling the already said, the cliché. The pharmacist Homais, Justin's employer (and, ironically, the youth's professional mentor), an archetypal male and the novel's most consistent oppressor, speaks and writes exclusively in formulaic, ready-made phrases. If Emma could only devise a fresh language, one (in her case) free of Romantic cant, she could then "translate from blackness, from darkness," to quote Duras, and bring forth her (woman's) story from the realm of the never-before-uttered, a region located at the antipodes of the cliché. Emma and her epigones reflect every woman's obscure but implacable need for self-definition through new words, her long-repressed desire to evade the demeaning restrictions of a discourse invented by and for men.

The impulse, or drive, to move beyond (childhood) silence and servitude toward (adult) speech and freedom receives full, unambiguous acknowledgment in Sarraute's *Enfance*. Paradoxically, however, given her gender, the autobiographer says nothing about the presumably different destinies awaiting male and female children. It seems that for Sarraute, while not for Flaubert or Malraux or Duras, in growing up (intellectually), regardless of sex, one can hope to grow in empowerment, to become, if not free, certainly freer than one was before. By contrast, implicit in Malraux, virtually explicit in Flaubert, both implicit and explicit in Duras, is the belief that, for women, gaining liberty entails changing gender, becoming (like) a man. More precisely, with these novelists, getting freedom means, first, acquiring the tongue of the (adult) male.

Yet at some deeper level in all three of the novels in question— *Madame Bovary, La Condition humaine,* and *Le Ravissement de Lol V. Stein*—rendering a particular woman's verbal inadequacy shades off into sketching the ineluctable impotence of humans generally, by highlighting the fundamental absurdity of an existence in which true communication is forever sought but never attained. At this same rather abstract level of observation, however, Sarraute's *Enfance*, with its perpetually self-doubting narratorial persona of time present, conveys a much more unsettling message about the frailties of human language than does any of the three novels. In this sense, and for this reason, Sarraute is the most disturbing of the four writers concerned. But then, of course, she is the one who wrote "Ich sterbe," whose recounting "je," whose primary narrating voice, dies again and again, from the story's first word to its last.

This brings us back to the question of *moralisme,* for Sarraute addresses, more directly than Flaubert or Malraux or Duras, issues that have concerned French moralists for centuries. Her scriptural enterprise goes straight to the heart of the matter, the matter in this case being, for want of a less loaded term, human nature, human nature in all its deluded splendor. In her novels, stories, and plays, Sarraute rips the mask off all chattering faces—whether men or women, victims or oppressors—to expose the ultimate treachery of our words and the murderous commotion going on beneath all social surface, inside all talking heads. Thus, despite the valorization of the rise toward speech-cum-emancipation that informs *Enfance,* when we place that work in the context of its author's other writings, we must wonder how far we have actually come from the nostalgia for the innocence of muteness that traverses the basically ungendered *La Peste.* Regardless of the many differences separating them, Sarraute and Camus stand together (and at a perceptible remove from Flaubert, Malraux, and Duras) near the center of the moralistic tradition, with both writers evidently longing for some asexual Eden of immediate, total, above all silent, communion. In this "age of suspicion," the practice of speech or writing (*l'usage de la parole*) has become, at least for moralists of a "purer" variety, a prime suspect in the "scandale" called living.

More obviously than their marginally less "pure" colleagues in this domain (like Flaubert, Malraux, and Duras), moralistic writers like Camus and Sarraute show every sign of operating on quite stable presuppositions about human nature. As noted in Chapter 1, with reference to Chamfort's popularity over the last half-century, much ink has been spilled during this period in the cause of demolishing traditional concepts of human nature, especially when such concepts are embodied in literary representations. (In this regard, Sartre may be viewed as only the most well known of recent adversaries of a universalist approach to human nature.) But as was argued in the discussion of Malraux and Camus and the notion of commitment in literature, the debate that pits a universalist against a particularist, or

an essentialist against an existentialist, view of human nature reduces an inherently intractable subject to a simple either/or propo-
sition that can only misrepresent it. Robert Alter's shrewd, insightful
comments on this important matter are especially helpful at this
juncture:

> It need not be claimed that human nature is fixed and un-
> changing, but after three millennia, sufficiently powerful con-
> tinuities persist in the literary representation of human
> realities to make us feel when we read that writers then and
> now are engaged with many of the same fundamental objects
> of representation. . . . The characters and life situations of the
> narratives of different eras speak to us not because they re-
> flect a knowledge which never changes but rather because
> they express a set of enigmas with which we continue to
> wrestle.[10]

Just how broadly relevant and revelatory these comments are becomes transparently obvious the moment we apply them first to
Camus and Sarraute; then to Flaubert, Malraux, and Duras; and finally to Gide and Proust.

Given their stature within the novelistic tradition, we may legiti-
mately assume that Gide and Proust incarnate (in Alter's words) the
"powerful continuities" that "persist in the literary representation of
human realities" even more successfully than the novelists reviewed
thus far in this chapter. Certainly, as we have seen, through their respective seminal fictions, these pioneers of the modernist age "express a set of enigmas with which we continue to wrestle" at a level
of subtlety in articulation probably unequaled before or since. Let us
now consider that achievement again, if only briefly.

In his wide-ranging, heuristic introduction to Proust's *On Reading
Ruskin,* Richard Macksey reminds us that "throughout his artistic career Proust was a stern if paradoxical moralist," and that he remained
to the core "the pitiless, illusion-free critic of human passions and
obsessions."[11] In his writings on Ruskin, Macksey further observes,

10. Robert Alter, *The Pleasures of Reading in an Ideological Age* (New York: Simon and
Schuster, 1989), 74, 76.

11. Marcel Proust, *On Reading Ruskin,* ed. and trans. Jean Autret, William Burford, and

"Proust's description of an interior struggle between the rival claims of esthesis and truth is cast in such a way as to suggest that it is an inevitable division for any deeply serious artist" (xl). Thus, despite their numerous temperamental differences, the English critic provided the French novelist with a virtual script for the drama taking place in every artist's soul, including his own.

In a bibliographical note appended to *On Reading Ruskin,* Macksey alludes to the way in which this struggle played itself out in Proust's oeuvre as a whole: "His life's work was literally as well as allegorically a vast palimpsest; revisions, hesitations and transpositions mark every stage of Proust's creative development. Like all his writings, the studies that Proust dedicated to Ruskin during the first years of this century constitute a complicated fabric of redactions, partial publications and internal quotations" (167). Macksey seems to be implying here (as well as elsewhere in his remarks) something very close to what my analysis of *Un Amour de Swann* illustrates, namely, that instances of quotation and repetition accompany Proust's recurrent interrogations of human nature to chart his inner journey, to endow an essentially spiritual quest with a specific material form.

In this connection, we might note, Macksey also points out in his introduction that "Proust, like Ruskin, could not bear to let a text enter the world without trying to recapture it through revision, marginal alteration, or cannibalization into some later project.... Like the author of *Praeterita,* he was to be engaged in a constant search to unite through successive revisions the living self and the writing self" (xxxviii, li). In the deepest sense, therefore, Proust conceived of living and writing as indissolubly linked, as a single series of acts in which recursiveness is all, in which always returning to the already said and done, in order to rework them, make up human existence. Coming to terms with incompletion—the last word, like the first word, being by definition unutterable in any case—is thus both his meekest admission of failure and his boldest pretension to accomplishment, an admission and a pretension that his oeuvre alternately laments and celebrates.

Phillip J. Wolfe, with introduction by Richard Macksey (New Haven: Yale University Press, 1987), xiv, 1. Subsequent page references to this work are in the body of the study, in parentheses.

During the long, sustained coda to *A la recherche* (i.e., throughout the entire last part of *Le Temps retrouvé*), the narrator, it will be remembered, experiences a muted, prolonged crescendo of realizations and recognitions. Significantly, all involve, in one guise or another, recursion wedded to illumination: for example, the narrator's fortuitous discovery of the past's total retrievability through involuntary memory; of his long-deferred vocation as a writer; of the creative potential of his suffering; his now seeing in Swann the inspiration for the book he will now write; his new understanding that his future readers will be thrown back on themselves to become the readers of their own lives. In Proust, critical self-awareness, hence ethical competence, thus develops apace with the increasingly lucid reformulation of prior discourse.

When one compares Proust's handling of citation with Gide's, one is immediately struck by the former's blatant foregrounding of the device itself, and by his turning the device into one of his novel's dominant themes, repetition. Phrases crucial to the plot and thematic structure of the narrative are repeated throughout *Un Amour* (and throughout *A la recherche*, for that matter). In the end, the very act of citation—or self-citation—will contribute as much to the text's impact on readers as will the substance of what is being reprised. Moral vision and scriptural design in Proust, although fated never to reach closure, move forward together, on equal footing and forever yoked.

As implied in the foregoing, unlike the situation obtaining in Proust, in Gide's fiction successive acts of quotation matter less than the quotations themselves. More precisely, material (or an author) cited in a Gidean narrative effectively signals to readers that texts other (and earlier) than the (new) one that we are reading exist and count for something. In our discussion of *L'Immoraliste* and *La Porte étroite*, for example, we noted the extent to which the palimpsest figure informs both novellas, where at almost any given moment the text we are reading can enclose (and hence disclose) or mask (hence unmask) another text. Still, the relentless drive to recover an all-warranting *Urtext*, variously dramatized in the two narratives, eventually uncovers, as we saw, only pure savagery or the abyss. In Gide, apparently, no ultimate textual source lies waiting to be discovered and deciphered by some saint-scholar-poet who would "justify the ways of God to man." It thus seems appropriate, if also

somewhat ironic, that in *La Symphonie pastorale*, his most conspicuously "religious" novella, Gide should have placed the whole problematical enterprise of reading, quoting, and glossing the Bible,
specifically the New Testament, at the heart of his narrator's doomed
search for self-understanding.

In *La Symphonie pastorale*, it will be recalled, a Protestant pastor,
minister to his flock in a remote mountain area of Switzerland, tells
the story of his catastrophic attraction for Gertrude, the blind waif
he has adopted. The narrator appears to expend as much energy
fending off remorse, hence responsibility for the fatal consequences
of his conduct, as he does seeking accuracy of detail in his recollection. In the end, we learn eventually, Gertrude kills herself, primarily
because of the pastor's guilty love for her.

At its most obvious and explicit level, the novella shows us how
moral blindness like the pastor's can wreak far more havoc than
physical blindness like Gertrude's. The pastor's self-deception, his
blindness to his own motives, derives from, and is buttressed by, his
highly selective citing of the Gospels (such as Christ's parable of
the lost sheep recorded in Luke and Matthew). When Jacques, the
pastor's eldest son and a student of theology himself, accuses his
father of choosing within the body of Christian doctrine only those
elements he finds congenial, the pastor adjudges Jacques "tradi-
tionaliste et dogmatique."[12] Their dispute turns heated and pro-
tracted, and complicating everything is their unspoken rivalry for
Gertrude's affections.

Just beneath the surface of the religious argument between father
and son are some of the thorniest ideological issues to have divided
Catholicism and Protestantism since the Reformation. The salient
bone of contention in this centuries-old debate, or at least the one
whose metaphorical power Gide, moralist-scriptor supreme, exploits
the most, concerns the question of the Bible's status as the sole authoritative text of Christ's teachings. According to the Protestant
model, individual conscience, nourished by frequent, reflective
reading of Sacred Scripture, is sufficient unto itself as a guide to the
Christian life. For Catholics, on the other hand, at least historically, in
order to lead such a life believers need the additional guidance of the

---

12. André Gide, *Romans: Récits et soties, oeuvres lyriques*, ed. Yvonne Davet and Jean-
Jacques Thierry, with introduction by Maurice Nadeau (Paris: Gallimard, 1958), 914.

Church fathers (e.g., Saint Augustine, Saint Thomas Aquinas), the pa-
tristic tradition of commentaries formally recognized by the Roman
Church. Locked in irresolvable conflict here are the opposing requirements of, on one side, authenticity, felt, embraced from within;
on the other, authority, imposed, accepted from without. This clash
of ideologies turns on the question of whether the light of faith and
the true way emanates from direct, unimpeded commerce between
the individual believer and the Bible in all its unencumbered, gloss-
free singularity, or whether that light comes from a necessarily double or twofold act of reading, the constant interplay and cross-
referencing of (original) text, the Bible, and (later) commentary, the
writings of the Church fathers. (In this, as in much else, Catholicism
imitates its venerable elder, Judaism, with the latter's pairing, in ped-
agogy, of Torah and Talmud.)

In *La Symphonie pastorale,* the pastor-narrator's stance, Protestant to the point of caricature, is underscored, thus obliquely criti-
cized, by his exclusive, unabashedly self-serving preference for the
gentler, more forgiving Gospels over the stricter, more exacting Epis-
tles of Saint Paul, the two parts of the New Testament most readily
construable as constituting the requisite combination (in miniature)
of sacred primary source and subsequent learned interpretation.
The whole thrust of *La Symphonie pastorale,* moreover, including
the final resolution of its plot, seems to favor the Catholic side in the
debate. After all, by the end of the story, Jacques, who loved Gertrude more unselfishly (presumably) than his father, has entered the
seminary to prepare for the Roman Catholic priesthood. As for the
pastor, whose obtuse bad faith endures essentially unimpaired to the
end, he stands implicitly condemned for his reprehensible and basically unexamined comportment. And yet, given Gide's own Protestant background, as well as his principled detachment (in keeping
with his famous "disponsibilité") regarding religion and theology,
something else, we suspect, must be involved.

The example of W. B. Yeats, Gide's contemporary and his fellow
writer of Protestant background also functioning in a predominantly
Catholic culture, may prove enlightening here. It will be recalled
that Yeats's celebrated poems, "The Second Coming" and "A Prayer
for My Daughter," included in his 1921 sequence *Michael Robartes
and the Dancer,* contain encomia of custom and ceremony that have
little to do with tradition-bound religious institutions and much to

do, it would seem, with matters secular.[13] For the Irish poet, apparently, ceremony consists in the respectful awareness, the knowing practice, and the conscious enrichment of the forms and conventions, including linguistic and literary ones, inside of which we may all, however ephemerally, redeem our works and days together. Gide would certainly consider such an ideal of always provisional but ever renewable innocence worth honoring; as a group, his novellas enact again and again the wise fallibility of just such a project. Thus, rather than promoting Roman Catholicism in *La Symphonie pastorale*, he is more likely supporting, through exemplification, a particular, entirely secular notion of ceremony, the lucid execution of steadily unfolding patterns of language and thought, patterns ever new, hence uncertain and in that sense unreliable, yet always rooted in a vital, thoroughly textualized past.

If ceremony preserves innocence in Yeats, and possibly in Gide as well, in Proust, as we have noted, habit, especially verbal habit, allows surprise, sporadic verbal deviation, to occur, while the dyad, the whole package, gives us an experience of controlled freshness that may well be indispensable for our inner balance. Without question, a comparable dialectical or generating process can be seen at work in all of the narratives treated in this study. Where Gide's novellas, for example, explore our linguistic inadequacies in relation to our incapacity for ethical inquiry, or where Proust dramatizes the inevitable, hypnotic (albeit fruitless) redundancies of self-analysis, Malraux and especially Camus suggest by their practice that even manifestly committed novels must problematize their instrument, while Duras and Sarraute give privilege to colloquy and dialogue in a foredoomed quest for moral certitude. In every case, both heart and tongue are fully and reciprocally engaged in the activity. As they have done since (at least) *Madame Bovary*, moralism and metalanguage thus combine in French fiction, in manifold, deeply gratifying ways, since 1900. Given the stylistic diversity and the wide historical lens represented by the novelists considered here, perhaps we may

13. W. B. Yeats, *The Poems* (*Revised*), ed. Richard J. Finneran (New York: Macmillan, 1989), 187, 190. Yves Bonnefoy's essay on, most notably, the rigorously secular salvation vouchsafed by Yeats's poetry seems especially relevant to the present discussion; see his introduction to W. B. Yeats, *Quarante-cinq poèmes de W. B. Yeats, suivis de La Résurrection*, ed. and trans. Yves Bonnefoy (Paris: Hermann, 1989), 7–31.

now view the blend of moralism and metalanguage they all achieve, however variously, as characterizing French fiction in our century.

Scanning back in time from our century, again our gaze falls to rest on Chamfort, the moment in the history of French moralism when *le vécu*, pulsating in dialogue, allied to incipient linguistic self-interrogation, suddenly enlarged that tradition, broke it open to forms at once looser and more exploratory than the maxim or the portrait. As noted in Chapter 1, the novel in particular was affected by this development. The moralistic and metalinguistic factors that we have seen operating in a series of varied, fundamental twentieth-century French narratives, for example, have their precursors, in embryo, in the following Chamfort *anecdote:*

> J'ai asisté hier à une conversation philosophique entre M. D... et M. L..., où un mot m'a frappé. M.D... disait: "Peu de personnes et peu de choses m'intéressent, mais rien ne m'intéresse moins que moi." M. L... lui répondit: "N'est-ce point par la même raison; et l'un n'explique-t-il pas l'autre?" "Cela est très bien, ce que vous dites là," reprit froidement M. D..., "mais je vous dis le fait. J'ai été amené là par degrés: en vivant et en voyant les hommes, il faut que le coeur se brise ou se bronze."[14]

The narrator lets us know early on here that he is recounting only that part of an overheard conversation that impressed him for its pith ("un mot m'a frappé"). The strain of cynicism and misanthropy, obligatory for traditional moralists, is palpable in this text. The first of the two interlocutors declares that the world, including especially himself, engages his interest but little, hence, by implication, deserves to be renounced. Woven into the second interlocutor's response to this avowal, however, we (along with the first interlocutor) discern a sly gibe aimed at the first interlocutor's amour propre, as well as an oblique foregrounding and even questioning of the instrument with which he is expressing his judgment: " ' ... et l'un

14. Sébastien-Roch de Chamfort, *Maximes et pensées, caractères et anecdotes,* ed. Geneviève Renaux, with preface by Albert Camus (Paris: Gallimard, 1982), 214–15. For an informative essay on Chamfort's writings, see Joseph Epstein, "Chamfort: An Introduction," *New Criterion* 10 (September 1991): 99–108.

n'*explique*-t-il pas l'autre?' 'Cela est très bien, ce que vous *dites* là,' *reprit froidement* M.D..., 'mais *je vous dis le fait*'" (emphasis added). Two devices at the close of the *anecdote*, parallelism-cum-alliteration and then terminal paronomasia, weld its moralistic and metalinguistic dimensions together: "'*en vivant* et *en voyant* les hommes, il faut que le coeur *se brise* ou *se bronze*'" (emphasis added). In effect, this brief dramatic narrative acknowledges and at the same time deflects all of our diffidence and frailty, both ethical and verbal.

Whatever else they are doing, Gide, Proust, and the other twentieth-century French novelists discussed here are ringing amplified changes on Chamfort's *anecdotes* for our age of uncertainty. As if fated by neoclassical tradition to carry the banner of Flaubert's post-Romantic project ever forward, they play out their utterly diverse lives as writers in an endless search for *les mots justes,* words at once right and righteous. The value of their quest derives, no doubt, from the vivifying power of the elusive equilibrium they are trying to reach.

Index

DATE DUE